WHAT TO DO WHEN YOU ARE FIRED OR LAID OFF:

A Complete Guide to the Benefits and Legal Rights You Need to Know to Get Back on Your Feet

By PK Fontana

WHAT TO DO WHEN YOU ARE FIRED OR LAID OFF: A COMPLETE GUIDE TO THE BENEFITS AND LEGAL RIGHTS YOU NEED TO KNOW TO GET BACK ON YOUR FEET

Library of Congress Cataloging-in-Publication Data

Fontana, P. K.
  What to do when you are fired or laid off : a complete guide to the benefits and legal rights you need to know to get back on your feet / by P.K. Fontana.
     p. cm.
  Includes bibliographical references and index.
  ISBN-13: 978-1-60138-287-0 (alk. paper)
  ISBN-10: 1-60138-287-1 (alk. paper)
  1. Employees--Dismissal of--Law and legislation--United States--Popular works. I. Title.
  KF3471.F665 2009
  344.7301'2596--dc22
                                      2009037951

Printed in the United States

PROJECT MANAGER: Carrie Speight
INTERIOR DESIGN: Samantha Martin • smartin@atlantic-pub.com
ASSISTANT EDITOR: Angela Pham • apham@atlantic-pub.com
JACKET DESIGN: Jackie Miller • sullmill@charter.net
EDITORIAL ASSISTANT: Scott Lavery

Printed on Recycled Paper

We recently lost our beloved pet "Bear," who
was not only our best and dearest friend but also
the "Vice President of Sunshine" here at Atlantic
Publishing. He did not receive a salary but worked
tirelessly 24 hours a day to please his parents.
Bear was a rescue dog that turned around and
showered myself, my wife, Sherri, his grandparents
Jean, Bob, and Nancy, and every person and animal
he met (maybe not rabbits) with friendship and love. He made a lot of people
smile every day.

We wanted you to know that a portion of the profits of this book will be
donated to The Humane Society of the United States. *–Douglas & Sherri Brown*

The human-animal bond is as old as human history. We cherish our animal companions for their unconditional affection and acceptance. We feel a thrill when we glimpse wild creatures in their natural habitat or in our own backyard.

Unfortunately, the human-animal bond has at times been weakened. Humans have exploited some animal species to the point of extinction.

The Humane Society of the United States makes a difference in the lives of animals here at home and worldwide. The HSUS is dedicated to creating a world where our relationship with animals is guided by compassion. We seek a truly humane society in which animals are respected for their intrinsic value, and where the human-animal bond is strong.

Want to help animals? We have plenty of suggestions. Adopt a pet from a local shelter, join The Humane Society and be a part of our work to help companion animals and wildlife. You will be funding our educational, legislative, investigative and outreach projects in the U.S. and across the globe.

Or perhaps you'd like to make a memorial donation in honor of a pet, friend or relative? You can through our Kindred Spirits program. And if you'd like to contribute in a more structured way, our Planned Giving Office has suggestions about estate planning, annuities, and even gifts of stock that avoid capital gains taxes.

Maybe you have land that you would like to preserve as a lasting habitat for wildlife. Our Wildlife Land Trust can help you. Perhaps the land you want to share is a backyard— that's enough. Our Urban Wildlife Sanctuary Program will show you how to create a habitat for your wild neighbors.

So you see, it's easy to help animals. And The HSUS is here to help.

2100 L Street NW • Washington, DC 20037 • 202-452-1100
www.hsus.org

DEDICATION

"My work is dedicated to Fred, Rudy, and Katie, who continue to support me, encourage me, and, most importantly, love me — no matter what. Also, to Clara and J.E., who truly meant it when they told me I could be whatever I wanted to be when I grew up!"

TABLE OF CONTENTS

Chapter 3: Reduction in Force (RIF) 45

Chapter 4: Closing/Bankruptcy 53

Chapter 5: Firing   **61**

Chapter 6: Have You Been Fired Illegally?   **71**

Chapter 7: Considerations for a Lawsuit   81

Chapter 8: Working with an Attorney to Challenge a Termination   93

Chapter 9: Surviving Unemployment   101

Chapter 13: The Job Hunt   145

Chapter 14: Résumés and Cover Letters   155

Chapter 15: The Job Interview   185

Conclusion   193

Appendix A: Glossary   195

FOREWORD

Losing a job can be one of the most stressful experiences a person can go through. Modern-day employees likely work half their waking hours, so a job is a large part of most people's lives. A natural reaction to job loss or even potential job loss is shock, thus many people fail to take steps quickly to protect their and their family's rights after termination — many do not know their rights and obligations. In this economy, every worker needs to know exactly what to do from the moment he or she is presented with a termination letter or severance package. That is why I am glad PK Fontana wrote her book, *What to Do When You are Fired or Laid Off: A Complete Guide to the Benefits and Legal Rights You Need to Know to Get Back on Your Feet.*

In this book, Fontana explains your rights and much more. She takes you by the hand gently, like an experienced friend or personal career counselor, and tells you exactly what to do from the moment you begin to think your job might end. She even advises you about the signs to look for to determine if your job is at risk.

If you choose to read this book before you are fired, you will learn exactly what to do to prepare yourself financially and legally before it is too late. If you have already been fired or laid off, you should have this book as your constant companion to wend your way through the financial minefields of benefits, government assistance, budgeting, and debts.

Once you have secured yourself financially, it is time to move on — and Fontana tells you how. Think you might have legal claims? She explains if and how to find a lawyer, what questions to ask, and discusses some of the potential claims you might explore with your attorney. Has it been a while since you were in the job market? You will receive advice on how to network, train, conduct your job search, and interview.

Some of my favorite parts of this book are the case studies in each chapter. Real people who have been right where you are share what happened to them, what they did, and how it worked out. These practical and true-to-life examples show a reader how others dealt with their own job dilemmas.

As a lawyer who has practiced employment law in Florida for more than 20 years, I have clients come to me to negotiate their severance packages, to get advice about non-compete agreements and employment contracts, to discuss discrimination or whistleblower suits, and to defend against suits by former employers. But my clients also need practical advice. This book is just what they need. It goes beyond legal advice, to the day-to-day matters every unemployed person must confront.

As the author of *The Writer's Guide to the Courtroom: Let's Quill All the Lawyers*, I know about good, clean writing. This book is written in plain English, so even the most stunned ex-employee can understand what he or she needs to do each step of the way.

By reading this book, you are taking the first step toward moving past the dreaded job loss and onto a new — maybe even better — stage in life. Good luck with your job search.

Donna M. Ballman, J.D.

President, Donna M. Ballman, P.A.

About Donna Ballman

Donna Ballman has been practicing law for more than 20 years, focusing primarily on representing employees and former employees. Her practice in employment law has been recognized by having been named one of the Top 500 Plaintiff's Attorneys in the U.S. by Lawdragon based upon peer ratings, a Leading Florida Attorney and Leading American  Attorney by American Research Group based upon a survey of attorneys, and a Top South Florida Attorney by South Florida Legal Guide based on a survey of South Florida attorneys. She was featured on the Forbes Channel's "America's Most Influential Women" program on the topic of severance negotiations and non-compete agreements. She wrote Behler Publications' *The Writer's Guide to the Courtroom: Let's Quill All the Lawyers*, a book that informs novelists and screenwriters about the ins and outs of the civil justice system, as part of its award-winning "Get It Write" series. She has also served on James Publishing's Editorial Advisory Board.

She has taught numerous CLEs and other seminars for organizations such as the National Employment Lawyers Association, Sterling Education Services, Lorman Education Services, Alison Seminars, the Florida Association for Women Lawyers, and community organizations. Ms. Ballman has published articles on employment law topics such as severance, non-compete agreements, discrimination, sexual harassment, and avoiding litigation.

Donna M. Ballman, P.A., can be found at **www.ballmanfirm.com**. The firm focuses on:

Employment discrimination: sexual discrimination, sexual harassment, disability, race, religious, national origin, color, pregnancy, sexual orientation, marital status and age discrimination claims, representation before EEOC, Florida Commission on Human Relations, and county Equal Opportunity Boards.

Negotiation of severance agreements: handling all aspects of severance agreement negotiations.

Employment litigation: whistleblower, non-compete, Family and Medical Leave Act, discrimination, advice, and litigation.

Non-compete agreements: advice regarding non-compete agreements; defense of non-compete enforcement suits and arbitrations; litigation to seek ruling from court on enforceability of non-compete agreements.

Alternate dispute resolution: Florida Supreme Court-certified circuit civil mediator; arbitrator for employment disputes.

INTRODUCTION

The business world is always changing. Giant corporations are bought and sold, and are even being supported by the federal government. Words like bailout, rescue package, and stimulus plan are now part of our everyday conversation. News of bankruptcies and layoffs cover the front pages of news Web sites and newspapers daily. Unemployment insurance is being upgraded and Employment Security Commissions (ESCs) are overwhelmed with the changes as well as with the number of new applicants each week. Job fairs entice hundreds — sometimes thousands — of applicants for relatively few available positions.

If you are among the newly unemployed, or you recognize the signs within your own organization that you may be laid off soon, you are not alone. Millions are facing similar situations. Unemployment across the U.S. reached a rate of 8.1 percent, or 12.5 million people, in February 2009, the highest since the early 1980s. But you are taking the right first step by reading this book. Here you will find information about your rights and your employer's obligations, as well as advice on where to turn for help, how to get back on your feet and start your job search again, and how to survive unemployment — financially and emotionally. The chapters will cover the many resources available to you through government agencies, non-profit organizations, and private support groups.

This book provides a simple outline of the types of unemployment and what each means to you in terms of rights, benefits, and obligations. The chapters are broken down into easy-to-follow sections beginning with preparing for unemployment, then guiding you through the various types of unemployment and the rights and obligations associated with each. There are helpful sections included on surviving unemployment and looking for your next job. Each chapter concludes with case studies from people who have been there before and experts who can help you along the way. The appendices break down laws by state, provide a glossary of commonly used terms, and give you further resources to investigate on your own.

The world of work is constantly changing. The time when a person could retire from the same company he or she started working for as a teenager has all but passed. The findings of the U.S. Department of Labor prove this fact by monitoring employment trends. Its Bureau of Labor Statistics looks at current unemployment rates and studies patterns over many years. Below are some of their findings:

- People hold about ten jobs in their lifetimes (though this estimate is based on limited studies).

- People experience unemployment almost five times during their working years. The better educated people are, the fewer times they are unemployed.

- The agency projects that in 2016, many older persons will be employed. Service-related jobs will continue to be important areas of employment.

Of course, when you are facing unemployment, these statistics will not offer much comfort. When you lose a job, you lose your health benefits and your income. It is natural to worry about how your family will overcome these detrimental circumstances. You may wonder how you will pay your mortgage, car, and credit card bills; how to put food on the table; and how to tell your children that Santa may not be coming this year. You may experience strong emotions: sadness, anger, frustration, hopelessness, and anxiety. These feelings can affect your health and your relationships with other people; they can make it difficult to find the energy and strength to get your life back together.

As you read through the information provided here, you will see that there are many options available to you, in your community as well as on a state and federal level. Resources abound for assistance with daily living expenses, utilities, and food. You can also receive help with finding a new job or creating your own job by starting your own business. Case studies at the end of each chapter feature expert advice and advice from people who have gone through this situation before.

Some people say that being terminated was the greatest favor they ever received. There is a brighter day ahead for you, and this book will help you find it.

Notes:

The information in this book is intended to educate you about employment issues. The information was accurate at the time it was written, but laws and other relevant factors change often. Please consult the most recent information using the resources provided. This book does not replace the need to speak with attorneys and appropriate agencies.

CHAPTER 1

Before You Become Unemployed

Losing a job does not typically come as a surprise to an employee, whether the loss is through a layoff or a firing. While you are still employed, watch for signs and do your homework. If your company is "restructuring" or making moves for budget reasons, such as cutting back on workers' hours or not paying their bills on time, the next step could be a layoff — or even a closing. Likewise, if you are receiving unfavorable feedback on your work performance or sensing that your supervisors are heading in a different direction, you may be in line for a dismissal.

You can be prepared for unemployment. This chapter will provide an overview of steps to take while you are still employed, such as increasing your savings and, of course, reading this book and other research materials to ensure you know your rights and your employer's obligations.

Watch for Signs

In challenging economic times, news of financial problems in the business world is splashed across Web sites, television news, and daily newspapers.

These resources can prove to be insightful for employees. By checking these sources, an employee of a struggling company can learn about the financial issues facing their employer. Keep up with the circumstances of the company you work with.

Pay attention to internal signs as well. Companies that are not doing well financially tend to increase the time they take to pay vendors — and sometimes do not pay them at all. Your amenities may be cut back. Pay heed if the company has canceled the annual picnic, if you are being charged for the once-free coffee in the break room, or if office supplies require more scrutiny and several layers of approval. Pay attention to keywords such as "tightening the budget" and "streamlining." These buzzwords usually mean cutbacks and, potentially, layoffs.

Your company may be searching for a buyer or partner. While this type of financial arrangement may be beneficial to the company as a whole, it does not mean that layoffs have been avoided. The new company may decide to consolidate staff or reduce overhead to make the combined venture more profitable. If your company is on the verge of a buyout or a merger, prepare for a change or work to make yourself invaluable to the organization. Often, though, even the most worthy of employees are laid off when the new owners review the financial statements and decide they need to reduce expenses.

Signs that you may be in line to be fired include the obvious, such as poor performance reviews, and the not-so-obvious, such as being left out of the communication loop on important decisions or not being invited to planning meetings. Speak with your co-workers to find out whether they have noticed anything or heard anything that might be a clue about a potential dismissal. Tread carefully when making inquiries. If the signs do not already exist, you certainly do not want to create any.

Prepare Yourself Financially

As soon as you start seeing the signs, begin considering what could be the inevitable. You may be stretched too thin already, but even a small amount put away each week will help if the time does come when you find yourself depending on savings. Do your research to find high-yield savings accounts, like those available with online banks. You want your savings to earn money, but you also have to be able to access it when it is needed the most. You may even want to invest in some long-term stocks or bonds to ensure you will have the money down the road as well but, first, determine your monthly and annual living expenses. Your living expenses will include bills, groceries, and any other expenses you incur. It is always a good idea to have enough money in your savings to pay for three months of living expenses.

You will have a more realistic idea of what your expenses are if you create a budget for everyday living. Act as though you are already unemployed when deciding how much you can spend each week. Watch for sales, use coupons and store discount cards, and make a list — and stick to it — when you grocery shop. Reduce or eliminate unnecessary expenses, such as restaurant meals. An easy way to build up a savings account is to calculate the money you will save each week with your new budget and deposit that amount into your savings account. You will find more detailed information about creating a budget — and sticking to it — in Chapter 11.

Investigate Other Possibilities

When you start to recognize the signs of an impending layoff, research other opportunities that might be available within your field. Be careful, however, not to jeopardize your current job any further. Do your research on your own time, using your own resources, until an official layoff has been announced. Ask co-workers, discreetly, whether you may list their names as references. They may need to list you as a reference as well. After a layoff, you might be able to take advantage of company resources to do your job search. Ask your human resource department about the services available to you after a layoff.

You should investigate opportunities to further your education. Speak with a representative from your local community college about their programs — and their options for the unemployed. There are many that enable the unemployed or underemployed to have their course registration fee waived for job-related classes.

Also consider investigating the possibility of doing work as a consultant or freelancer, or even starting your own business. However, if you do take on any extra work, be careful not to jeopardize your current position. With this extra income, you can start increasing your savings and laying the foundation for what might have to become your full-time job. Your local community college can also help you with small business advice, most of which is available at no charge. You will find more detailed information about starting your own business, and the resources available to you, in Chapter 14.

Prepare Yourself Legally

Know your rights and your employer's obligations. Do your research on the local, state, and federal level so you will be prepared if your employer does not provide the benefits it is obligated to provide or does not do so within the schedule required. If you believe you are about to be fired and suspect that it may be an illegal termination, you may need to consult with a lawyer. Later, we will go into more detail about the legalities of being fired or laid off.

Prepare yourself by gathering all the information you can about your employer, the status of your job, and your employer's obligations should you lose your job. If you are still employed but suspect that something may be happening within your company, begin documenting anything that might seem out of the ordinary. Particularly if you suspect you are going to be terminated, with or without cause, start a journal in which you write a description of any suspicious behavior on the part of supervisors or co-workers. Remember to date each entry and keep the information factual.

Gather information on continuing your health insurance, life insurance, retirement plan, and other job-related benefits by consulting with your company's human resources office. You can approach the subject by asking the hypothetical question, "In case of a layoff, what happens to my . . . ?" or you can request to see the employee manual's.

Being prepared is the best front line against unemployment battles. The best-case scenario is that you will not need to have all this information — the additional savings, the reduced budget, and the other items discussed here; however, if the signs are pointing toward a layoff or firing, preparation will definitely be your key to surviving a job loss.

CASE STUDY: LISA BRAITHWAITE, M.A.

Public Speaking Coach and Professional Speaker
E-mail: lisa@coachlisab.com
Telephone: 805-207-7647
Web site: **www.coachlisab.com**

Today I own and operate a business as a public-speaking coach and professional speaker. I enjoy helping others build skills and confidence as speakers. I also offer seminars and workshops on public speaking, PowerPoint design services, and a public speaking e-course. But just a few years ago, I underwent three layoffs from non-profit organizations in four years.

The first layoff was a shock. I really thought I was indispensable and, in fact, the position had been created for me. I also felt hurt that the board would choose my position to eliminate over other positions and staff who were newer. I was not the only staff person let go, but it still felt personal. I had planned on going away for a family reunion with my husband, but as I was given a week's notice, I had to stay home by myself and deal with closure alone. I was fortunate to find another non-profit job within three months, but that organization soon failed, and everyone lost their jobs. We were all surprised to hear the organization was out of money but had a sense of camaraderie over being let go together. The third time, I was almost relieved, as I was not happy at this job and needed the kick in the butt to get out of there. However, they gave me five weeks' notice. So I sat around in my office for five weeks, rearranging files and cleaning my desk. It was brutal.

I applied for unemployment each time I was laid off. One time, I was unable to get it because I had a part-time job running the nonprofit I had founded, and they assumed I would not look for a full-time job (they were right).

My husband and I discovered that we were able to live on one salary fairly successfully by the third layoff, which was surprising because we live in an expensive southern California city. But the first two times were more difficult, and we racked up a bit of credit card debt.

I think we changed our lifestyle in subtle ways that did not feel like deprivation. We ate out less, and my husband started cutting my hair — he had always wanted to try it. He has been doing it for four years now, and I receive compliments everywhere I go.

CASE STUDY: LISA BRAITHWAITE, M.A.

I used my contacts and networking to find new jobs, and I suggest that others do the same. Call everyone you know and put the word out that you are job hunting. Not all of the leads will pan out, but it helps you feel like you are being productive. It is also a great way to catch up with people you have not talked to in a long time.

After the third layoff, I was fed up and decided to go out on my own. I initially started a jewelry business because I had been making jewelry for many years, and it seemed like a quick and fairly easy business to start. I also went through a 14-week women's self-employment training program. Eventually, I started my current business and cannot imagine ever going back to working for someone else.

Through all these changes and challenges, I have learned that no one is indispensable. Keep improving your skills. Keep learning and growing. Keep making contacts and building relationships in the community, even if you feel secure in your job. You never know when you will need to draw upon your resources.

I still feel shocked at having endured so many layoffs, but I realize that I was meant to work for myself all along, and that it was a good thing that I was forced to make that decision.

CASE STUDY: JOHNNY "THE TRANSITION MAN" CAMPBELL

DTM, Accredited Speaker
Owner, Speak On It
E-mail: Johnny@transitionman.com
Telephone: 888-255-8626
Web site: **www.transitionman.com**

I call myself "The Transition Man" because I have been through five corporate downsizing events. From my troubles, I have found a new career and business for myself and have a way to help others who are struggling with employment and other issues.

I worked in insurance and was OK with my job for many years. But when I was promoted to corporate trainer, I really found my niche. So, when this job was phased out, I took it personally. I was bitter, and I felt management had back-stabbed me. In my opinion, losing a job I loved so much felt like losing a loved one. I tried to discuss the termination with the manager and show him why it was a mistake, but I had no documentation of my good work record. He just glared at me and told me his decision was final.

I did receive unemployment while looking for a job. The unemployment system is tough, but not because of the little amount of money they pay you. It is sitting there explaining why you failed and what happened. It is re-living this pain over and over again. That beats you up because every month you have to check in to tell them if you are succeeding or failing in your job search.

In order to survive, I gave up my apartment and rented a room in the basement of a house. The money I had saved was for a rainy day, and this was a storm. I did everything I could to reduce my expenses. I did not eat out; I really counted my pennies.

Although I was broke and feeling bad, I had a friend who was always trying to get me to attend Amway meetings with him. He told me that joining this group would help me solve my financial problems. I attended, and the meeting was awesome. The people were high-energy, excited, and filled with the possibility that their tomorrow would be better than today. Although I never joined them, I attended their meetings every week for three months. I used the meetings as therapy to help me get over my negative feelings about losing my job.

After a while, I let go of the bitterness and finally accepted that I was a good person in a bad situation. I think the breakthrough happened when I finally removed my personal identity from the job.

CASE STUDY: JOHNNY "THE TRANSITION MAN" CAMPBELL

In other words, I stopped letting the job define me, and I started defining myself. By doing that, nothing can bring me down because I know who I am and what I want out of life. I began evaluating my prior job duties and experiences and realized that public speaking would be an ideal career choice for me.

Since 2000, I have been speaking on topics such as dealing with change, difficult people, and generational issues. I have written five books and appeared on television and in several movies. I currently hold the honor of being an Accredited Speaker, a designation given by Toastmasters International that is held by only 58 professional speakers in the world for excellence in public speaking. Upon receiving this honor, I became the first African-American under the age of 40 and the youngest person in the world to hold this designation.

I am very proud of my accomplishments, but the biggest thing I am proud of is being invited back twice a year to that same unemployment office I once received benefits from to hold workshops to help others deal with the pain of losing a job and to move on.

My tips for dealing with job loss:

1. Accept the reality that you have lost a job. I spent months being bitter and regretful.
2. Do not hide from people; begin to network with people at social events, fairs, and malls. The more you are out around people, the less you will feel isolated.
3. Never give up on your dream for a better life.
4. Ask for advice, not help. When you lose your job, you need advice on how to bounce back. Help is what you need when you are hurt.
5. You must work every day toward your dreams. The fight is won in the daily battles.
6. The activities you do toward your dream must be measurable, so you know if you are making progress.
7. Pick a career based on your talents, passions, and expertise. The best thing I did was that I figured out what I did well and started looking for a career that offered me the opportunity to do that. The worst thing you can do is take on a job where the expectations are unclear. If expectations are unclear, how will you be able to achieve the results the employer wants?

CHAPTER 2

What are your Rights, Benefits, and Obligations?

In this chapter, we will discuss and define the terms used in later chapters to describe your rights as an employee and your employer's possible. We will discuss the WARN Act (the requirement for notice), COBRA, severance pay obligations, obligations regarding continuing education and retraining, as well as other considerations on both the employee's and the employer's part. Again, specific rights and obligations are determined by the type of unemployment, as well as the size of your employer's company. Each will be discussed in detail in the following chapters.

Unemployment Insurance

If you have become unemployed through no fault of your own, you will likely qualify to receive unemployment payments. The amount of the payments and the length of time for which you will be eligible to receive them will vary depending on your situation and your work history. Benefit amounts tend to be "based on a percentage of an individual's earnings over a recent 52-week period — up to a state maximum amount," according to the U.S. Department of Labor. The first step in determining whether you qualify for unemployment insurance is to find your state's employment security commission or unemployment insurance office. Contact information for each state is included in Appendix C.

There are a number of ways to qualify for unemployment payments:

- If you have been laid off
- If you were part of a business closing or bankruptcy
- If you lost your job because you were fired without cause. Your case will probably be reviewed to determine whether you became unemployed through no fault of your own

You may not qualify for unemployment benefits:

- If you quit your job
- If you were fired with cause.

Whether or not you believe you will qualify, you should apply for benefits. As the unemployment situation changes, eligibility rules also change. And you certainly will not be eligible if you do not apply.

Once you are approved for unemployment insurance, many states require a one-week waiting period before issuing unemployment payments. Once you are determined as eligible, check with your state agency to determine when your benefits will begin. Knowing when to expect payment is significant, especially when planning your unemployment budget.

While you are receiving unemployment benefits, you will be required to actively look for a job. You also must report to the agency on a regular basis. This may be in-person, by phone, or through the Internet. You will be asked about your job search, any money you have earned, your availability for work, and whether you have accepted or declined a job offer.

Your unemployment insurance benefits will likely continue for 26 weeks if you continue to report regularly; however, many changes have been made in early 2009 to the extended benefit program, and you may be eligible to receive payments for a longer period. Your state's unemployment insurance agency will provide you with the information regarding your benefits and the period of time for which you will be eligible, according to the updated regulations.

Unfortunately, if you were employed as one of the following, you are likely not covered by unemployment insurance in most states:

- Farm workers
- Those working on 100-percent sales commission
- Casual domestic workers and babysitters
- Newspaper carriers under the age of 18
- Those employed by family, such as a child working for a parent or an adult employed by a spouse or adult child
- Employees of religious organizations
- Some corporate officers
- Elected officials

Again, check with your local unemployment office to determine whether you are qualified.

Living Assistance

Another unemployment benefit that unemployed persons may qualify for is living assistance. Living assistance is the technical term the government uses to refer to what we commonly call welfare or public assistance. Living assistance payments are funded through the state and tend to be sent to recipients monthly. These payments are low. For example, in Alabama, a family of four could receive up to $245 a month. These payments vary by state, however, and are not the only programs available that provide assistance. Qualified persons may also receive Medicaid or Medicare coverage and food stamps. Often, an adult is limited to a total of 60 months in the living assistance program during his or her lifetime; thus, these programs are not the most ideal long-term solution to unemployment.

Each state administers its own living assistance program, and each state uses its own name for the program. Temporary Assistance for Needy Families is a common name. Other examples include North Carolina Work First, California CalWORKS, and Iowa Family Investment. These programs are managed by state and local social services departments or human services departments. Although each state sets its own rules, the following are general guidelines that apply to most locations. To receive living assistance payments, you must:

- Be responsible for a child under the age of 19 or be pregnant
- Have no or low income
- Be unemployed, underemployed, or losing a job soon
- Have the legal right to live in the United States and live in the state in which you are applying

Most states require that participants enroll in some type of training and/or work program to continue to qualify to receive living assistance payments. These programs are designed to help people move on to earning money as quickly as possible so that they can leave the living assistance program.

Notification — The WARN Act

In some cases of mass layoff and plant closings, companies must follow the Worker Adjustment and Retraining Notification Act (WARN). This law requires that workers in certain situations be given 60 days notice of the job loss.

The WARN Act applies to all employees in companies that:

- Have at least 100 full-time workers (those hired in the last six months and those who work less than 20 hours weekly are not included in the count)

  OR

- Have at least 100 workers who work a combined total of 4,000 or more hours each week

AND

- Are private for-profit firms, private nonprofit organizations, or quasi-public organizations (separate from standard government agencies)

The WARN Act applies in these types of layoffs:

- A plant is closing and laying off at least 50 workers.
- There is a mass layoff, which can mean releasing between 50 and 499 full-time employees at one job site, such as a single plant or operational center, and the number laid off is at least 33 percent of the total number of full-time workers at the site.
- Five hundred or more full-time workers at one job site are laid off.

The WARN Act applies to employees who:

- Lose their jobs — but not to those who quit, retire, or are fired for cause
- Are laid off for more than six months
- Have their regular hours cut by more than half during each month within a six-month period

The WARN Act does not apply to employees who:

- Strike or are locked out in a labor dispute
- Are hired on a temporary basis

- Consult with or provide contracted services to the company but are not employed by the company
- Work for federal, local, or state governments
- Quit, retire, or are fired for a cause

The WARN Act says that when a company plans a mass layoff or plant closing, it must give all affected workers a written notice 60 days in advance with this information:

- Whether the layoff is permanent or temporary
- The date of the closing and the date you will be laid off
- "Bumping rights," if that is part of the company's structure (this means employees' seniority would play a role in who is laid off, and more often applies to union workers)
- The company contact person for more information

If the company fails to give notice, even though it is required to according to the WARN Act, employees may be awarded payments equal to back pay and the company may be fined. More information about your right to pursue legal action against an employer for not providing proper notice is discussed in Chapter 7.

Most employers will also notify local resources such as community colleges, Rapid Response teams, and other agencies indicating that they are facing a significant layoff, so these organizations can begin preparing to assist the laid off employees.

Notes:

If the closing or layoff is due to unusual circumstances — such as a natural disaster or other conditions beyond the company's control — or if advance notice will harm a troubled firm's efforts to find new capital funding and/or business to keep it in business, the WARN Act does not apply.

Health Insurance — COBRA

The Consolidated Omnibus Budget Reconciliation Act (COBRA) requires all employers with 20 or more workers to offer ongoing health insurance when jobs are lost for any reason. Your coverage can be extended for up to 18 months at the group rate of the company. Most states also have extended health insurance laws that apply to companies with fewer than 20 employees. A list of those states and their qualifications can be found in Appendix C, Resources by State.

While retaining the coverage, especially at the lower group rate, can be important, your out-of-pocket cost will rise. Many companies pay a portion of the premium for their employees, but when you are laid off or fired, that benefit ends. This means you will be paying the entire premium, which could amount to several hundreds of dollars each month. That amount may difficult to pay if your only income is unemployment compensation.

But you may have other options for health insurance. If your spouse is covered under a plan through his or her employer, you may qualify to be added to that plan when you lose your job. Although dependents are generally only eligible to be added during what is called the "open enrollment" period for the employer, there are special circumstances allowed in which dependents can be added at other times. Depending on your spouse's plan, losing your job may be considered a special circumstance for you to be eligible to be added to that plan. For more information about the COBRA act, see the government Web site **www.dol.gov/cobra.**

Trade Act

The Trade Adjustment Assistance (TAA) and Alternative Trade Adjustment Assistance (ATAA) programs are known as the Trade Act. The TAA program helps retrain workers whose jobs were lost due to foreign competition. Eligible workers may receive help in finding new jobs. They may also receive funds to help in the job search and relocation and assistance with health insurance. Some persons may qualify for training and educational services.

For those who lost their jobs after age 50 due to foreign competition, additional assistance may be available. The ATAA program helps older workers who may not benefit from re-training by supplementing their incomes if they must take a new job at a lower wage. For more information, visit **www.doleta.gov/tradeact/benefits.cfm#2**.

Job Search Assistance

Your state's Employment Security Commission (ESC) or Unemployment Insurance (UI) office will likely provide resources you can use to search for a job once you are unemployed. The ESC or UI offices have job listings provided to them by employers, many of whom choose to only advertise open positions through those offices.

One-Stop Career Centers

In addition to unemployment insurance offices, most states also have JobLink or One-Stop Career Centers designed specifically to help the unemployed find work. Rapid response teams generally go on-site to assist a company and its employees in the case of a mass layoff or plant closing. The Rapid Response program partners with the One-Stop Career Center program. These offices provide a wide range of employment-related services, including:

- Access to computers, phones, and other office equipment
- Job placement and career counseling services
- Education and training services
- Counseling for coping with the stress and financial strain of unemployment

There are more than 2,000 centers across the country. Find a local One-Stop Career Center online at **www.servicelocator.org** or by phone at 1-877-US2-JOBS (1-877-872-5627).

Some states have additional laws, regulations, or ordinances that apply in the event of a plant closing. Your Rapid Response office can provide information. In addition, some states offer supplementary assistance beyond that required in the WARN Act. For example, some states mandate that employers provide laid-off workers with severance payments and/or other benefits.

Severance Pay

Many companies provide severance pay for employees involved in a layoff, restructuring, or business closing. For those who receive severance packages, the actual payout can vary widely, depending on the company, the employee's position, and the length of service. A common rule of thumb is to give two weeks' pay for every year of employment. You may also receive payment for unused vacation leave. All these payments will have tax withheld, just like a regular paycheck.

Other Components of the Severance Package

In addition to monetary severance pay, other benefits or services may be included in a severance package, such as re-training or assistance in finding another job. This may be provided through employment placement services or by way of offering company resources to employees who are about to be laid off. Often, a company will make available its computers, printers, and even telephones to employees to aid them in finding another position.

Timing of Payment

Your employer chooses how to make the severance payment. It may be in installments, according to the regular pay schedule, or it may be a lump-sum payment.

State laws specify when the final paycheck must be paid. Some states require employers to include pay for unused vacation in the final paycheck. About half of the states expect the last paycheck to be given within two to three days; most others allow it to be paid on the next regular payday.

What Are Your Options?

It is crucial that you learn as much as you can about the options you have once you are laid off or fired, realizing that your rights and your employer's obligations are determined by the type of unemployment you have experienced. Check with the local and state authorities to be sure you have the most current information when you are determining whether you have received the appropriate benefits. Laws and regulations change rapidly, particularly with the drastic changes in unemployment taking place at the time of this book's publication.

Types of Unemployment

There are many circumstances through which an employee might become unemployed. In the early 21st century, those circumstances usually involve a company that is struggling just to stay in business. In such a situation, although the company might cut back on other expenses, employees can be cut back and laid off as well. Some companies try not to lay off mass numbers of valuable employees and may institute temporary measures known as furloughs. When a business goes completely bankrupt, though, or decides it is time to close its doors, all the company's employees will find themselves in the same situation you may be currently facing.

The types of unemployment can be broken down into three basic categories:

1. Reduction in force — layoffs, restructuring, furloughs
2. Closing/Bankruptcy
3. Firing — with and without cause

In the following chapters, we will examine each of these types of unemployment, defining them in legal and practical terms and explaining how each is affected by federal and state laws.

CASE STUDY: MARY ELIZABETH BRADFORD

President, The Career Artisan
Web site: **www.maryelizabethbradford.com**

As a career marketer, coach, and consultant, I am sometimes asked about the benefits of recruiting firms. Recruiting firms are typically independent agents who are hired by companies to find qualified candidates who match their needs for particular positions. A recruiter's job involves scouting for talent or persons who are qualified, scheduling interviews for the company, and helping to negotiate a job offer. A recruiter may also be responsible for checking references and background checks. Through all these changes and challenges, I have learned that no one is indispensable. Keep improving your skills. Keep learning and growing. Keep making contacts and building relationships in the community, even if you feel secure in your job. You never know when you will need to draw upon your resources.

What can a recruiter do for you? Recruiters are paid by clients who want to find that person who exactly fits their requirements. If you are looking to build on your previous industry experience, you have a solid job history, quantifiable achievements, and a good academic background — you may be a very attractive prospect to a recruiter. Recruiters can and do work with candidates who have been laid off or fired, although they will need to thoroughly understand the conditions that led to your situation.

CASE STUDY: SELMER PETERSON

Owner, Thoughts Forward Inc.

E-mail: selmer@thoughtsforward.com

Web site: **www.thoughtsforward.com**

Would you believe I was laid off after nearly 40 years with the same company? That is what happened to me in 2005; I was an upper-level manager in the information services department.

You may be surprised to learn that I did not have any negative feelings about this. I looked at it as an opportunity for positive change from the moment that I walked out of the building shortly after learning that my position had been eliminated. I have a strong faith in God, and I had watched scores of others go through the same ordeal and had observed that the vast majority ended up better after the transition. I had confidence that this would work out well for me, too.

The excitement was in waiting to see how it transpired. Probably the biggest concern that anyone has when going through this experience is telling your spouse. In my case, I came home and left the car in front of the garage instead of parking it in the garage. My wife came home an hour later, saw the car, and came into the house. Her first comment was, "So you got fired. There are several bags of water softener salt in the car. Would you bring them in?" In other words, she took it very well.

The second thing that we did was take a vacation to visit my family in Northern Minnesota for about a week to get into a different environment and have time to reflect. Prior to going on vacation, I had sent a couple of e-mails. The first e-mail was sent to my former employees. I had been in the habit of sending them a "thought for the day" message, so I took the opportunity to send one last e-mail to ensure they knew I cared for them and was proud to have worked with them. I have continued contact with my former colleagues. I also e-mailed those who had let me go. I let them know I realized how difficult it was for them and that I did not have hard feelings.

A very good thing that my previous employer does for displaced employees is to purchase them time with a firm to help displaced employees regroup and plan for the future. I found this very helpful because I had never had to develop a real résumé or actually interview for a job. They provided me the skills that I needed to enter this new world with confidence.

Probably the best thing I was able to do was maintain a sense of humor about the whole thing. For example, one of my managers at the old firm contacted me several weeks after the restructuring to let me know that if the company posted my former position, he would like to apply for it.

CASE STUDY: SELMER PETERSON

I was able to inform him that they had already posted the position, and that he should apply for it immediately. He called back an hour later and asked if I would be a reference for him to apply for my former position, which I gladly did.

Because we had saved money through the years and I received a generous severance package, I did not have to replace my income immediately. Eventually, I started my own business, Thoughts Forward Inc., to do business as an independent information technology consultant, doing work similar to what I had done as an employee. We also became involved with real estate investment in a small way and now own several properties. Best of all, I now work fewer hours, earn more, and can contribute more to charitable causes.

Through this experience, I have learned things that I would consider changing if I were still employed. First, we were frequently advised to pay off the mortgage so that we would have equity in the home and no monthly house payments. I would strongly consider keeping the home mortgaged to the hilt and investing any built-up equity into a rainy day fund. I would do this because the day you receive notice of employment termination is likely to also be the day you no longer qualify for a loan of any kind.

Second, I would consider carrying my own health insurance instead of the employer's policy. Again, once you are terminated, your monthly insurance premiums rise significantly, and you have a finite window to find new insurance. Any number of health issues can make a person or family uninsurable, so the safe thing to do is to have your own insurance that you have already qualified for. We were fortunate in that we were able to get insurance, and we were able to get a mortgage when we needed it.

If you are facing unemployment, I hope these tips will help you:

- Keep a positive attitude. It is a lot more fun that way, and it also helps you to be successful in your transition.
- Establish a network of associates. They can be very encouraging. I learned that the "Club of Former Employees" was alive and well. By this, I mean that anyone who had previously worked at my former company was extremely eager to assist and encourage me as I transitioned.
- I started an e-mail newsletter so I could share current events with the network. I received many positive comments from it. My only regret is that I have not kept it going.

CHAPTER 3

Reduction in Force (RIF)

Layoffs, furloughs, and cutbacks are terms used to describe a company's reduction in force. If your job is affected by a company's reduction in force, you have certain rights and benefits available to you through the company itself, as well as through federal and state resources. Temporary layoffs, often referred to as furloughs, are discussed in this chapter as well. Many companies, such as auto manufacturers, are turning to furloughs as a way to reduce costs but keep employees from being laid off permanently.

Reduction in Force

Reduction in force, or RIF as it is commonly known, is the formal term used to mean that a company's workforce will be cut and employees will be laid off. Other terms used to describe this situation include downsizing and corporate restructuring. No matter the term or phrase used, the result is that a number of jobs will be eliminated to save the company money or because of changes in business conditions. RIFs are common in a challenging economic environment. When an employer is faced with a tightening budget, payroll is often seen as a viable area to cut. It is legal when it is conducted in a proper manner.

The method for reducing employees may be spelled out in union or employment contracts, or in company policies outlined in employee handbooks. Sometimes, the last person hired is the first to be released. But if an employer is handpicking those to layoff, laws related to discrimination and civil service will apply. They state how a reduction in force must be handled. If a company does not consider these factors when deciding who will lose jobs, it leaves itself open for lawsuits.

Layoff/Restructuring

Layoffs occur when a company informs its employees that their jobs have been eliminated. Layoffs often involve a number of employees but can also apply to one or two people whose positions are targeted for elimination. A mass layoff is usually the result of financial difficulties within the company.

A restructuring involves reorganization of the company and its positions. Restructuring can occur when a company is bought by or is merged with another company, and duplicated positions need to be eliminated. A company might also restructure to try to be more efficient and eliminate positions that are considered overhead and not contributing directly to the profits of the business. Administrative and middle management positions are often cut during a restructuring, but other positions may also be eliminated in order to streamline business operations and reduce expenses.

Temporary Layoffs/Furloughs

To reduce costs but forestall the need for mass, permanent layoffs, many companies are choosing to place their employees on temporary furloughs. An employee on a temporary layoff or furlough is not paid for the period of time he or she is not working. Furloughs tend to be for a set period of time, such as a week or month, after which employees are called back to their jobs and start receiving regular paychecks again.

Furloughs are common among some major manufacturers that extend their planned shutdowns, causing temporary layoffs. During Christmas 2008, most of the major automobile companies in America — already facing serious financial challenges — extended their planned holiday shut-down, beginning it several weeks prior to the original annual schedule. Their employees were furloughed and not paid for those extra weeks but were able to return to their regular jobs when the plant reopened. During their extended unpaid time off, they were considered unemployed.

Your Rights and Resources

If you are laid off or "RIF'ed" as part of a reduction in force or larger layoff, you should qualify for unemployment insurance payments. Check with your local employment security commission office or unemployment insurance office to determine your level of eligibility.

Temporary Furlough

If you are on a temporary furlough, you may qualify for unemployment insurance payments for that period. Although there usually is a one-week waiting period for payments, special considerations are sometimes made for temporarily furloughed employees who may only be unemployed for a few weeks. As in the case of the automobile company that enforced an extended temporary layoff, an exception was made regarding the waiting period. No matter what your circumstances are, always research your rights.

Permanent Layoff

If you have been laid off permanently, you should also be able to continue your health insurance coverage through COBRA. Check rates carefully for COBRA coverage. When your employer is no longer paying its share of the health insurance premiums, your share will increase significantly. Your employer-paid health insurance should continue either through the end of the month that you are laid off or through the end of the following month, depending on how your payroll deduction system works. Consult your human resources department for the exact dates your coverage will end without COBRA continuation.

Your Employer's Obligations

Your employer has certain obligations to which they must adhere when they are considering reducing their workforce. Your employer's specific obligations depend on a number of specific circumstances. When a company downsizes, undergoes a corporate restructuring, or implements a reduction in force, the Worker Adjustment and Retraining Notification Act may apply. The requirements for the act must be met for workers to receive advance notice and other benefits. If the company does not meet the requirements regarding the number of employees and hours worked by each, though, the 60-day notification period is not required.

If the company is laying off part of its workforce, it cannot choose whom to lay off based on certain factors, including age. The federal Older Workers Benefits Protection Act can help those over the age of 40 during a reduction in force. If the company is trying to cut costs, it may consider releasing workers with the highest pay and, often, these are the most long-term and older employees. The Older Workers Benefits Protection Act bans firing workers solely because of their age. If the company is simply laying off the highest-paid employees due to budgetary reasons, for example, and can show it is not discriminating based on age, then the Protection Act does not apply.

If you have invested through your employer in a retirement benefit account, such as a 401(k) or pension plan, you are protected by the Employee Retirement Income Security Act (ERISA) of 1974. Essentially, ERISA states that the funds you invest in retirement plans through your employer will still be available to you if you are laid off or even if the company closes. ERISA does not require your employer to pay out your retirement benefits in one lump sum. In fact, if you do receive the retirement benefits as one payment before you reach the minimum age required for retirement fund distribution (usually 59 ½), there could be significant tax liabilities for you.

Your employer should provide you with a summary plan description as well as an individual benefit statement that shows your benefits, how they are calculated, and the specific value of your retirement benefits, including how much you have earned in the retirement account.

CASE STUDY: CHERYL SMITHEN

Strategic Marketing and Public Relations Consultant
E-mail: cheryl@charlestonpr.com
Web site: **www.charlestonpr.com**

I have been laid off twice since 2001. Each time, changes in company strategy or economic conditions were the reason. In each case, I have realized that there is something better or something that will take me to the next level just waiting to be found. It is up to me to find it. When this happened in 2001, it was a career first — and a huge shock.

The second layoff was a bit frightening because I had relocated for the job and I had not received any money from the sale of my old home because it was still unsold. But I did see the writing on the wall, so it was not a complete surprise. I focused on staying positive, not talking about it with any negativity. I tried to recognize that a business owner has to do what is best for the business, not necessarily what is best for me. I have to do what is best for me. I make sure (now and then) to exercise, stay positive, use my faith, and use my brain. I take every opportunity to read and learn about the newest trends and techniques in my industry. In a way, this time is like being in an incubator. I am growing and learning and getting ready for the next opportunity.

By surviving these periods of unemployment, I now know that I can make things happen. The experience reinforced my belief in personal responsibility as one of the most important character traits. I also learned that you can be working in a job and believe you love it — and actually be suffering from terrible stress, as I was at one point. There is no one to blame when you are laid off. This is a free market economy, for the most part, and good things happen to people who take personal responsibility and get out there to make connections and find opportunities. I also learned to never stop learning. Take the time off as an opportunity to learn more and develop more so that you are more valuable.

I believe that we all should expect at least one job termination during our working lives. Save money and maintain a financial cushion so that you can have something to fall back on during your time out of the work force. Use your connections to find temporary or freelance work. Be creative. Stay focused. Maintain the discipline of work. For example, I get up, dress, go to my computer every morning, and work a regular work schedule. If I do not have freelance work to complete, I focus on reading and learning new activities or gaining business intelligence that might lead to new clients/jobs. Surround yourself with positive people, and avoid negativity.

CASE STUDY: TERRI ZWIERZYNSKI, MBA, OWNER

Solo-Entrepreneur.com Inc.

Web site: **www.Solo-E.com**

Along with thousands of others, I fell victim to the dot-com bust in the early 2000s. I was laid off after six years as an internal management consultant.

I knew in advance I was going to be laid off, so I figured the emotional stuff was all over. But it turned out to be a huge adjustment. I was diagnosed with depression and got medication and treatment shortly thereafter. Otherwise, to cope, I used humor; I still tell people today that I "graduated" from the old firm. Layoffs had been going on for five months by the time I was let go, and I knew I was in danger. My husband and I looked at all our expenses and income and considered our options. We used my unemployment compensation and our cash savings to help replace my income; eventually, we sold some of our stocks to invest in the solo business owner resource business I later started.

My support group was the others I had worked with who had also been let go. We went to lunch monthly for a while. I also had a close friend who got laid off a few months after I did. The biggest factor in moving on was making the decision to start my own business and finding help to do that.

It seems that just about everyone gets laid off at least once in their lifetime. The whole notion of staying at one company for a long time is dead. And it is not like it was when my parents were working; being laid off no longer has the stigma that it once did. In fact, for me, being laid off was a great thing. I had been talking about starting my own business, but the chances that I would really quit a good job to start a new business with a 6-year-old and a 3-year-old were slim. Getting laid off pushed me to really get started.

CHAPTER 4
Closing/Bankruptcy

When a company shuts its doors, it may not have the financial abilities or the legal obligations — depending on the type of bankruptcy involved — to provide employees with additional pay or benefits. However, there are federal and state regulations and funding sources that provide displaced workers with benefits when their employer shuts down operations completely. Specific rights, obligations, and resources available to an employee affected by a business closing or bankruptcy are discussed in this chapter.

Business Closing/Bankruptcy

When a business closes completely, all its employees are laid off. The company may have chosen to go out of business, to cease operations totally, to move to a distant location in another state or another country, or may have been forced to close for financial reasons.

Corporate bankruptcy generally takes one of two forms: reorganization under what is known as Chapter 11, or complete liquidation under Chapter 7.

The "chapters" refer to chapters in the Bankruptcy Code. If your company files for Chapter 11 bankruptcy, it usually intends to continue operations under the court's protection. The company will reorganize its structure and financial situation to attempt to run business operations more efficiently. However, reorganization generally involves layoffs, as the company tries to eliminate expenses and save money.

If your company has filed for Chapter 7 bankruptcy, it will no longer operate as a business and will have to lay off all employees. If you have been laid off from a company that has declared Chapter 7 bankruptcy, you should check with your benefits administrator or human resource representative to determine what effect the liquidation will have on your benefits.

Your Rights and Resources

Just as with the other types of layoffs discussed in this book, if you lose your job because of a business closing, you should qualify for unemployment insurance payments. You will have to register with the local unemployment insurance office or employment security commission.

If you have invested money in a retirement account through your employers, this investment will be safe and transferable in the case of a business closing. Instead of withdrawing your money from your retirement account, roll it over into another retirement account, such as a 401(k), to avoid having to pay taxes on the retirement benefits. However, unless the business decides to provide you with your retirement benefits in a lump sum, you should be able to leave it in the original account. Retirement accounts are not often maintained by the business itself but rather through a financial institution, such as a bank or investment firm. If you do not have a 401(k) or other retirement account, but you do participate in a traditional pension plan, also known as a "defined benefit plan," your money is protected through the Pension Benefit Guaranty Corporation, a federal corporation.

You will be able to continue health insurance coverage through COBRA; however, COBRA payments tend to be much higher than your payroll contribution was for health insurance. The COBRA premiums include the amount the employer was paying as well as your contribution. For families, the premium can be quite high and often unaffordable when your only income is unemployment insurance. You may qualify for state medical benefits through programs such as Medicaid — depending on your income level — once you begin receiving unemployment benefits.

Your Employer's Obligations

The WARN Act states that a company that meets the requirements for workforce size of at least 100 workers that is laying off at least 50 of those workers has to give employees 60 days' notice. In the case of a company of more than 100 employees closing its doors completely, or going bankrupt, it is also required under the WARN Act to provide 60 days' notice to all of its employees that it is going out of business.

In addition to providing unemployment insurance benefit payments to workers who have been laid off, the following states offer assistance and severance programs in the event of a plant's closing:

Alabama
Alabama offers an educational and financial assistance program for laid-off workers with debts.

Alaska
Alaska offers employment and training programs to those who may be unemployed within six months.

Colorado
Colorado provides customized job re-training.

Connecticut
Connecticut requires employers to pay for existing group health insurance for terminated workers and their dependents for 120 days or until workers become eligible for other coverage.

District of Columbia
The District of Columbia requires providers that take over service contracts to hire the workers used by the previous provider.

Florida
The Workforce Florida program offers counseling, training, and placement to terminated workers in the business community. State agencies must give hiring preferences to those in the commercial saltwater fishing industry who are displaced due to certain changes in law.

Georgia
There are no laws pertaining to plant closings; however, the labor department's statewide career centers offer assistance, office equipment, and workshops.

Hawaii
Employers must supplement unemployment compensation to equal the former wage for four weeks. The state offers training for displaced workers.

Louisiana
Those who lose jobs because of technological changes or avoidance of state environmental laws are provided with services through the Displaced Worker Retraining Program.

Maine

Employers must give one week's severance pay for each year of employment for those who worked three or more years.

Maryland

When more than 25 workers are laid off, on-site unemployment insurance filing, re-training, and job placement services will be provided.

Massachusetts

When a company that employs 50 or more workers is sold, the new owner must give two weeks' severance pay for each year worked for workers who were employed for at least three years. The Department of Workforce Development offers reemployment assistance programs. Those who have worked for a company for at least one year may receive up to 13 weeks of reemployment assistance benefits.

New York

State assistance is available to facilitate continued operation of the plant as an employee-owned enterprise.

Ohio

State assistance is available to facilitate continued operation of the plant as an employee-owned enterprise.

Oregon

Professional technical training is offered to displaced workers.

Pennsylvania

Workers are eligible for customized job training and living assistance while in the program.

Rhode Island

Employees may continue health insurance at group rates for at least 18 months.

Texas

Funding is available to communities, programs, and businesses that assist or hire laid-off defense workers.

Utah

Laid-off defense workers are eligible for retraining benefits.

Washington

Laid-off workers in the aerospace, thermal electric generation, and forest products industries may receive training and counseling.

Wyoming

Occupational transfer and retraining programs are available.

CASE STUDY: CAROL HOENIG

Owner, Carol Hoenig Publishing Consultant Inc.
Web site: **www.carolhoenig.com**

I was laid off from my job as an event planner when the chain bookstore for which I worked downsized its marketing department. For the first 30 minutes, I had a meltdown, since I had recently bought my first house as a newly divorced woman on my own. I could not imagine how I was going to manage.

After the initial meltdown, I took advantage of the timing. My novel, *Without Grace*, had just received a glowing review on the very morning of the day my job was eliminated. Due to the unsettling climate of the store, I had been tempted to quit and try to go out on my own, but was afraid of failure. Within hours of being let go, I decided to test the waters to see if I could secure some work as a freelancer, and by that afternoon, I had managed to do so. I also decided to take the time to promote my book and go on a tour along the Eastern seaboard. I was soon making more money than I had been making when working for someone else.

Eventually, I incorporated and am doing so well, I may hire an assistant. My business combines different aspects in the publishing industry, such as writing, consulting, editing, and publicity. Now I set my own hours and do what I love. Being pushed out of my comfort zone definitely brought a change for the better.

CASE STUDY: SAMANTHA SILVUVITCH

Marketing and public relations professional

Due to poor business conditions, I was laid off from my Director of Marketing job. I found it hard not to take it personally. The owner of the company was a lifelong friend, and I found the way that I was discharged to be particularly hurtful, although I had a sense that a layoff was eminent. But I had already begun to think about going out on my own and  was beginning another business. So I suppose the timing was not so bad; I had already made some financial and lifestyle adjustments.

Having said all that, I must emphasize that getting laid off is not easy. For me, there was a feeling of a loss of self because so much of what and how I think of myself has been tied to my work. Loss of the work, loss of contact with co-workers, and so on can be a discouraging experience. When it happens, I believe the best thing to do is surround yourself with supportive friends and family, and seek help if you do not have a strong support network. It takes a bit of time to recover. But, when you do, you can move forward to something new, and, who knows, maybe more exciting or fulfilling.

I did draw unemployment for the allotted time period. I remember going to the required orientation and thinking, "Am I the kind of person who would take unemployment?" It was an emotionally difficult decision, but an easier decision from a financial point of view. I felt the unemployment payments would carry me over until I had either found another job or my second business would begin to contribute some income. So, I swallowed my pride and signed on the line to get my unemployment check.

If you are working for friends and/or family, remember business is business; friendships and family are more important and should be carefully considered. I wish that I would have been able to get in touch with my feelings more quickly. If I had, maybe I would not have lost a friendship as well as a job.

CHAPTER 5
Firing

If you are fired from a job, you may have rights in regard to challenging the dismissal, even though you may not be entitled to certain benefits, such as unemployment compensation. The rules for determining whether a firing is legal are determined by each state, although there are certain established federal laws concerning terminations. If you believe you were fired due to illegal discrimination, you have legal recourse for challenging the decision and may even have the right to pursue a judgment against the company.

In general, all states are considered to fall under the "employment at-will" regulation, which gives employers much more leeway in dismissing an employee, with or without cause. However, there are many exceptions to the employment at-will rule. Montana is the only state that adheres to an employment at-will policy only during an employee's probationary period. Other states adhere to the policy throughout the probationary and full employment period, but recognize exceptions to the employment at-will rule, such as discrimination as defined under federal law, agreements made under an employee contract, and an implied agreement called the Covenant of Good Faith and Fair Dealing, recognized by 11 states.

This chapter will examine your rights and your employer's obligations if you are fired.

Firing

If you have been singled out to be dismissed, with or without cause, you are being fired. Being fired is different from being laid off or furloughed in that there is usually a direct connection between you, your job, and your dismissal. Reasons for your dismissal might be job performance or conduct. There is always the possibility that your dismissal is not for any particular reason at all, which is often legal within certain parameters. Or you may be fired illegally as a result of discrimination or employer misconduct.

Firing with Cause

Firing with cause means that some action on the part of the employee led to the termination. If you have broken a company rule or "misbehaved" in some way, you may be fired with cause, or fired for a good reason. Some examples are:

- Lying on the job application
- Leaving the job site without permission
- Interfering with the workflow by participating in a work slowdown or stoppage
- Misuse of company equipment, such as phones or supplies
- Doing personal chores during the workday, such as making personal phone calls
- Drinking alcohol or taking illegal drugs at work
- Committing a crime, such as stealing on the job or threatening others
- Harassing others
- Discriminating against others

Sometimes a person is fired with cause for problems directly related to work. This may mean:

- Not meeting the standards of the job, such as not reaching the production goal
- Too many absences
- Not following directions or orders, or insubordination

Firing without Cause

If your employment classification is what is known as employment at-will, this means you can be dismissed at any time, for any reason. Unless company policy, your contract, federal law, or state regulations require it, your employer does not have to give a good reason for your dismissal. Within certain parameters, employers can let a person go for any random reason. Most workers can be terminated without a good reason and without being given advance notice. However, there are many exceptions to the employment at-will rules. If you are employed in a state that recognizes those exceptions, or if the employer breaks a federal law, you may have been wrongfully discharged.

Wrongful Discharge

Some types of terminations are against the law and are called wrongful discharges. Examples of wrongful discharge include:

- Breaking an employment contract, or firing someone who has a legal contract spelling out terms of employment.
- Breaking a union contract.
- Firing a whistleblower, or someone who has reported serious violations of the law at the company that present a danger.
- Letting someone go because of her personal or political activities outside of work hours.

- Firing someone who refuses to break a law or public policy when asked to by the employer. This may include refusing to commit a criminal act, but it also may involve a role of civic or public duty. For example, it is against the law to fire someone because that worker had jury duty. The public policy term can mean legal rights, too. For example, it is illegal to fire someone because he or she filed a workers' compensation claim.

- Illegal discrimination.

Illegal Discrimination

It is illegal to fire a person because he is part of a protected group. For example, the Federal Age Discrimination in Employment Act prohibits discrimination against workers aged 40 to 64. This means you cannot be fired just because you fall in that age group; that age group is a protected group. You can be fired for other reasons, but not simply because of your age. If your boss says she is letting you go because "50-year-olds cannot do this kind of work," she has discriminated against you on the basis of age. Other federal anti-discrimination laws include:

- The Older Workers Benefit Protection Act: An employee's age cannot be used as the reason for discrimination in benefits; older workers cannot be singled out during a staff reduction process.

- The Americans with Disabilities Act: A person who is qualified for a job and uses a wheelchair cannot be fired because she is disabled.

- The Rehabilitation Act (Sections 501 and 505): Prohibits discrimination against disabled persons who work for the federal government.

- The Civil Rights Act: Bans discriminating against workers because of their race, color, religion, gender, or national origin (sexual harassment and pregnancy discrimination are banned as gender discrimination).

- The Civil Service Reform Act: Prevents discrimination.

- Genetic Information Nondiscrimination Act: This is the most recent addition to forms of prohibited discrimination, which became law in May 2008. The act bans health insurance companies from using genetic information to set premiums or determine enrollment eligibility. Employers cannot use genetic information in hiring, firing, or promotion decisions.

Your Rights

You may be able to collect unemployment insurance payments even if you have been fired. The key phrase for determining whether you will be eligible for unemployment insurance is that you have experienced a job loss through no fault of your own. If you were fired for a specific reason that is directly related to your performance, you will probably not qualify for unemployment insurance payments. When you complete the application for unemployment benefits, you will be asked how you lost your job. Generally, there will be an opportunity to offer an explanation if the reason is anything other than a layoff or business closing. Regardless of the reason for your job loss, you should apply for unemployment benefits. They may deny your request, but you will not know until you try.

You may also have the right to challenge your termination or even file a lawsuit against your employer. More details regarding your rights and the steps you may need to take if you feel you have been discharged illegally are provided in Chapter 6.

Your Employer's Obligations

In most situations, your employer has an obligation to follow a process of documenting your work habits and performance. You should be allowed the opportunity to review any write-ups or performance appraisals and possibly even receive counseling on your performance prior to being fired for a particular reason. If you feel you have not received the proper treatment and have been fired unjustly or even illegally, you may have options for recourse. The following chapter provides guidance as to what to do if you feel you have been fired illegally.

An Employer's Obligations in a Termination with Cause

Most companies have written policies on discipline and termination for misconduct. When a boss identifies a problem with an employee's work performance or conduct, reputable firms will follow the discipline policy to the letter. Implementing this practice protects the company from being sued for not following its own rules.

A discipline policy might include:

- A verbal warning when the problem first occurs (for example, telling you to get to work on time in the future); in some cases, multiple verbal warnings may be given
- Written warning or warnings if the problem continues or if the offense is serious
- Suspension or firing if the situation is not corrected

These steps should be documented in the worker's personnel file. Workers should be asked to sign a statement that they received a written warning. This process lets the worker know there is a problem that threatens his job. It also provides a paper trail of evidence demonstrating that the boss has addressed the situation a number of times and has tried to work with the employee. The documentation helps an employer prove that there is a reason to fire an employee because efforts to correct the situation have not been successful.

Most employers will tell you the reason you are being fired and back it up with the documentation mentioned previously. If you sue the company, they have evidence that it was a fair and legal dismissal because of the problems and attempted solutions. If the employer does not provide you with a written statement explaining why you were fired, try to get one. Having the employer's statement of the cause will help if you decide to fight the termination.

Some states have laws requiring employers to provide terminated workers with service letters. Service letters are written statements providing certain details of employment, which may include the reason for termination. Each state outlines what information may be disclosed, who can receive the information, and other requirements; it differs from state to state. If your state has no service letter law, check with your state's department of labor to determine whether other regulations exist that can help you obtain a statement.

If you cannot get a written explanation in the ways outlined previously, you can send your former employer a letter of understanding. State the facts as you understand them, and ask that you be sent a letter correcting any misinformation by a certain date.

Sample Letter of Understanding:

May 2, 2008

Ms. Former Boss
XYZ Corp.
123 Main St.
Anywhere, Any State 00000

Dear Ms. Boss:

I am writing to clarify the reasons for my termination on May 1, 2008. It is my understanding that I was terminated due to the relocation of Plant #1.

If this is not correct, please notify me in writing by May 15, 2008.

Best regards,
Joe Employee
456 Pine St.
Anywhere, Any State 00000

A letter of understanding will provide the documentation you may need to pursue legal action, to prove to future employers that you were let go through no fault of your own, or to qualify for benefits such as fee waivers for retraining courses at community colleges.

An Employer's Obligations in a Termination Without Cause

If you are fired without cause, the employer is not saying you did anything wrong or failed to perform the job satisfactorily. He or she is ending your employment at-will for any number of reasons that do not reflect on you.

It may be a layoff situation or a change in the business plan. Your employment may be ended at any time, for any reason under the employment at-will model. If you are in an employment at-will situation, it is legal for your employer to let you go without a good reason, with the exception of a case where you are being discriminated against. An employer's obligations for discharged workers not in an employment at-will situation, as well as examples of illegal discharge, are discussed in the next chapter.

Your employer may choose to reveal the reason behind your job loss or may simply indicate that the company can no longer employ you. Many bosses will explain the reasons to you to help protect the company against your challenging the termination. It is beneficial to have a written statement for your records; if you do fight the discharge, it is essential documentation.

CASE STUDY: RUTH JONES

Family law attorney

Yes, I am an attorney, but I am not writing about employment law. You see, I was fired myself.

In 2002, I was let go from a non-profit law firm. I was very upset and hurt at the time, but considering the organization and discussing the situation with co-workers helped me realize it was not completely personal. I was told the reason for the discharge was that some other employees who questioned some of my decisions did not think of me as a "go-getter." I found that the organization itself was in transition and also realized some personality conflicts contributed to the situation.

As the firm was undergoing challenges, other attorneys and clerks were let go or departed voluntarily at the same time that I lost my job. One attorney later became a judge, so obviously, she was a competent attorney. That helped me realize a lot of the problem was with the organization. In addition, I had a personality conflict with one of the attorneys who had issue with my performance. For example, she had worked there before, and shortly after her re-hire, she began to go through my cases to see whether there was anything she should be working on.

CASE STUDY: RUTH JONES

While my discharge was not illegal, I felt it could have been handled better. I could have been given a chance to improve. The other employees who had issues with me could have discussed the situation with me before approaching the manager of the organization. After I was dismissed, I contacted the manager and asked that the firing be put on the books as a voluntary separation, and  he agreed. I contacted the other attorneys in the unit I had been part of and asked them to use professionalism and not disparage me among other area attorneys in our field of law. They agreed to act accordingly and, though I still felt wronged, it helped to have this assurance from them.

Looking back on the situation, I realize that I should not have taken for granted that everything was going well. I should have stayed on top of the pulse of the place and considered my feelings toward the job and other people's feelings and attitudes about me.

On the bright side, I had done some independent legal work prior to taking this job, so I was able to generate some business on my own. I continued to work on my own for a few years until I found a position in a firm with which I was more compatible.

Of course, it is best to avoid the termination in the first place. If you begin to feel out of sync with other employees or supervisors, address the issues right away. Address personality differences and conflicts, perhaps suggesting ways each employee's strengths could be used. Keep your supervisor in the loop, even if the nature of your work is independent. If there are conflicts, keep brief notes about them in case the subject comes up later. If you do get fired, be gracious and calm. It may help to write out your feelings before you talk to anyone at the place of employment. Most people have suffered a similar loss at some point, and it probably will not cost you your career. I now see that my termination was a good thing because it brought me to my current job.

CHAPTER 6

Have You Been Fired Illegally?

When you have been fired, your first reaction may be that your employer is wrong to let you go. You may not agree that there was a justifiable reason for the firing, and you are understandably upset and probably uncertain about your future. "How could he fire me? I have kept this department running for years. He will be sorry." Those thoughts quickly lead to the idea of challenging the termination. It is so unfair that it must be illegal, you may assume.

Before deciding that you have been illegally terminated, it is wise to let the emotions of the moment settle so you can focus on the facts. Let the reality of the situation — and the law — guide your decision as to whether you have grounds to challenge your termination, rather than the raw emotions you feel in the moment that you are discharged. You may think the reason you were given for being discharged, if there was one, was not the true reason you lost your job. Maybe the proper procedures established by your employer were not followed. Examine the situation closely and objectively before deciding whether your employer was truly wrong in firing you. Here are some points to consider when determining whether the termination was legal.

Can You Sue Your Former Employer?

How do you know whether you have a case for suing your former employer? First, your situation must fall into one of the categories covered under the law. If an employment contract was broken, or if you believe you were fired based on a protected trait, you may have a case. Second, you must have facts to prove your termination was unjust. If your employer said you were fired for one reason, but you believe it was because you are more than 40 years old, you must have evidence to support that grievance. The types of evidence that might be needed include: employment records; statements of disciplinary action, such as written warnings; and your notes concerning the employer's actions while you were employed, among others.

The following types of employment are the main exceptions to the employment at-will regulations.

Employees Under Contract

If you had an employment contract, review it carefully. What does it say about termination? If it says you cannot be fired for any reason, you may have been discharged improperly. If it says that a discipline process must be followed before firing, was it followed and documented? Does the contract say that a certain amount of notice must be given? Many employee contracts will provide details of a progressive discipline policy that must be followed before termination. Under such terms, the employer will be required to conduct reviews and evaluations, and perhaps even a series of warnings or lesser disciplinary actions, before firing an employee. If any of the conditions of the contract were not followed, you may have reason to believe that you were discharged improperly.

Union Workers

If you were a union worker, your dismissal must follow the terms agreed to by the employer and the union. Study the union handbook, or talk with a union official to determine whether the correct procedure was followed. The collective bargaining agreements of most unions say that members can only be discharged for cause. A progressive discipline program must be followed. This means a series of warnings and opportunities to improve must be given.

Union members may challenge, or "grieve," a firing or disciplinary action. Speak with a union official about the grievance process. Review your union agreement for the terms of employment and discharge. Often, there is a limited time period in which the grievance must be filed, so do not put this process off. The grievance will be reviewed and may be settled by an arbiter — a neutral person who is knowledgeable in employment law. If the case is decided in your favor, your job may be reinstated, and you may be given back pay for the time you were out of work.

Government Workers

Employment at-will rules do not apply to government workers. A government employee is considered to have a property interest in his job and so is protected by the 5th and 14th amendments, which prohibit any government entity from depriving individuals of "life, liberty, or property." Government employees can only be terminated for cause, after a disciplinary program has been followed. The disciplinary process may include a series of verbal and written warnings and/or suspensions. You should become familiar with the employee handbook and established personnel policies to determine whether the proper procedures were followed.

Whistleblowers

The Department of Labor (DOL) has spelled out the protections afforded whistleblowers in the workplace in "Whistleblower Protection Provisions Enforced by OSHA," a chapter in the DOL's *Employment Law Guide.* The guide details who is covered under the protection, the basic provisions, and requirements of whistleblower protection, employee rights, and compliance assistance available.

Workers who report practices on the job that are illegal or harmful to the public cannot be fired for that reason. For example, if you think you were let go because you alerted the Occupational Safety and Health Act (OSHA) agency about a violation at your job or because you told police that your boss was stealing payments made to the company in cash, you may have reason to believe you were discharged illegally. Some states protect workers who report any violation of the law. Others limit protection to those who question only certain practices; only labor laws or environmental regulations might be included.

If you believe you have been discriminated against or that your employer has retaliated against you for reporting safety or health concerns, you may file a complaint with OSHA. For workers in the trucking industry, the Surface Transportation Assistance Act (STAA) gives you the right to file complaints with OSHA if you believe that your employer has discriminated against you for reporting safety concerns or for refusing to drive under dangerous circumstances or in violation of safety rules. Employees in a number of other industries, including airline, pipeline, public education, and securities, also have the right to file complaints with OSHA if they feel they have been discriminated against or retaliated against for reporting violations.

Information concerning additional anti-retaliation statutes is available in the DOL's Employment Law Guide, describing the statutes enforced by different department agencies, such as the Wage and Hour Division of the Employment Standards Administration, the Employee Benefits Security Administration, and the Mine Safety and Health Administration.

Basic Provisions/Requirements

According to the DOL, the employee protection provisions listed above generally prohibit an "employer" or any "person" (the definition of which may vary from statute to statute) from discharging or otherwise discriminating against any employee with respect to the employee's compensation, terms, conditions, or privileges of employment because the employee engaged in specified "protected" activities. Protected activities are essentially those associated with reporting a violation or participating in the investigation or proceedings related to enforcing these statutes.

The Energy Reorganization Act of 1974 (ERA), the Wendell H. Ford Aviation Investment and Reform Act (AIR21), the Sarbanes-Oxley Act (SOA), and the Pipeline Safety Improvement Act (PSIA) specifically cover an employee's internal complaints to his or her employer, and employees who express safety or quality assurance concerns internally to their employers are protected under the other whistleblower statutes.

Employee Rights

An employee who believes that he or she has been discriminated against in violation of any of the statutes listed above may file a complaint with OSHA. Complaints must be filed:

- Within 30 days after the occurrence of the alleged violation under the OSH Act, the Clean Air Act (CAA), the Comprehensive Environmental Response, Compensation, and Liability Act (CERCLA), the Solid Waste Disposal Act (SWDA), the Federal Water Pollution Control Act (FWPCA), the Safe Drinking Water Act (SDWA), and the Toxic Substance Control Act (TSCA)
- Within 60 days under the International Safety Container Act (ISCA)
- Within 90 days under the AIR21, the SOA, and the Asbestos Hazard Emergency Response Act (AHERA)
- Within 180 days under the STAA, the ERA, and the PSIA

Investigations/Penalties/Sanctions

The process of investigating a complaint of discrimination or retaliation begins when OSHA receives your complaint. Then OSHA notifies the employer and, if conciliation fails, conducts an investigation. Where OSHA finds that complaints filed under the OSH Act, the AHERA, and the ISCA have merit, they are referred to the Solicitor's Office for legal action. Complaints under these three statutes found not to have merit will be dismissed.

Where OSHA finds a violation after investigating complaints under the other statutes listed above, it will issue a determination letter requiring the employer to pay back wages, reinstate the employee, reimburse the employee for attorneys' and expert witness fees, and take other steps to provide necessary relief. Complaints found not to have merit will be dismissed.

Use caution when filing complaints. Be sure you have a good case to present to OSHA. If you are found to have filed a frivolous complaint or one filed in bad faith, you may be liable for attorneys' fees up to $1,000.

Compliance Assistance Available

More detailed information, including copies of regulatory and interpretative materials, may be obtained from the nearest OSHA office. A list of district offices is provided in Appendix C. Additional compliance assistance information is available from the OSHA Web site, **www.osha.gov**, or by contacting OSHA's help line at 1-800-321-OSHA (1-800-321-6742).

Public Policy

If you believe you were let go because of something related to public policy or civic duty, you were possibly illegally terminated. For example, if you were required to serve in the military as part of the reserves or when recalled into active duty, you cannot be terminated for fulfilling your civic duty. Likewise, if you have been called to jury duty, you cannot be fired for responding to the summons. Employees are also protected from being fired for refusing to participate in illegal activities, such as falsifying documents. And, under the public policy umbrella, a worker is protected against being fired for participating in outside activities, such as religious or political events.

After reading through this information and determining that you may have been terminated illegally, your next step will be to seek legal recourse. You may want to investigate filing a lawsuit against your former employer.

CASE STUDY: MARY GREENWOOD

Attorney and author

I have worked in human resources, the legal field, and have served as an arbiter, mediator, and union negotiator for more than 25 years. From those experiences, I have written two books, *How To Negotiate Like A Pro* and *How To Mediate Like A Pro*. I have worked with employers and people who have lost jobs.

Over the years, I have seen employers make their share of mistakes when terminating employees. I would say the biggest mistake in firing or laying off workers is taking action too quickly.

CASE STUDY: MARY GREENWOOD

Many times, I was called when action had already been taken and it was too late for me to give meaningful advice.

Lack of proper documentation would make a close second. Sometimes I would be told something vague, like, "Mr. A has a bad attitude," without the specifics to show that he violated a specific policy. Not following procedures is part of the lack of documentation. Employers must show that a policy was violated and, usually, that there was progressive discipline.

In a lay-off situation, an employer could build good will if he or she explained to the employees what was happening in a timely fashion and offered job counseling and tried to help the employees find other employment, either at the same locale or outsourcing. Employers know this is a bad time and want to be part of the solution. Telling employees to clear out their desks at the end of the day is totally unnecessary and just makes the employees angry.

Workers easily make mistakes surrounding termination, as well. The biggest mistake is probably getting angry when they first hear of the job loss and possibly saying something in anger that they might regret later. Employees must be levelheaded at a time when they are most likely scared, angry, and frustrated. If it is a layoff, an employee should try to buy some time or see if he/she can transfer to another area or even take a demotion. An employee has to rethink all the angles. Ask if the employer will provide training or outsourcing. See if something can be negotiated with the employer.

If a worker believes the termination was a wrongful discharge, file a union grievance if he/she is in a union. There are time limits, so it is important to file promptly. There may also be some type of grievance or appeal process for non-union members. My first advice is to tell someone to keep a diary of everything that has been said about the discharge. What was the employee told? What were previous incidents? When were the various meetings and who was present, with dates and times?

Someone considering a wrongful discharge lawsuit should remember that it can take a long time; be prepared to commit up to three years to the process. A suit can be expensive, especially if you lose. The process is likely to be emotionally draining.

Those who choose to take legal action should form a partnership with their lawyers to help them be successful. Keep diaries of everything concerning the discharge. Be totally truthful with the attorney so he/she does not get surprises from someone else's testimony. Be polite and respectful at any meetings or hearings, and dress professionally. Do not hesitate to ask your attorney to answer your questions and address your concerns; open communication makes a better working relationship.

CASE STUDY: EVA ROSENBERG, ENROLLED AGENT

Owner, TaxAnxiety Inc.

Web site: **www.TaxMama.com**

I dropped out of high school to start working for Services Unlimited, creating part-time job openings for students at the University of California at Los Angeles (UCLA) and the University of Southern California (USC). That was not a bad thing because I had already been accepted to UCLA with a California State Scholarship. I spent the first half of my life finding jobs for people, or for myself, just for the fun and variety of working with different companies. Somewhere along the way, the jobs turned into accounting and tax positions (perhaps after the B.A. in Accounting, and to support the costs of the M.B.A in International Business). So now, after a healthy career in taxation, I am teaching other tax professionals how to get licensed by the Internal Revenue Service and to build their own businesses or to find jobs in the tax industry.

My company also works with individuals and businesses on tax matters and financial planning. When a client loses a job, we know it and try to help. But too often, they do not let me know until they have been unemployed for weeks or months. But when they do tell me, I ensure that they file for unemployment benefits, or with the Labor Board, if applicable. Sometimes, the best option is to start a business, in which case we provide guidance and assistance to help get the business up and running.

My first suggestions for unemployed clients include ensuring that you have sufficient financial resources to cover your expenses for the next three months, so you are free to select a job you want, rather than to accept one due to your desperate straits. Start the unemployment filing process to generate some back-up revenue in case you do not get the job offer of your dreams in the first week. Since you do not want to deplete your assets, look for sources of freelance or part-time revenue to cover your fixed living expenses.

When it comes to coping with the situation, I say just face up to it. Tell your family what is going on. Do not tell them it is going to be all right. It might be, but, in today's economy, it may take months, or over a year, to get back to the same level of earning, if ever. Your family will need to be a part of the solution; they will need to cut their spending and start taking up some of the slack. Do not hesitate to have your children start picking up part-time work. That is good for them. It improves their own self-esteem and it makes them feel they are valuable members of the family.

Cancel subscriptions or monthly charges for things that are not really being used. Check your credit card bills for automatic charges you are not even paying attention to.

CASE STUDY: EVA ROSENBERG, ENROLLED AGENT

If you own a home with a lot of equity, get a home equity line of credit (HELOC) on the house immediately. Draw on that to cover your bills and house payments when your unemployment income and savings run out. Getting the HELOC while you can still show recent income is easy. Two months later, it will be almost impossible or very expensive. If you are driving a vehicle with a high monthly payment (over $500), replace it within a month after job loss. Frankly, at that level, it is even cheaper to rent a car when needed for job interviews than to maintain that payment.

As you begin your job search, look at the reality of your business, profession, or industry. Is it collapsing? Over the years, I have seen several industries collapse. Aerospace engineers faced massive layoffs in the 1970s. Teachers in southern California were laid off in the 1980s. Keypunch and switchboard operators disappeared in the 1980s and early 1990s. Entertainment jobs and manufacturing moved offshore in the 1990s. The printing industry collapsed in the 1990s with everyone having color and laser printers at work. The dot-com boom bottomed out in the early 2000s. If your industry may be the next one on that list, start looking for an alternate reality. If you are a key player in your industry with a good reputation and contacts, you have a great possibility for rehire in that field. If not, move on to an industry that is not likely to disappear. A few of these include tax preparation (we know the IRS is not going away), health care, services for senior citizens, and online businesses.

Speak to your religious or spiritual leader (and spouse). They know a lot about their congregation. I got a job with a national Certified Public Accountant firm by speaking to my rabbi's wife. Talk with "the invisible people," such as your banker, barber, dry cleaner, doorman, gardener, house cleaner, and waiter. You may be surprised at whom they know and what they pick up listening to their customers.

Before sending out résumés, do a thorough search for your own name on the Internet, especially in connection with your jobs over the last ten years. See what your employers will find when they look you up. How will your online image reflect on your desirability as a job candidate? If there are a lot of unsavory pictures and/or postings, remove them if you can. If not, quickly create about 100 new postings or pictures to a variety of venues, sites, social networks, and blogs to replace the bad ones. The newer ones should surface first and make the old ones harder to find.

If you were fired from your last job, tell the truth and be prepared with a good, concise story to explain the situation. Do not leave blanks in your work history. Time spans of more than a month or so between jobs looks like drug problems or jail time to an employer — or, worse, a job you do not want them to know about.

CHAPTER 7

Considerations for a Lawsuit

If your situation is covered under the law, and if you have or believe you can obtained evidence, you may have a potentially successful case for a lawsuit. However, even if it seems clear that you have been improperly dismissed, you should thoroughly consider the situation before filing a lawsuit.

You may need to sue to recover income that is lost, which is an important consideration. But remember that lawsuits are long and drawn-out. You will have to wait for the result. In addition, there will likely be out-of-pocket expenses that you may be required to pay upfront. Even if your attorney will be paid out of any award you receive, costs of depositions and expert witness fees may be billed to you. Even if you lose the case, you are still responsible for those payments.

The process of suing will be stressful. Will your family support you through that period? Are you healthy enough to withstand the pressure? Sometimes suing can make it more difficult to find another job. Other employers may want to avoid the chance that you will later sue them if they hire you. You may choose to delay the case until you have a new job or try to settle with the old employer without going to court.

Consider whether the company can pay an award if you win one. If the firm has financial troubles or is a small operation, it may be impossible to collect an award. Although there are cases in which a wronged worker is awarded millions of dollars, the allowed compensation varies in different types of cases. If a jury is involved, it is difficult to know what dollar figure jury individuals may award you. Attorneys' fees, expenses, and taxes will be deducted from any monies you are given.

There are many positive results that may come from a lawsuit if you and your attorneys successfully prove that you were terminated illegally. The following describes many of the common, potentially valid reasons for lawsuits and the positive results they may mean for you.

Employment Contracts

If a worker had an employment contract and was fired before the contract's time period was up, the worker may be awarded "benefit of the bargain" damages. This means the employee receives all the pay she would have gotten if she had not been fired. For example, if you had an employment contract that stated you would work one year and earn $100,000, but you were fired after only six months, you could be awarded the $50,000 you would have earned if the boss had honored the contract.

Improper Notice Under the WARN Act

Chapter 2 addressed the WARN Act, which requires a 60-day notice of certain types of layoffs. If proper notice was not given, the case can be taken to the U.S. District Court. If the court agrees that proper notice was not issued, each employee involved is awarded a payment equal to back-pay and benefits for the number of days the employer was in violation of the act, up to 60 days. If an employee sues and wins, the company must pay the employee's legal costs. If the employer did not give proper required notice to a unit of local government, the company may be fined up to $500 a day for each day of violation.

Discrimination

An employee who was found, through a lawsuit or court action, to have been illegally terminated due to discrimination may be awarded:

- Back-pay (also known as economic damages)
- A return to his old job
- Front-pay (the difference between what you expect to earn after the case is closed until a future date, and what you would have earned had you kept your old job — also known as economic damages)
- Reasonable accommodation (a change in the job, facility, and/ or equipment to adapt for workers' needs; for example, providing a wheelchair ramp to allow a disabled worker to be employed or adjusting work schedules to permit a worker to attend religious services)
- Lawyers' fees, court costs, and expert witness fees
- Other remedies that "treat" the damage done by the discriminatory termination

If a worker can prove that the discrimination was intentional, he or she may be entitled to compensatory damages, sometimes referred to as pain and suffering. This may include lost wages, future lost wages, and mental distress. Mental distress relates to how the discrimination affected the worker as a human being and includes the physical and emotional outcomes of poor treatment.

Punitive damages may be awarded if a company ignored regulations concerning discrimination and acted as though it were "above the law." It can be difficult to prove to a court's or jury's satisfaction that a company not only discriminated, but also did so in an irresponsible manner. You will need concrete evidence, such as an employer's discriminatory statement — preferably heard or documented by a third party. For example, if your supervisor states that he cannot work with women, and that is why he is terminating your employment, then you may have evidence that you were discriminated against intentionally and in an irresponsible manner.

In some discrimination cases, the amount of compensatory and punitive damage awards is limited. For example, cases filed under the Civil Rights Act are limited according to the number of employees a firm has. For companies with up to 100 workers, the limit is $50,000; from 100 to 200 employees, $100,000; from 200 to 500 workers, $200,000; and for companies with more than 500 employees, the limit is $300,000. Other limitations may apply in cases involving other federal or state laws.

Filing an Equal Employment Opportunity Commission Complaint

If you believe your termination is a direct result of discrimination, the first step in suing under a federal discrimination law is to file a complaint with the Equal Employment Opportunity Commission (EEOC). There is no cost for this, and you can do it yourself by contacting the local EEOC office or agency chosen in your state. A list of the appropriate offices in each state is provided in Appendix C.

The EEOC is responsible for enforcing the protections against discrimination regarding employment decisions based on covered traits. People who have those traits are a "protected class." Protection is given for:

- Age (40 years or older)
- Gender (this category includes sexual harassment and pregnancy discrimination)
- Race
- Religion
- National origin
- Disability
- Genetic information

There are exceptions in each category, and not all employers are bound to the laws protecting these groups. There are some categories that the EEOC does not enforce, but to which many federal, state, and local governments do extend protection. These regulations ban discrimination based on:

- Marital status
- Sexual orientation
- Being a parent
- Political affiliation

If you fall into one of the protected groups, this does not mean you cannot lose your job. It means it is against the law for you to be discharged simply because you belong to that group.

The EEOC office can tell you when the complaint must be filed. If your state has an agreement to accept claims of federal violations, you have 300 days from the date you were fired to file that claim. If not, you have 180 days.

The EEOC office will use your form to write-up a charge, which you must sign. EEOC then has 180 days to investigate. But it may take a long time to have the charge placed, and this is where an attorney can help. He or she may be able to draw up the charge right away and get things moving.

Expect the investigation process to be slow; rarely can the EEOC meet the 180-day deadline and issue the paperwork — called notice of right to sue — that you need to file the case in court. Because of that, you can withdraw the claim early, and often the EEOC will issue the notice. But that means you will bear the cost of the investigation because the EEOC will end its study of your case. This is another matter in which a lawyer can advise you of the best course in your situation. You will find information on hiring the right lawyer in the next chapter.

The Process of Challenging a Termination

The process of challenging what you believe to be an illegal termination should be carefully completed. If you are unsure what you should do first, keep reading. The following is a list of the steps to be taken when you have decided to challenge your termination, to file a claim with the EEOC, or to file a lawsuit against your former employer.

1. File a claim with the EEOC or contact your local civil rights office. If your former employer broke an employment contract, that will not be necessary.

2. Work with your attorney to prepare your case. The pre-filing stage is the process of gathering all documentation possible. Your attorney will investigate to determine whether there is a valid case.

3. Your lawyer will then write your former employer about why you are working with a lawyer and the facts supporting your claim. It will also state that unless the employer offers an acceptable settlement, you will file a lawsuit. Often these letters do not convince the company to settle with you, so most times, the case goes to the next step.

In some cases, you must exhaust all administrative remedies before going to court. This may also involve filing a complaint with a civil rights enforcement agency. The agency will conduct a free investigation, which can be helpful to you and your attorney. It will then present a ruling that your case is or is not backed with sufficient evidence to proceed. If the agency agrees with your claim, it will help you and the company to come to an agreement on a settlement. Whether successful or not, you will receive a right-to-sue letter. If unsuccessful, you can take your claim to court.

4. At this point, your attorney will file a complaint or your claim with the court. A summons, or order to appear in court, will be served to your former employer. The company will have a certain amount of time to file a court appearance. It is not unusual for the company's lawyer to ask for an extension on this time requirement.

5. Discovery requests come next. Your attorney and your former employer's attorney will ask for documents relating to the case.

6. The next step is depositions. Lawyers for both sides will question those who have information about the case. Depositions are usually taken in a lawyer's office and are recorded and then transcribed.

Now that all the information has been gathered, your former employer may ask for a summary judgment. Your former employer, the defendant, will have his or her attorney state that your case is so weak that it should not go to a jury and the judge should dismiss it. To fight this, your lawyer will show that there is considerable evidence to prove your claims. About 25 percent of cases are dismissed at this point.

Also at this point, many cases will be settled. In a settlement, both parties agree to a certain dollar amount or to other conditions that are mutually agreeable so the case does not have to proceed to trial. However, if your case is not settled then, you will move to trial. You will need to be present in court during the trial and may be asked to testify, but your lawyer will help you plan your statements in advance. A jury will be selected, and each lawyer will present their case.

After the jury gives its verdict, certain administrative motions will be filed that allow the judge to correct any errors made at trial. This process can take several weeks or months. The judge may decide to take away the jury verdict or order a new trial. You and the defendant will have a certain time in which to file an appeal.

An appeal by either side can be a long process. The earlier decision can be approved, modified, or reversed by the appellate judge. If it is reversed, often referred to as "struck down," the case may be sent back to the trial court for a new trial.

At any point during these legal proceedings, either side may ask for a settlement. Your lawyer will help you decide whether an offered settlement should be accepted, based upon the strength and value of the case and other factors, such as your stress and health concerns.

Deciding on a Settlement

It may be better for a fired worker to settle for compensation than to risk going to court. If you lose the case, you do not receive any payment from the company, but still must pay your lawyer and cover-related fees. In a settlement, you may be able to negotiate things other than money; a jury can only award financial compensation. For example, you may get the employer to agree to provide a good reference. Each case is different, so look to an attorney for guidance.

An attorney also will advise on determining a settlement amount. Factors may include:

- The amount of money you have lost or will lose
- The seriousness of the employer's offense
- The degree to which the worker has suffered
- A jury's anticipated reaction to the worker and the employer
- The chance of the worker winning
- The size of the employer's business

When you decide to work with a lawyer to pursue legal action against your employer, you will need to consider carefully a number of factors involved in choosing the most appropriate lawyer. You will also need to know what to provide your lawyer to ensure that he or she has all of the information necessary to move forward with a solid case. The following chapter provides guidance on working with a lawyer to pursue your case.

CASE STUDY: ELIZABETH PARKER KENTUCKY

Communications professional

I was laid off due to the company's financial troubles. I was actually very dissatisfied with my job and was thrilled to be let go because I had wanted to quit for months. But unforeseen events in my personal life soon overshadowed my employment situation.

I was scheduled to go on a cruise just five days after the layoff, so I decided to enjoy the trip and deal with my unexpected unemployment upon my return. The unfortunate situation for me was just after returning from the cruise, my father passed away. Shortly after that, I received, as his beneficiary, his life insurance payout, so that actually was a blessing financially. Dealing with his death and settling the estate was difficult and emotionally draining, so my job situation went to the back burner.

I did go to the unemployment office and set up a meeting with a counselor. They were very helpful, but I was surprised at how small my check was going to be.

CASE STUDY: ELIZABETH PARKER KENTUCKY

Since I had a lot of saved vacation time, and it was paid out in my severance check, I had to wait several weeks for a check from unemployment. They counted the number of weeks my severance check covered before benefits started.

The layoff itself was handled very poorly. There were multiple typographical errors in the discharge letters. My letter referenced me as a "he" in some parts of the letter. Others received letters saying they would get two or three months' severance when they meant two weeks. The ones getting the two or three months were upper management folks being discharged. It was handled so abruptly, but I think they thought they were being discreet. The folks getting laid off got e-mails directing them to meetings with human resources with about 15 minutes' notice. When others did not get the message, folks started questioning what was going on. It was a mess then and is still regarded as a mess by those who were laid off and the ones who were not. It left quite a negative impact on the employees.

The company actually called me to come back after about six weeks because they were then understaffed in the department. I was very reluctant to return to work because of my prior dissatisfaction, but after eight weeks and some salary negotiation, I decided to go back and could still continue looking for another job. Health insurance was one of the main reasons I went back.

Through this experience, I learned everyone may be replaced or discharged at a moment's notice (literally, in my case). Always try to expect the unexpected. Always be prepared to exit, even when things seem to be going along smoothly. While it is not for everyone, I would also recommend considering branching out on your own and being your own boss. That is easier said than done, but at least you would know where things stand in your own business. If it does not work out, you could always go back to the regular workforce.

A job loss can be an opportunity to assess where you are in your life and career and determine if this is the time to look at something new. Do not dwell on the negative of being let go, but consider what the new possibilities may be. Meeting with a career coach can help with your résumé and guide you to the next steps. Networking with folks in your field can be critical.

CASE STUDY: CATHERINE LANG-CLINE, CSP AND KRISTEN HARRIS, CSP

Owners, Portfolio Creative Staffing
Telephone: 614-839-4897
Web site: **www. portfoliostaffing.com**

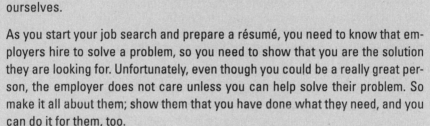

Portfolio Creative Staffing is a firm that specializes in connecting clients with creative talent in the Central Ohio area. It services a niche market of advertising agencies, marketing and creative departments, design firms, and other related businesses. Our clients are looking for freelance or permanent artists, writers, and marketing professionals. In addition to helping others find work after job losses, both of us have survived unemployment ourselves.

As you start your job search and prepare a résumé, you need to know that employers hire to solve a problem, so you need to show that you are the solution they are looking for. Unfortunately, even though you could be a really great person, the employer does not care unless you can help solve their problem. So make it all about them; show them that you have done what they need, and you can do it for them, too.

Create a skill and background summary at the top of your résumé that pulls together your key experience, skills, and what you have to offer an employer. Include success stories for each position. Instead of just describing what you did or your job duties, show how you were successful by increasing sales, reducing expenses, providing improved services, or increasing visibility. Do not just say you did something — show why it mattered. Tailor your skill summary and success stories to what the potential employer may be interested in as much as possible. Really play up all of the things that you have done to specifically address the job description, if you have one.

Have someone else read it. If it does not make sense to them, it will not make sense to a potential employer. "Fresh eyes" will also help you find any typo errors. Errors and misspellings are the kiss of death, so do not put all of your faith in a computer's spell check function.

Statistics say 80 percent of jobs that are filled are not advertised. That means all of the postings you see are only 20 percent of the jobs that people are actually hired for. Definitely apply to openings you see posted, as those are viable jobs companies are hiring for. But also contact companies you are interested in even if they do not post openings, work with recruiters, talk to friends and family that may have connections — look under every rock you can for opportunities.

CASE STUDY: CATHERINE LANG-CLINE, CSP AND KRISTEN HARRIS, CSP

Be open to options and where they may lead. A temporary position may lead to full-time; a slightly lower-level position may get you into a company with the opportunity for promotion. Look at all of the factors, not just what is on the surface. Ask yourself if this opportunity will get you where you are going, or at least keep you on the right road to your destination.

Go to meetings, events, job search workshops, seminars — anywhere you may meet people in your industry with connections. And invite people you meet out for coffee to chat one-on-one. A lot of people will say yes, and are willing to help someone out. Connect through organizations related to your industry by attending meetings, keeping tabs on the Web site, or volunteering to help at events. You will find more specific job postings on industry-specific sites, including postings that often are not on the large job boards.

In this Internet age, no one has an excuse for not researching a company prior to an interview. Know what they do, something interesting about them, maybe recent news or a new endeavor they are getting into. Ask questions about the company. Be engaged and engaging; you are interviewing them as much as they are interviewing you.

Interviewers may ask you when you left your last position, so be prepared with an answer. Do not let it strike fear in you. Remember that most people have lost a job themselves, or at least know someone who has. Just keep the information short and to the point, then move on to why you are there. Be honest, but do not go on about it; the more you talk about it, the more they will have questions about the situation. If it was a mutual agreement and you left on good terms, say so. If it was a disaster, just say it was not a good fit and you are moving on to better things.

Show that you fit in at the organization with which you are interviewing. Dressing the part is one way, but you have to also show that your personality fits as well. Try to mimic the behavior of the interviewer. If they are serious, be serious; if they are casual, be casual. If they have a photo of their kids or dog or boat on their desk, make a connection with them and ask them questions about those things. Mention you have kids the same age, that you give to animal rescue, or just a simple line like, "Is that your boat? When I was a kid, we had a lot of fun on my dad's boat." And leave it at that — because the connection has been made. This makes you stand out. Someone who is more qualified but has less of a connection (or personality) may be passed over for someone who is a better fit all-around.

Finding a job is your job right now, so treat it that way, and work hard at it every day. In more difficult economic times, it may take longer or be harder to find, but that job is out there — you just have to find it.

CHAPTER 8

Working with an Attorney to Challenge a Termination

If you have decided to challenge a termination, you may wish to hire a lawyer. In some cases, you can begin the process yourself; however, facing your former employer in court may not be something you want to do alone. The required documents and procedures are complicated and difficult to complete. The thought of hiring an attorney may seem like a tough task; chances are, you do not know a lawyer who specializes in employment issues. This chapter will reveal ways to find possible attorneys, how to choose the right one, and what information he or she will need to evaluate your case.

How to Find the Right Attorney

There are several ways to find attorneys:

- *Word of mouth:* If you know someone who has worked with a lawyer on employment issues, ask her what lawyer he or she would recommend.

- **Legal clinics:** The Legal Aid Society or a law school in your area may be able to make a referral. Some organizations like this may provide low-cost or even free legal services.

- **Legal rights organizations:** Groups that work for legal rights may be a referral source. Examples are groups for gay and lesbian persons or the National Association for the Advancement of Colored People (NAACP).

- **Workers' organizations:** Associations for specific types of workers may be able to provide information. Examples are professional groups for accountants and the National Association of Working Women.

- **Unions:** Union workers may contact their union and partnering groups for assistance.

- **Legal associations:** Groups for lawyers, such as the National Employment Lawyers Association (NELA), can refer you to a local attorney specializing in employment. Call 415-296-7629 or go to **www.nela.org**.

- **Legal Services Corporation:** A federal government branch that provides civil legal assistance to low-income Americans. A listing of each state's legal services office, with contact information, is provided in Appendix C.

Questions to Ask Before Hiring an Attorney

The process of challenging a termination will likely be expensive and take a great deal of your time. It may take months, or even years, to resolve. Considering this schedule, it is important to be certain that the lawyer you choose is someone you can work comfortably with and who will pursue your best interests.

Once you have a list of several possible lawyers, make appointments to talk things over. Some attorneys may wish to do part or all of this over the phone. That can save both of you time and money. This is important to lawyers and should be to you, too. Sometimes the initial consultation is free, but be sure to ask so that you know what to expect. Other questions you should ask include:

- What is your experience in employment law?
- Have you handled other cases similar to mine?
- What were the outcomes of those cases, and what is the potential outcome of mine?
- Do you have any alternatives to suggest, other than filing a lawsuit against my employer?
- How long do you think it will take to resolve my case?
- What are your rates?
- Will I be billed, or will you take the case on a contingency basis?
- What do you think the total cost will be for my case?
- Are there others in the office, such as junior attorneys or paralegals, who can handle some of the paperwork to reduce the costs?
- How will you keep me updated as to the progress of the case, and how often?

When speaking with an attorney, realize that both of you will be evaluating each other and the chance of success with your case. The lawyer will not be willing to take your case, especially on a contingency basis, if he or she does not believe you can win. Contingency means you do not pay up-front; the lawyer is paid out of any settlement you are awarded. If you do not win a monetary award, you will be responsible for paying the lawyer fee after the case has concluded.

You will be spending plenty of time and money with your lawyer, so hire one with whom you feel confident and comfortable. Look for an attorney:

- Whom you are comfortable talking with and who talks to you in a way that is understandable
- Who gives you adequate time to explain your situation
- Who answers your questions completely and patiently
- Who has experience with cases similar to yours

Be prepared when you go into the meeting with your potential new lawyer. Write out the important facts of your case. State what you wish to achieve — a financial settlement or a return to the old job.

What You Need to Provide Your Attorney

To represent you successfully, your attorney will need certain items of information from you. It is important to provide complete documents and facts as quickly as possible so that your attorney has all the ammunition he or she needs to prove your case.

Some things you may be asked for:

- A narrative or written statement of exactly what happened. Include as many facts, details, dates, and names as possible.
- Your employment contract, if you had one.
- All written disciplinary notices you received.
- Any other memos or documents your employer gave you about any part of your employment and/or termination.
- Any notes you took on happenings in the workplace.
- Your employee handbook, if you had one.

Your lawyer will tell you which additional items he will need to be able to successfully pursue your case. Working with the right attorney and providing accurate documentation may lead to a winning case against your employer. Whether your lawsuit succeeds or not, however, you will still need to provide for your family and yourself once you have become unemployed. The following chapter will help you learn how to survive unemployment by taking advantages of the many resources available to you.

CASE STUDY: D. JILL PUGH, J.D.

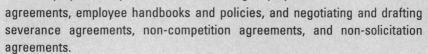

Member Washington State Bar
Law Office of D. Jill Pugh
Telephone: 206-325-2801
Web site: **www.EmploymentLawWA.com**

I have practiced employment law in Seattle since 1994. I represent individuals as well as businesses, handling traditional employment disputes as well as drafting employment agreements, employee handbooks and policies, and negotiating and drafting severance agreements, non-competition agreements, and non-solicitation agreements.

Over the years, I have seen both employers and employees make serious mistakes when dealing with terminations. The biggest mistake employers make is giving inconsistent or even false reasons when they terminate workers. It is best for the employer to be straightforward and truthful, and when the reasons for a termination change over time or can be shown to be false, it supports a legal inference that the real reason was illegal.

There are two big mistakes that employees make in dealing with job loss. The first is to react out of anger and emotion and make threats, either about suing or "taking down the company." Those statements, even if the employee does have a good legal case, inevitably come back to haunt them and damage their credibility in a later legal action. It virtually never scares any decision-maker at the employer's company into changing their mind, and can be used later to create an impression that the employee is a "hothead" or "moneygrubber."

The second mistake is also related to acting out of emotion; they destroy everything they have that relates to their former job. For example, some clients hold a bonfire, or just throw out everything that had anything to do with their previous employment.

CASE STUDY: D. JILL PUGH, J.D.

As long as it is something they legitimately and legally were in possession of from their former job, an employee should hold on to these things until they make a final decision about pursuing legal action.

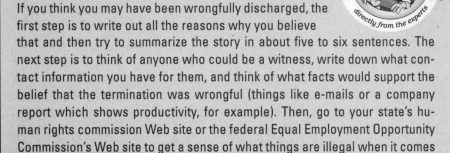

If you think you may have been wrongfully discharged, the first step is to write out all the reasons why you believe that and then try to summarize the story in about five to six sentences. The next step is to think of anyone who could be a witness, write down what contact information you have for them, and think of what facts would support the belief that the termination was wrongful (things like e-mails or a company report which shows productivity, for example). Then, go to your state's human rights commission Web site or the federal Equal Employment Opportunity Commission's Web site to get a sense of what things are illegal when it comes to terminations. Finally, contact an attorney for advice.

The most important thing you can do to help your attorney in a wrongful termination case is to be 100-percent truthful and not conceal any "bad" facts (like arguments with co-workers, a conviction for driving under the influence of alcohol, or filing bankruptcy). It is also helpful if they stay in contact with friends from their old employer to keep up on what is going on there. However, it is extremely important that if they do keep in contact, they do not discuss the case with them. If you think a discharge is coming, it is very helpful if you contact an attorney before things progress further.

Before initiating a wrongful discharge suit, you need to know that it is a lengthy process that is expensive and very invasive of your privacy. You will have your life turned inside out and upside down for 18 months to two years, and employment law is a very political area of the law, so even with the best possible facts, you might not prevail. I have had clients who have gone through trial and won, yet said if they had to do it over again, they would not. Imagine how the folks who do not win feel.

It is not in your best interest to pursue a wrongful discharge claim under any of these circumstances:

- If you are extremely emotionally fragile, perhaps have had severe post-traumatic stress disorder, for example. The process can be harsh, and I have had clients who decided it was not worth it, or that they would be too damaged by it.

- If you were engaged in some sort of serious "bad act" while at your former employer. For example, if you assaulted a co-worker, stole from the company, or gave company secrets away.

CASE STUDY: D. JILL PUGH, J.D.

- If you work in a very small community. This is not a hard and fast rule, but the smaller the business community, the more likely future employers will view you with suspicion as a potential liability since you have sued a past employer.

- If you get a much better paying job right away. The largest component of damages for most wrongful termination claims is lost wages, and if the new job is better, there are virtually no damages.

In general, be extremely careful before signing contracts of any kind. Be wary of severance agreements, especially if the employer does not want to let you take it home to read and think it over. At the other end of the employment relationship, be careful when signing documents at the start of employment; in most states, non-compete agreements are valid and can hinder your ability to find work later.

There is a constant tension between the interests of business and the interests of employees, and there is a general misconception by the courts that employment claims really are just making the courts into a "super human resources department." The U.S. Supreme Court has recently issued two key decisions regarding unlawful retaliation that were very favorable to workers; however, in the last session, it issued at least one decision that was so unfavorable that members of Congress attempted to correct it with legislation this last session (the bill failed). This is an area of law where the laws of the individual states really matter; you could have a scenario with the same facts end up with opposite results in different states.

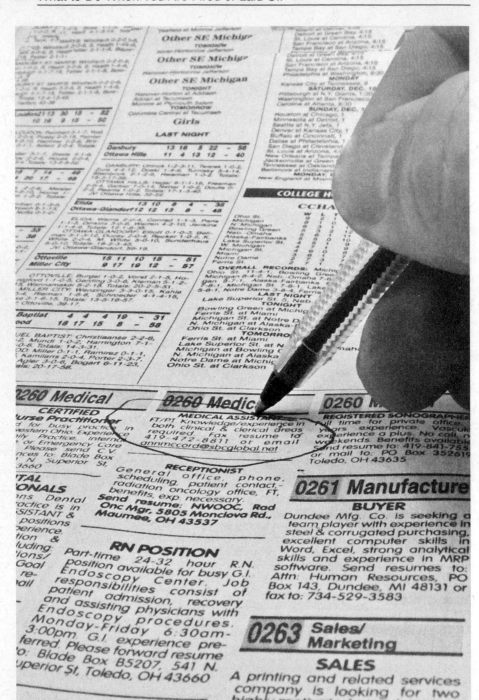

CHAPTER 9
Surviving Unemployment

There are many resources available to the unemployed to help with budgeting, paying bills, dealing with health insurance issues, and managing the daily struggles involved in losing a steady paycheck. As the unemployment rate rises, more organizations are stepping forward to help. Likewise, more businesses are willing to work with the unemployed to help you set up reasonable plans, to pay your utility bills, and even restructure mortgage and car payments.

Whether you were laid off or fired, choose to pursue legal action or not, you must cope with being unemployed. This is a difficult time for many people. You are experiencing an emotional upheaval: anger over being let go, loss of self-esteem and self-image, and perhaps depression. You may be feeling worthless as a person, a spouse, and a parent. You may feel you have disappointed your parents. You are likely worried about your finances and health insurance. This chapter will offer you the help you need to deal with your feelings toward your unemployment.

Getting Help

With unemployment rates rising across the country, a number of programs have been created or expanded to assist the growing number of unemployed people, just like you, who need help paying bills and providing health coverage for their families. The following provides information about where to turn when you need that assistance.

Health Insurance

The Children's Health Insurance Program (CHIP) was reauthorized in February 2009 and will be funded through 2013. CHIP provides health insurance and dental insurance coverage for uninsured children and pregnant women in families with incomes too high to qualify for most state Medicaid programs, but too low to be able to afford private insurance. If you are receiving unemployment insurance payments, your income may fall above the threshold for eligibility for Medicaid in your state; however, the income levels for the CHIP program have been raised significantly with the reauthorization, and most unemployed families will now qualify.

There may be some out-of-pocket expenses with CHIP, in contrast to Medicaid coverage, which does not charge patients anything out-of-pocket. However, any costs to patients covered by CHIP would be limited. The amount of expenses incurred by CHIP recipients can vary by state, but states cannot impose charges that exceed 5 percent of a family's total income while the child is enrolled in the program.

If your income is extremely low, even with unemployment insurance payments, you may qualify for Medicaid. As with the CHIP coverage, regulations and qualifications vary by state. To qualify for Medicaid, you will need to meet certain eligibility requirements. The Department of Health and Human Services lists the following as "mandatory eligibility groups:"

limited income families with children who meet certain eligibility requirements in the state's Aid to Families with Dependent Children (AFDC) plan; Supplemental Security Income (SSI) recipients; infants born to Medicaid-eligible women; children under age 6; and pregnant women whose family income is at or below 133 percent of the federal poverty level. In addition, states are required to provide Medicaid coverage to children born after September 30, 1983, until they are 19 in families with incomes at or below the federal poverty level.

You may also be eligible for Medicaid if you fall within certain other categories, based on your age, any disabilities, and your income and resources. You should apply for Medicaid coverage if you have limited income and resources.

Mortgage Assistance

A new program for homeowners who are at risk of losing their homes was established in October 2008 and runs through September 2011. The HOPE for Homeowners Program provides new, 30-year, fixed-rate mortgages insured by the Federal Housing Administration (FHA) if you are eligible to participate.

To be eligible for the HOPE for Homeowners Program, you must meet the following eligibility criteria:

- The home is your primary residence and you have no ownership interest in any other residential property

- Your existing mortgage was originated on or before January 1, 2008, and you have made at least six payments

- You are not able to pay your existing mortgage without help

- As of March 2008, your total monthly mortgage payments due was more than 31 percent of your gross monthly income

- You certify that you have not been convicted of fraud in the past ten years, have not intentionally defaulted on debts, and did not knowingly provide false information to obtain your existing mortgage

Another new program, Making Home Affordable, may be able to help you with a loan modification for your mortgage. To find out whether you are eligible, answer certain basic questions:

- Is your home your primary residence?

- Is the amount you owe on your first mortgage equal to or less than $729,750?

- Are you having trouble paying your mortgage? (An example of a qualifying reason is because of your reduced income.)

- Did you get your current mortgage before January 1, 2009?

- Is your payment on your first mortgage — including principal, interest, taxes, insurance, and homeowner's association dues, if applicable — more than 31 percent of your current gross income?

To answer these questions and determine whether you are eligible for a loan modification, visit the program's Web site at: **www.makinghomeaffordable.gov/modification_eligibility.html**.

If you are unemployed and facing foreclosure, seek help through the HOPE for Homeowners Program or the Making Home Affordable program. Contact your lender, another FHA-approved lender, or a housing counselor to apply or for more information. Housing counselors are also available to provide you with the information and assistance you need to avoid foreclosure. Foreclosure prevention counseling services are provided free of charge by nonprofit housing counseling agencies working in partnership with the federal government. You should not pay a private company for foreclosure counseling services.

Assistance with Utilities

Many states offer assistance with utilities for the unemployed. These state agencies receive federal funding for their programs through the Low Income Home Energy Assistance Program (LIHEAP). LIHEAP does not provide assistance directly to individuals but allows state agencies to help low-income families with paying their utility bills. LIHEAP has been operating since 1982 with the purpose of assisting "low-income households, particularly those with the lowest incomes, that pay a high proportion of household income for home energy, primarily in meeting their immediate home energy needs." The program encourages priority be given to those with the "highest home energy needs," meaning low-income households with a high energy burden and/or the presence of a "vulnerable" individual in the household, such as a young child, disabled person, or frail, older individual.

Some forms of assistance available to low-income households through State LIHEAP programs include: financial assistance toward a household's energy bill, emergency assistance if a household's home energy service is shut off or about to be shut off, and a range of other energy-related services that states may choose to offer, such as weatherization improvements, utility equipment repair and replacement, and budgeting counseling.

Unlike some Federal programs, eligibility guidelines can vary greatly among LIHEAP grantees. LIHEAP eligibility criteria include income levels and whether recipients fit into categories such as SSI or food stamp recipients. The LIHEAP statute establishes 150 percent of the poverty level as the maximum income level allowed in determining LIHEAP income eligibility, except where 60 percent of state median income is higher. Income eligibility criteria for LIHEAP may not be set lower than 110 percent of the poverty level. If you have lost your job and are living on unemployment insurance payments or no income at all, apply with your state office to determine your eligibility for utility payment assistance through LIHEAP. A list of state offices is provided in Appendix C.

Food Stamps

The program once known as the Food Stamp program has recently undergone a name change and has expanded its services for low-income families. The Supplemental Nutrition Assistance Program (SNAP) provides assistance to low-income families who have trouble affording groceries. SNAP also provides information and education on nutrition, one of the reasons it recently changed its name from the "Food Stamp" program. To be eligible for SNAP benefits, you should meet certain guidelines regarding your resources and income. SNAP uses the family's gross income, which should be no more than 130 percent of the Federal poverty level, and their net income, which can be no more than 100 percent of the poverty level. Families receiving Supplemental Security Income (SSI) or Temporary Assistance for Needy Families (TANF) benefits do not have to meet the income requirements. You will also have to register for work and participate in an employment and training program to be eligible to receive SNAP benefits.

Receiving SNAP benefits

States issue SNAP benefits through local state or county offices to households that are eligible to receive them. Traditionally, they issued paper food stamps, but increasingly, states issue the benefits through Electronic Benefit Transfer (EBT). Eligible participants will receive an electronic card, which is similar to a bank's debit card. You can pay for your groceries at authorized food stores — which includes almost all food stores — by using the card at the checkout counter. The cost of the groceries bought is deducted from your account automatically.

The amount of benefits the household gets is called an allotment. To determine the amount you are eligible to receive through the SNAP program, your household's net monthly income is multiplied by .3, and the result is subtracted from the maximum allotment for the household size to find the household's allotment. SNAP households are expected to spend about 30 percent of their resources on food.

The SNAP Web site, **www.snap-step1.usda.gov/fns**, provides the following table to enable you to calculate potential benefits you might receive, depending on your income:

Benefit Computation	Example
1. Multiply net income by 30%. (Round up)	$1,163 net monthly income x .3 = $348.90 (round up to $349)
2. Subtract 30% of net income from the maximum allotment for the household size.	$668 maximum allotment for 4 - $349 (30% of net income) = $319, **SNAP Allotment** for a full month

If you apply for benefits after the first day of the month, benefits will be provided from the day the household applies. SNAP benefits are available to all eligible households regardless of race, sex, religious creed, national origin, or political beliefs.

Many factors are involved in determining eligibility for the allotments for each family. If you are unemployed and your income has been severely reduced, apply for SNAP benefits. To see whether you qualify for a SNAP allotment, you can use the SNAP Pre-Screening Eligibility Tool on their Web site at **www.snap-step1.usda.gov/fns**. To apply for benefits, visit your local office to complete an application and a face-to-face interview. You can find your local office through your state's toll-free number. A list of toll-free numbers for getting information on each state's SNAP benefits is provided in Appendix C.

Assistance with Debts

If you anticipate difficulty in making credit card, car, or other loan payments, contact the creditor right away. Some companies have programs to assist customers who have lost their jobs. The creditor may give you a grace period, accept interest-only payments, or extend the loan's term. The key is making arrangements before you are behind on payments.

If you fall behind on many bills, you may wish to consult a credit counselor. A credit counselor can help you work with lenders to work out payment arrangements. The sooner you talk with someone, the easier it will be to get yourself back on the road to financial stability. Because credit counseling is required to file for bankruptcy, the U.S. Department of Justice offers a list of approved counseling services on its Web site: **www.usdoj.gov/ust/eo/bapcpa/ccde/cc_approved.htm**.

Tips for Choosing a Credit Counselor

The Federal Trade Commission offers guidelines for selecting a credit counselor in its publication, *FTC Facts for Consumers, Focus on Credit.*

Places to find a credit counselor:

- Private companies
- Universities
- Credit unions
- Military bases
- Housing authorities
- U.S. Cooperative Extension Service
- Consumer protection agency

Once you have found the credit counselor that suits you, ask him or her some important questions, such as:

- What are your services?
- Are information and educational materials available at no cost? If not, consider another group.
- Will you help me create a plan for avoiding problems in the future?
- What are your fees?
- What if I cannot afford your fees? If the counseling service will not work with you if you cannot pay, look for one that will.
- Are you licensed?
- What are your qualifications?
- Are your employees paid more if I sign up for certain services? If yes, this is not a good firm for you.

It is important to investigate their background. There are some places that will assist you in finding any complaints against the credit counselor:

- State Attorney General
- Consumer Protection Agency
- Better Business Bureau

Coping Emotionally and Physically

Communication is more important than ever when you are unemployed. Difficult as it is, you must tell your family and friends about the situation right away. Putting it off will not make it easier. Honest conversations about your unemployment, your feelings, and the effects will benefit you and your family. Communicating your problem will give you an emotional outlet and will allow your loved ones to offer to help in any way.

Your family members may be concerned about the consequences in their own lives. Those concerns, along with anger, disbelief, and discouragement, are normal for an entire family. A spouse may be worried about meeting expenses, and children may fear losing their home or being unable to attend college. Discussing these feelings and making a plan together gives everyone confidence and hope. It is important to address the concerns of your family as well as your own concerns.

A few days of feeling sorry for yourself and sleeping your days away are all right, but to cope and move on, you need to take some steps toward your new life. While you are unemployed:

- Wake, shower, and dress at a reasonable time.

- Establish a schedule for yourself. Plan to spend a part of each day in positive activities, such as those discussed below.

- Spend time with other people. Visit friends, attend meetings, and volunteer your services to charitable groups. Resist the temptation to drop out of sight. Others can encourage you and may be able to assist in your job search.

- Reward yourself. When you complete a job-searching task, treat yourself by going to a park or dropping into your favorite coffee shop.

- Protect your health. Exercise is a great stress reliever. Eat properly and get the right amount of sleep.

- Explore something that has always interested you. Take a class or join a hobby group.

- Keep a journal to record your feelings. Writing helps organize and clarify your thoughts. Brainstorm the possibilities for the future.

Using these techniques and others you find effective will help you deal with unemployment in a healthy way. Remember that this is not permanent, and you are not alone in this.

CASE STUDY: WENDY MCGRATH

Former business owner

In the mid-1980s, I was the first woman in Illinois to receive a small business micro loan. With that financing, I began a gymnastics business that thrived for 20 years. Ironically, as I got closer to retirement age, my working life took a kick in the teeth.

At age 64, I sold my company because of poor health. The arrangement was that I would be a salaried employee of the new firm for two years and would receive buyout payments on the first, second, and third anniversaries of the sale.

CASE STUDY: WENDY MCGRATH

The new owners closed the company after 11 months and, because of an oversight on my part (trust, actually), I received nothing for a company I had owned for 20 years. Not only was I let go, but my retirement nest egg was gone. I became severely depressed, had thoughts of suicide, and sought medical help at the local health department, as I had no income at the time. Later, I was able to collect unemployment, which the new owners contested!

I immediately canceled everything that was not a necessity: newspaper, cable, Internet, cell phone. Because the company had dissolved, I could not go on CO-BRA for health insurance and had to go into the state insurance program, which ran $1,200 a month. Because I was not yet 65, I could not collect Medicare for another year. Additionally, to receive full Social Security benefits, I would have to wait until I was 65 and 11 months old. Early benefits would entail a loss of $500 a month — not a lot to some folks, but the world to me at that point in my life.

Probably the hardest thing to do was to go to the unemployment department; there was a stigma about collecting unemployment, even though I knew I was entitled because I had paid in to the program for the 50 years I had worked. Still, I felt like a loser, and the personnel at the unemployment office did nothing to alleviate that feeling. During the six months that I collected unemployment, I only met one employee who seemed to enjoy his job.

On a more positive note, I took classes in finding a job offered by the unemployment office. I took classes online with educational tutorials in Excel, Microsoft Word, and PowerPoint. I attended a week-long class at the Latter Day Saints Employment Resource Services, which is a national program set up to help people get back into the workforce. You do not have to be a member of the church to participate; anyone can go to the center and use their fax machines and computers and browse through the want ads that were posted on a bulletin board. I was amazed at the number of people who had Ph.Ds and were executives from all walks of life.

Of all the places I went, this organization was the one that gave me the courage to not give up. I was surprised to learn of all the groups who offered help, including youth groups; senior groups, such as Seniors4Hire; community career centers; and community colleges.

I signed on with a temporary agency and picked up work assignments that lasted a week or two each time. The best part of that was that I was able to familiarize myself with the workplace.

CASE STUDY: WENDY MCGRATH

I had owned my company for 20 years and had not been an employee for that long. Stepping into a temp job also bolstered my confidence and made me realize that 65 was not too old to do a good job. I also did some secret shopping assignments to help make ends meet.

Ultimately, one of my temp assignments turned into a permanent, full-time position. I enjoy what I am doing, and it is never boring, but it is hard to remember to be an employee and not the boss. At a time in life when many people are retiring, I had to redesign myself to fit into a whole new profile and to accept that there are no free rides in life.

If you are dealing with unemployment, I urge you not to be afraid to ask for help. Do not take no for an answer, especially at the unemployment office. Present your case and be patient. Keep busy; get up every day just like you were going to work, because you are: You are working on finding employment. There is nothing more demoralizing than feeling unwanted. No matter how old you are — or how much money you have — you must feel good about yourself and useful. Do not be afraid to try new things. I learned so much working for the temp agency. I did things I never expected to do in my life. What a great challenge.

CASE STUDY: MICHAEL R. NEECE, CHIEF STRATEGY OFFICER

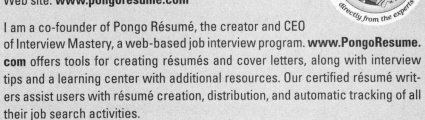

Pongo® Résumé
367 West Main Street
Northborough, MA 01532
Telephone: 508-393-4528
Web site: **www.pongoresume.com**

I am a co-founder of Pongo Résumé, the creator and CEO of Interview Mastery, a web-based job interview program. **www.PongoResume.com** offers tools for creating résumés and cover letters, along with interview tips and a learning center with additional resources. Our certified résumé writers assist users with résumé creation, distribution, and automatic tracking of all their job search activities.

I suggest that when faced with a job loss, you follow these initial steps:

1. Take inventory of your talents: Use a structured approach to inventory the many talents you have demonstrated through paid employment and unpaid volunteer efforts.

CASE STUDY: MICHAEL R. NEECE, CHIEF STRATEGY OFFICER

2. Take time to rest: We all work very hard and often feel overwhelmed with the difficult balance between work, family, and personal time. Unemployment offers time for rejuvenation.

3. Invest in your health: Without health, nothing else is possible. When employed, we often neglect regular exercise in favor of other priorities. Unemployment is a time when our health is more important than ever. Healthy and active people project better during interviews, have the energy to invest in a job search, and overcome the challenges that often accompany times of unemployment or under-employment.

4. Avoid the honey-do trap: Completing tasks around the house is not a job search. It feels better because there are tangible results of your efforts, but it does not help in finding work. Job search is full-time and should be treated with the importance it requires.

5. Cultivate your support system: The job seeker needs emotional support from family and friends. Too often, well-intentioned family members put destructive pressure on the job seeker in an attempt to encourage and support. If the job seeker does not get required support from family, cultivate emotional support from friends and other relatives.

Emotions during this time are profoundly affected by the assumptions you make and the actions you take (or do not take).

1. Many job seekers feel ashamed that they got laid off, assuming that only marginal performers get laid off. This is a false belief that harms the individual who makes this assumption; most everyone gets laid off. Whether you get released from a job or not is not always related to job performance.

2. Motion creates positive emotions, and the lack of physical motion generates negative emotions. Job seekers often isolate themselves at home attempting to secure their next job by writing their own résumé, posting to online job boards, and submitting résumés to online job postings. This online-only approach leaves job seekers frustrated with the total disconnection with real humans and feeling like the world is against them.

CASE STUDY: MICHAEL R. NEECE, CHIEF STRATEGY OFFICER

Résumé writing tips:

1. Include an objective if you are seeking a position that is different from your most recent job.

2. Use descriptive titles versus your assigned title. Assigned titles are often not reflective of the actual responsibilities. Help the résumé reader understand your experience rapidly by using descriptive titles.

3. Avoid using the phrase "Responsible for ..." Instead, begin each sentence with an action verb.

4. Functional résumé format is often more effective than the traditional reverse-chronological format.

5. Customize the résumé for each position you apply for.

6. Always include a cover letter.

7. Two pages is a good length for a résumé. The one-page résumé rule was never effective.

As the former "Interview Master" for **www.Monster.com** and the creator of Interview Mastery, I have scores of interview tips. Below are several of the most important.

1. Prepare: Research the company, position, and the interviewers. Evaluate yourself by taking an inventory of your hard skills and soft talents.

2. Ask questions throughout the interview to ensure you are communicating effectively and staying aligned with what the interviewer wants to learn about you.

3. Ask two questions at the end of every interview.

    a. What strengths do you feel I bring to this position?

    b. What concerns do you have about my background?

CASE STUDY: MICHAEL R. NEECE, CHIEF STRATEGY OFFICER

4.   Do not discuss salary until near the end of the selection process. Discuss specific salary numbers after the company has decided they want to hire you. Until that time, you have no negotiating leverage, and discussing salary can only eliminate you from further consideration.

5.   Practice answering the most common interview questions and the questions you are afraid of.

As you search for your next opportunity, use online resources and social media Web sites, such as Facebook®, to cultivate professional contacts. Make contact and meet people either face-to-face or voice-to-voice. Many job seekers make the mistake of only using social media sites for networking efforts. Effective networking is best done human-to-human. Thirty-seven percent of new positions are secured through professional contacts and networking efforts. At best, only 17 percent of new jobs are found through applying to online job postings.

CHAPTER 10
Budgeting

When you are out of work and there is no steady paycheck coming in — other than perhaps an unemployment insurance payment — you should create and stick to a new budget for your household. Take stock of your living expenses; you will be living on a smaller amount of money for a time. This is serious, but there are many things you can do to stretch whatever savings, severance pay, or unemployment compensation payments you may have. To do this, determine how much money you must have to meet your living expenses. Then, explore ways to find that amount each month.

Whether you are already unemployed or you see it as a future certainty, you should work on a budget now to ensure you have enough to survive unemployment. Your new budget may require drastic cuts, such as eliminating cable television services or reducing your cell phone plan. When you begin the process of looking for another job, however, you will need certain communication tools, such as basic phone service and perhaps even Internet access — although you can often use the public library's computers for free. Decide how much you can afford and how the cost of those tools can be reduced.

You will also need to plan ahead for a worst-case situation; decide which bills get priority if you lose your income, and if unemployment insurance does not kick in on time or is not sufficient to cover your basic monthly bills. Unless you have access to public transportation, a car will be necessary when job hunting, so your car payment should be made. Look at your rent or mortgage payments to determine if you can refinance a mortgage to bring down the payment or find a less expensive home to rent. Now is the time to make those crucial financial decisions, when you have time to weigh the options.

Analyzing Your Monthly Expenses

You may have no idea how much money you spend each month. Of course, you know the amount of your rent or mortgage payment, but you may be surprised to learn how much you spend at the grocery store, the coffee shop, and the video rental store. While employed, a few lattés may not be a problem, but it is surprising how quickly those treats add up. When your income is reduced, small expenses can make a difference in covering the basic needs.

The first step is to look at your spending over the last few months. Go through your checkbook or bank statement. If you use a computer-based financial management system, such as Quicken or Microsoft Money, you can run a report that will show all your spending. Your expenses will need to be entered into cost categories to provide this report. Check with your computer software program for instructions. Remember to include cash purchases that may not be recorded in a checkbook. Jot down every dollar spent or keep receipts, and encourage all of your family members to do the same. By keeping track of even the smallest expenses, you will be able to develop a full picture of your monthly spending. If you do not have access to a computer program, you can simply record your expenses on the form below:

Present Monthly Expenses *(Using a pencil is suggested)*	
Item	**Amount**
Rent/mortgage	
Car payment	
Health insurance	
Car insurance	
Life insurance	
Homeowners'/renters' insurance	
Groceries/dining out	
Telephone/cell phone	
Electricity and/or natural gas	
Water/trash/sewer service	
Medical expenses	
Entertainment (cable television, events, vacations)	
Clothing	
Child care	
Charity	
Gifts	
Car/transportation expenses (gas, maintenance)	
Newspaper/magazine subscriptions	
Household services (such as cleaning and lawn care)	
Personal services (such as hair and nail salon)	
Memberships (such as health club and golf club)	
Other	
Other	
Other	
Other	
TOTAL	

Without thinking about the total, look at each item again. Can anything be eliminated? If so, erase that item and subtract the dollar amount from your total.

Analyzing Your Monthly Income

The next step is to determine how much income you will have for the present. It is tempting to think that you will find a new job quickly, but it takes most people several months to get back into the workforce. Many factors affect your return to the workforce; if the economy is poor or the unemployment rate is high, it will take longer to get hired. If business is booming in your area, chances are you will be re-employed more quickly. It is best to plan on several months of unemployment. When you have an action plan in place, you will feel more confident and able to conduct a successful job search. Use the form below to record your monthly income as it is today. Do not add any savings or other funds you may be able to access if necessary. These items will be addressed later.

| Present Monthly Income ||
Source	Amount
Unemployment compensation	
Spouse's income	
Rental/investment income	
Other	
Other	
TOTAL	

Compare your monthly expenses to your present monthly income. Do not panic if the expenses are higher than the income; there are ways to bring those figures closer together while you are unemployed.

Reducing Expenses

One way to balance the budget is to reduce expenses. When you looked at your monthly expenses, you had an opportunity to review them for possible reductions. Take another look now if you wish.

If you need to reduce expenses further, consider these ideas:

Housing. If you rent, can you get a roommate or find a less expensive place? When you consider moving, think about the costs of reconnecting utilities, deposits, and transportation of your belongings. You may also lose the deposit you placed on your old home. If you have a mortgage, a roommate may be the better option. If it becomes difficult to make your house payment, contact your mortgage company right away. Lenders and brokers may be willing to give you a grace period, accept interest-only payments, or make other arrangements to keep you in your home. No matter what, pay your mortgage first. Losing a home can damage your credit for many years.

Food. Eliminate or reduce restaurant meals. Make specialty coffee at home. Save on groceries by planning meals ahead and making shopping lists. Include sale items in your menus. Try store-brand products. Use coupons for brand-name items you must purchase.

Utilities. Set your heating thermostat lower or your air-conditioning control higher; a few degrees will make more difference in your bill than in your comfort. Your water heater also can be reset at a lower temperature. Turn off lights and appliances when not in use.

For more savings on utilities:

- Clean or replace your heating and air conditioning filters at least once a month.

- When using exhaust fans in your bathrooms and kitchen, turn them off no longer than 20 minutes after you are done in those rooms.

- In the winter, keep your curtains and shades open on south-facing windows to allow sunlight to come in and help heat your home.

- In the summer, keep those curtains and shades closed during the day to keep out the heat from the sun. Only run your dishwasher when it is full. Clean as much off your dishes as possible before loading them in the dishwasher.

- Instead of using the drying feature on your dishwasher, let your dishes air-dry.

- Wash clothes in cold water and only when you have a full load.

- Clean your dryer's lint filter each time you use the dryer.

- Do not over-dry your clothes; test and adjust drying times so the dryer is not running excessively.

- Check your dryer vent to be sure it is not blocked or clogged and can operate efficiently.

Transportation. You can reduce your transportation costs while unemployed by using available public transportation, walking, or biking. If these options are not feasible (and may not be while you are going on interviewing or visiting prospective employers), you can also reduce the costs associated with driving your personal car by following these tips:

- Do not let your car idle excessively. Warming up your car in the winter is actually best done by driving it slowly for a few miles rather than letting it idle in the driveway.

- Drive within the speed limits and avoid sudden starts and stops, which waste gas.

- Clean your car inside and out. If you have been carrying around boxes of personal items retrieved from your former office, the added weight can reduce your gas mileage.

- Check your tire pressure regularly to ensure that they are inflated properly. Also check your alignment and the tire tread to be sure you are getting optimum performance.

- Use the proper motor oil, as recommended for your car.

- Check fluid levels regularly, particularly engine coolant and transmission fluid.

- Change your car's air filter regularly.

- Combine trips to get the most out of your mileage when running errands or going shopping.

Other areas. You can save money on entertainment costs by taking advantage of local museums and galleries that offer free admission. Take your family to a park or area historic site. Borrow books and movies from the library (be sure to return them on time to avoid late fees). Some additional money-saving tips include:

- If you have a cell phone, disconnect your landline telephone. Savings: *$30+ per month*

- Increase the deductibles on your car and home insurance. Savings: *$10+ per month*

- Use tap water instead of bottled water. Savings: *$10+ per month*

- Instead of taking clothing to a dry cleaner, use one of the at-home cleaning products. Savings: *$10+ per month.*

CASE STUDY: JULIE LENZER KIRK

Author, president, and CEO, Path Forward International
E-mail: Julie@julielenzerkirk.com
Telephone: 301-916-5126
Web site: **www.julielenzerkirk.com**

Part of my work is helping people to start their own businesses. Many of my clients come to me after a layoff and decide to start a business rather than looking for another job. They are tired of leaving their futures in the hands of others. I help them to come up with an idea for a business or put into action an idea they already have.

When people come to me after a job loss, I advise them to acknowledge that they may be going through a grieving process. I tell my clients to go ahead and have their pity party, serve tea, then move on. One of the best ways to do that is to make a ceremony of getting rid of something from your former job, like throwing away your business cards. That is a liberating act. I tell them that it is what it is, and they can decide how they react to make it either a positive experience or a thoroughly negative one. Putting the wheels in motion to take control of your own destiny by starting a business is great therapy. In times when jobs are difficult to find, starting a business may be the best option. The key is to find a need and fill it.

Sometimes people feel they do not have the skills necessary for operating an independent business, but most of us are more prepared than we think. My book, *The ParentPreneur Edge: What Parenting Teaches About Building a Successful Business*, demonstrates many of those "hidden" skills.

Some of my clients, after starting a successful business, see getting laid off as one of the best things that ever happened to them. It took that little nudge for them to take a chance at following their dreams.

CHAPTER 11
Generating Additional Income

The second part of living with reduced earnings is to find additional funds to cover your expenses until you find employment. You may be surprised to find that you have or can generate more income than you think. Here are some strategies that will help increase your income:

Sell your items. It is unlikely that you can uncover buried treasure in your backyard or a small fortune beneath your sofa cushions, but there may be funds available elsewhere. You may earn a sizeable payback by holding a yard sale. Do you have a stamp collection or memorabilia you can part with? These items can command high dollars from local collectors or eBay shoppers.

Ask family members for a loan. Consider asking your parents or other family members for a short-term loan. Use caution when deciding on this option. Although your relatives may want to help, borrowing money from them can strain the relationship. If a family member wishes to give you a monetary gift, make him or her aware that gifts more than $11,000 will add to the giver's tax bill.

Take a cash advance from a credit card. It is a costly move because of transaction fees and possibly high interest rates. However, if you have a no-interest account, this would be less risky.

Look at your assets. If you own stocks, extra vehicles, boats, a second home, or other valuable property, consider cataloging these items and evaluating their worth. This list may give you peace of mind in knowing that you do have a cushion to fall back upon, if necessary.

All of the previously mentioned techniques can help you develop some income while you are unemployed. There are some options, however, that you should not consider. One of them is taking money from your 401(k). When you lost your job, you may have received information about a retirement and/or 401(k) account. If you have been working and saving for years, the account balance may be quite high. It is tempting to withdraw those funds for living expenses, especially if you are not close to retirement age. However, you can never make up for the lost accumulated interest if you withdraw the funds or borrow against them. Withdrawing early also carries a penalty and taxes.

There are cases in which retirement funds can be withdrawn or borrowed without penalty, such as medical expenses, first home purchase, and college costs. But most of the time, touching your retirement funds is a bad idea. Evaluate all other options before considering taking money from your retirement.

Additional options for generating income while you are unemployed include the following.

Home Equity Lines of Credit

If you have established a home equity line of credit, you may access those funds. This action may put your house at risk, however. Use caution and careful deliberation when considering funding options related to your home and mortgage.

In some cases, refinancing your home may be helpful. If interest rates are lower than when you purchased the house, refinancing may lower your monthly payments. Consider the pros and cons carefully, and remember that refinancing will include closing costs. Sometimes, the closing costs can be included in the loan amount so you do not have to pay the expenses out-of-pocket. Refinancing may also extend the length of your loan, even though the amount you will have to pay each month will be less.

Part-Time or Temporary Work

Accepting part-time or temporary work during your unemployment has many benefits:

- You are supplementing your unemployment compensation and any other income. Although your earnings must be reported to the state employment compensation office and will be deducted from your benefits, you may be able to extend your eligibility.

- If your state designates a maximum benefit amount, you may be able to collect unemployment for a longer time period by supplementing it with other earnings.

- Your work may lead to permanent job possibilities.

- Part-time work helps you maintain a schedule and a positive outlook.

It may hurt your pride to accept work that is not of the quality or pay level of your former job, but the benefits outweigh those concerns.

You may be able to earn money through a hobby. Do you have a skill such as sewing, cooking, or woodworking that could be offered to others for a fee? If your skill or former employment lends itself to contract or freelance work, you may be able to find work with local companies. Writers, editors, designers, graphic artists, attorneys, accountants, and many others often contract with one or more firms to provide services from home. Many people have started small businesses when unemployed that grew into successful, permanent ventures.

Monthly Budget

You have reviewed your expenses, ways to reduce those costs, and ways to generate income. You now have many ideas about how to manage your finances until you land a new job. Seeing your options and possibilities may help you realize that you can meet the challenges before you. Now you can develop a monthly income and expense budget.

Revised Monthly Income	
Source	**Amount**
Unemployment compensation	
Spouse's income	
Rental/investment income/savings	
Part-time/temporary work/hobby income	
Loans/gifts	
Other	
Other	
TOTAL	

Revised Monthly Expenses	
Item	**Amount**
Rent/mortgage	
Car payment	
Health insurance	
Car insurance	
Life insurance	
Homeowners'/renters' insurance	
Groceries/dining out	
Telephone/cell phone	
Electricity and/or natural gas	
Water/trash/sewer service	
Medical expenses	
Entertainment (cable television, events, vacations)	
Clothing	
Child care	
Charity	
Gifts	
Car/transportation expenses (gas, maintenance)	
Newspaper/magazine subscriptions	
Household services (such as cleaning and lawn care)	
Personal services (such as hair and nail salon)	
Memberships (such as health club and golf club)	
Other	
Other	
Other	
Other	
TOTAL	

Do the income and expense figures balance? If not, try cutting expenses further. Think about selling assets, if necessary. Remember, you have several tools to see you through the period of reduced income.

Handling Your Taxes

When you are unemployed, perhaps the last thing on your mind is taxes. But planning for April 15 is still important. Taking action now can help avoid problems later on. Contact your tax or financial consultant, if you have one. This person can not only advise you on tax matters, but can also assist with the financial picture.

Continue having taxes withdrawn from any checks you receive and file income tax returns on time. Have the same percentage withheld from unemployment compensation and paychecks as you did when you were employed. It may seem difficult when you are struggling to make ends meet, but it can help prevent your having a large tax bill later. No matter what, file your federal income tax returns, even if you cannot pay any balance that is owed. The same is true if your state has an income tax. The bright side to filing your taxes on time is that you may have a refund coming.

If you owe taxes and cannot pay the total, make a payment toward what you owe by April 15. File an extension by April 15; this gives you until October 15 to save the rest of the payment. Once you have enough funds, file the return and make the payment. If you cannot pay by October 15, file the return and include Form 9465. Form 9465 is a Request for Installment Agreement. On the form, outline a payment plan that will cover the tax due in a reasonable amount of time. The Internal Revenue Service (IRS) accepts realistic payment plans. This will be a stressful time for you, but taking care of your responsibilities on time is just one of the ways you can start to take back control of the situation.

CASE STUDY: B.L. LINDSTROM

Computer Application Systems Consultant and Author

Telephone: 480-699-0313

Web site: **www.SomeplacElse.tv**

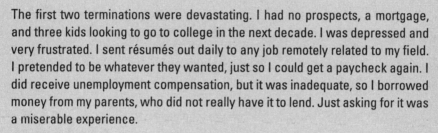

I spent 25 years in corporate America in the computer systems field. Between 1984 and 2002, I lost six jobs. In my opinion, all of these losses occurred due to mismanagement, corporate greed, and favoritism. For example, I faced mandatory pay cuts, forced relocation without adequate compensation, and job elimination when new officials were elected.

The first two terminations were devastating. I had no prospects, a mortgage, and three kids looking to go to college in the next decade. I was depressed and very frustrated. I sent résumés out daily to any job remotely related to my field. I pretended to be whatever they wanted, just so I could get a paycheck again. I did receive unemployment compensation, but it was inadequate, so I borrowed money from my parents, who did not really have it to lend. Just asking for it was a miserable experience.

I have never really come to a place of acceptance of these circumstances. Job after job just kept disappearing. I kept thinking there was something wrong with me, but now I know there is something wrong with a process that does not see the value of full employment. Employees are the most expendable asset of any corporation, especially when the stock price is plummeting and executives are under intense pressure to cut expenses.

Eventually, I started my own consulting business and even wrote a novel, partially based upon my experiences in the corporate world. My advice to others is to get out of debt and never assume that your employment situation is stable. Start your own business before things change.

CASE STUDY: JENNIFER BOURGOYNE

Founder and designer, Czela Bellies CesareanWear

Web site: **www.czelablue.com**

Today, when I think of the manager who sat there tearfully with me on September 2, 2005, and laid me off, I say, "Thank you from the bottom of my heart," But I certainly did not feel that way at first.

Newly married and nine months pregnant, the timing could not have been worse. My husband had recently been laid off, too. The crushing blow was that once I went through all my exit paperwork, I realized that my last day of extended insurance coverage would end the day before my scheduled c-section delivery date. That was a big shock to our system, and one that was especially insulting because I had been an award-winning employee with years of seniority. Maybe I was not as special as I thought I was. Another painful aspect was that my manager who had to fire me had indeed become a great friend through the years. I know it was also terribly hard for her, but her hands were tied. I found myself comforting her, letting her know I would be all right. That is the thing: I really, really loved my job. I stuck with the company through so much, and I absolutely loved our technology. I was truly mourning the loss of the job for months. I still feel like I will probably never have another team of people to work with that was such a well-oiled machine, and there was such absolute fun in the workplace.

My husband double-timed his job search and started a good position a few days before our son was delivered. The new health insurance kicked in the day of his birth.

With a new baby, I did not have time to fret over the job loss, but I was fretting over clothing. Everything was so uncomfortable, hitting right at the incision site. I researched for about a year, and determined that I just had my own "a-ha" moment and set out to design and manufacture the first comfortable and fashionable underwear for recovering c-section moms. My product, Czela Bellies Cesarean Wear, available at **www.czelablue.com**, has really been well-received across the globe. I never dreamed that I would be a stay-at-home mompreuner, and now it has actually happened.

Ironically, I even had studied at a fashion institute, but never had the opportunity to pursue that field. I am grateful for the job loss and caesarian section that allowed me to live the dream I had wanted since the age of nine.

CASE STUDY: JENNIFER BOURGOYNE

Getting started in a business is difficult. I found these to be some of the keys to being successful:

1. Do your homework. Research, research, research. We are so fortunate to be living in the Internet age where so much good information is at your fingertips. What will differentiate your business or product from the others?

2. Do not be afraid to talk about your vision with others. Often, this is exactly how things really get into motion. I have found that so many people have ideas that they are afraid to discuss with anyone else for fear of someone stealing their business idea — although, of course, you want to protect yourself. I have found that doing this alone was exhausting. If it were not my own vision or passion, I would not want to go through this process.

3. I am not a naturally comfortable networker. However, I did join an international organization called Ladies Who Launch, and I have to say, genuinely, that the benefits of this group are immeasurable. Ladies Who Launch has given me the opportunity to get media exposure I would not have had access to otherwise. It is not your typical women's networking organization. This is a powerful and thoughtful movement.

4. Be ready to take some financial risks. This was and continues to be difficult for me, but no pain, no gain, right? Every little step along the way to building your business will have a new cost associated with it. At some point, you have to stop being afraid to invest in yourself. It could potentially change your life.

5. Develop some thick skin. Not everyone will love your product. Some people will hate your branding. Learn to identify the difference between opinions and actual strategic advice.

6. Do what you love, take one thing at a time, and keep focused

CHAPTER 12

Networking, Support Groups, and Other Resources

You are not alone in your unemployment or in your search for a new position. A wide variety of support groups and networking groups are available to you, as are a number of quality education and training resources such as community colleges and career training centers. This chapter will guide you through the numerous resources — many funded on the federal and state levels — that can help you revise or create a résumé, search for jobs more effectively, and learn or re-learn interview techniques and job-search etiquette.

Networking

It has been said that most jobs are found through networking. True or not, it is a vital part of your job search. Use your contacts to find out about potential new opportunities and to spread the word that you are job-hunting. Networking contacts can include family, friends, and people whom you only "meet" through an online networking group. Contact anyone you know in the business world about your search. This may be a former co-worker who has moved to another company, a vendor or provider you worked with in your old job, or a former classmate who has business connections. Some companies have employee referral programs in which existing workers help recruit new ones. If you know someone who works for a company that interests you, ask whether he can refer you for consideration.

Web sites that are geared toward business people, such as LinkedIn^SM, can help you connect with others in your industry who can help spread the word to their contacts about you. More informal Web sites, such as Facebook® or Twitter^SM, can also help you make new connections; however, these are generally used more for personal communication among family and friends. Be sure your Web site posts are professional, regardless of which networking site you use. Potential employers may be watching your page to learn more about you.

Other organizations can be helpful, too. Get in touch with alumni groups representing your college or former employer. Organizations of "former AYR Corporation workers" are becoming more common and may include people working in your field and previous coworkers. Professional groups, such as those specific to a certain field or demographic, can keep you up-to-date on your industry and offer networking opportunities. Being active in groups, meetings, conventions, seminars, and Web sites related to your industry can be important to your well-being and your job search.

Networking is effective because people like to hire workers who have been recommended by others they like and trust. It is the same principle as telling a friend about a good movie. A referral to a potential employer can make the difference between getting in the door or not, but once in, it is up to you to sell yourself.

Support Groups

Whenever anyone is dealing with a hardship, it is important to have a strong support system. You may want a shoulder to cry on and someone who will listen. Having a person who acts as your cheerleader can encourage your progress. Most of all, you may need to know that you are not alone. It is important to remember that many more people have survived unemployment and are now back at work — many of them in situations that are better than their old jobs.

Support groups can connect you with others coping with job loss. Groups vary in their structure and focus. Some are intended to bring together job seekers for support and educational purposes; others concentrate on networking and sharing job leads.

A well-run group can help you come to terms with your situation and move on. Most are free and provide you with the sense of community you once felt in your workplace. A support group may lead you to new employment, but even if it does not, it can offer you the skills and confidence to find your next opportunity. A listing of support groups by state is online at **www.job-hunt.org**.

Training Resources

If you feel you need assistance in finding a job, or if you need training to be qualified for a change in careers, you may have a number of options. Training resources for the unemployed and underemployed have received increased funding to accommodate the growing number of unemployed individuals, just like you, who need a little help in finding a new direction in their career paths. Following is additional information on resources available to you in your community, at no or reduced costs.

Workforce Investment Act (WIA)

WIA authorizes training for dislocated workers through a federally funded program. According to the WIA Web site, at **www.doleta.gov/usworkforce/WIA/Runningtext2.htm**, for dislocated workers, services will be provided through the "One-Stop" system, and if certain individual training is need, workers can choose a training program that most benefits them based on their individual training accounts.

WIA categorizes services as "core" and "intensive." Core services, available to all adults, include:

- Job search and placement assistance (including career counseling)
- Labor market information, which identifies job vacancies; skills needed for in-demand jobs; and local, regional, and national employment trends
- Initial assessment of skills and needs
- Information about available services
- Follow-up services to help customers keep their jobs once they are placed

Intensive services available through the WIA are specifically designed for the unemployed who are not able to find jobs by taking advantage of the core services. Intensive services include:

- More comprehensive assessments
- Development of individual employment plans
- Group and individual counseling
- Case management
- Short-term pre-vocational services

In cases where qualified individuals receive intensive services and are still not able to find jobs, they may receive training services that are directly linked to job opportunities in their local area. These services may include occupational skills training, on-the-job training, entrepreneurial training, skill upgrading, job readiness training, and adult education and literacy activities, in conjunction with other training.

Individuals participating in WIA training opportunities will be able to:

- Receive a preliminary assessment of their skill levels, aptitudes, abilities, and support service needs

- Obtain information on a full array of employment-related services, including information about local education and training service providers

- Receive help filing claims for unemployment insurance and evaluating eligibility for job training, and education programs or student financial aid

- Obtain job search and placement assistance, and receive career counseling

- Have access to up-to-date labor market information, which identifies job vacancies and skills necessary for in-demand jobs and provides information about local, regional, and national employment trends

One-Stop Career Centers

Established under the WIA, One-Stop Career Centers are designed to do just what they say — provide a single location (one-stop) for job seekers. You can review job listings and receive career counseling under one roof. Employers also use One-Stop Career Centers to find skilled workers who are job-ready. One-Stop Career Center program offices provide a wide range of employment-related services, including:

- Access to computers, phones, and other office equipment
- Job placement and career counseling services
- Education and training services
- Counseling for coping with the stress and financial strain of unemployment

There are more than 2,000 centers across the country. Find a local One-Stop Career Center online at **www.servicelocator.org** or by phone at 1-877-US2-JOBS (1-877-872-5627).

Community Colleges

Community colleges are a convenient, inexpensive resource for college-level courses as well as vocational training of many types, including cosmetology, culinary, and automobile mechanics. Employers in your area may work with a community college to help train workers for jobs they need to fill. Those who successfully complete the training are virtually guaranteed a job. Most educational programs you attend will have a job placement service to assist you in finding employment when your course of study is complete. Often, registration fees are waived or reduced for unemployed and underemployed students. Classes are often offered during both the day and evening, so you can work your schooling around your schedule. Look into what programs your local community colleges have to offer. You may find that this is a great opportunity to get into a career you will really love.

CASE STUDY: GAYLE LYNN FALKENTHAL, APR, MS

Accreditation in Public Relations, Master of Science /
Mass Communication
Owner, Falcon Valley Group
E-mail: info@falconvalleygroup.com
Telephone: 619-997-2495
Web site: **www. falconvalleygroup.com**

I spent 15 years in broadcasting, which is a notoriously fickle business. I saw people laid off and fired all around me. Yet I never, ever lost a job. My employment was incredibly stable. I then made a career change to public relations. In less than four years in that field, I was laid off from three different senior management positions.

The first layoff had to do with a very politically charged civil lawsuit against me as part of an attack on my publicly elected boss. It was a complete surprise and incredibly shocking. It is never nice to be sued, after all, much less lose a job because of it. It also took place two days before my 40th birthday, so there was more than a little sense of a true life passage there. That case was later dismissed after 18 months of litigation. The second and third layoffs were not as high-profile; they were simply due to budget cutbacks.

I am not one to sit around at home feeling sorry for myself. My coping mechanism is to take control of my destiny and my future by taking action. The more people who knew about my situation, the more people there would be in my personal network available to possibly help me with a referral, reference, or good advice. I have always gotten tremendous benefits in my life, personally and professionally, from being aggressive about networking and being thoroughly engaged. You never know who you might meet that can help you. I got my first senior public relations job by volunteering on a political campaign. I got the next job from a personal referral from a fellow member of a volunteer board of directors for a charitable organization. I got the job that followed due to being well-known to them through nine years of previous volunteer work. So, not a single job came from answering an ad or applying with a herd of people. I was the only person interviewed — and the only person hired.

During the second layoff, I was fortunate enough to be provided the services of an executive career coach. It was a fantastic experience, and I learned a great deal from him. I met with him regularly, and I came out so much the better for that particular layoff. During this time, I threw myself into volunteer public relations work that got me out of the house, was active in my professional organizations, and started picking up some freelance assignments.

CASE STUDY: GAYLE LYNN FALKENTHAL, APR, MS

By the third time I was laid off, I had enough experience working independently to feel confident I could make a go of starting my own business. I did so on February 8, 2004, and I have never looked back.

The financial aspects of the job losses were not too tough, as I am a frugal person, and I have never lived beyond my means. I applied for unemployment. I pay plenty of taxes, and I had no qualms with accepting legitimate support.

What made things truly difficult was that my husband (at the time) was also laid off three months after I was laid off the second time, in September 2002. He remained unemployed for 18 months. He took it very hard, became depressed, and did very little to find a job. Contrasting with my approach, it caused major tension — so major that we eventually ended up getting divorced in May 2007.

If you have lost a job, remember that there is no shame in being laid off, or even fired in many cases. These things happen to a lot of good people, often through no fault of their own. As Norman Vincent Peale said, "Life isn't what happens to you, but what you do with what happens to you." Do not hide yourself away. This is the time to call upon everyone you know: colleagues, friends, family, former classmates, and social contacts. And if you have been a good and generous friend and colleague to them when you were not in need, they will be there to reciprocate when you are. Be your own best advocate. Do not be shy about getting out there and engaging in every possible conversation you can that leads to a discussion about job opportunities.

While you are looking, make yourself useful and help someone else. Donate your skills to a good cause. It will help you stay sharp, give you a reason to get out of bed in the morning, and make you feel productive. It will allow you to put your talents on display; think of it as a living, breathing, movable résumé. Today, virtually all my business comes from referrals. I have more business than I can handle, and I do not do any marketing. It is all from networking, contributing to the community, and working hard on staying visible.

Throughout these changes, I have found that I love my work. But work does not define us. I also learned that life is full of possibilities, but it is all too easy to be bound by habitual, singular thinking, rather than to open ourselves up to all the grand options available to us. It is exciting when life takes you in a different direction than you expected. It might feel uncomfortable or scary, but taking a chance usually does. I learned that I am really good at getting a job. Now I am the person dozens of colleagues call weekly to ask for advice on careers. If I ever changed professions, I would think seriously about becoming a career coach.

CASE STUDY: LESLEY GATES, M.S.

Senior Human Resources Professional through
the National Society for Human Resources Management
Founder and owner, Gates to HR, LLC
E-mail: lesley@gatestohr.com
Telephone: 480-626-5636
Web site: **www.gatestohr.com**

I am a human resource consultant offering human resources solutions for small-through medium-size companies. Throughout my career, I have managed hundreds of voluntary and involuntary terminations and served as a resource to help individuals cope with job loss. Depending on the situation, this can include explaining the reasons for the end of employment, presenting any severance agreements and/or career transition assistance offered by the company, coordinating outplacement job fairs, communicating job search resources, and preparing letters of reference. Many times, I was simply a friend for the departing employee — someone he or she could talk to while dealing with unemployment issues.

My advice to you is to view your job loss as a chance to pursue your true passions and dreams. It just takes determination, planning, and persistence.

Contact local universities and colleges, especially those with a curriculum in your discipline of interest, to learn more about on-site or online continuing education courses. There are a myriad of online assessments, many of which require a fee. You can also pursue self-development books and periodicals at the library or bookstore that cover your field of work or industry of interest. For a more personal approach, speak with career and life coaches. Your next career move may be identified through discussions and exercises involving personal reflection and goals setting.

Here are some of my favorite job search tips:

- Read the local news and business publications for business notices that may have information about a company's staffing status.

- Contact staffing agencies and search firms that have a niche in the industry or position you are interested in.

- Attend networking groups, such as through your local chamber of commerce or state work force connection office.

- Use the Internet as part of your valuable job search tool. Besides job listings, a number of sites provide free tools like fax services, e-mail accounts, networking opportunities, and free Web space for your online résumé. LinkedIn[SM] (**www.linkedin.com**) is also becoming an increasingly popular site for networking and job postings.

CASE STUDY: LESLEY GATES, M.S.

In times of economic slowdown, finding a new job may be especially difficult. Remember to network as much as possible. Most job leads and résumé submissions come from people whom you already know. Moreover, many employers offer referral programs to encourage their employees to help them find qualified talent.

Follow up every interview with a thank-you note. E-mail is OK, but a personal, handwritten note is recommended. Take the extra step to show prospective employers that you appreciate their time and that you have continued interest in the opportunity.

Your résumé is the first impression you will make on a potential employer. Learn the basics of résumé architecture, which includes selecting the appropriate format. There are a plethora of career and employment books available in libraries and bookstores. Plus, many job board Web sites, like Monster and CareerBuilder[SM], offer useful information and templates that are easily edited. Whenever possible, provide measurable and objective data about your financial and/or business impact to the organization, versus generic task information that often reads like a job description.

When you are invited for interviews, remember:

- Having knowledge about a potential employer gives you a competitive edge over job seekers who do not. Research companies you plan to interview with. Resources like Hoovers.com, Securities and Exchange Commission filings, business directories, and news sources can all provide valuable background information about specific businesses and industries.

- At interviews, wear professional attire, even if the work environment offers a business-casual dress code. There will be plenty of opportunities to wear casual attire once you have secured the job.

- Come prepared with questions. This can include questions about the company organizational structure, the culture, opportunities for growth, or inquiries about the pros and cons of the position. Be honest and stick to the facts. If the departure from your former employer(s) was involuntary, keep your responses short, simple, and non-derogatory.

CHAPTER 13

The Job Hunt

A job search can be complex and varied; not one search is better or more effective than the others. It is best to use a variety of techniques to find a new position quickly. The U.S. Department of Labor offers some helpful tips on conducting an effective job search.

Essential Elements of an Effective Job Search

When searching for a new job, you want to find the position that best meets your needs, both financially and for your career goals. In today's challenging economic and employment environment, you must sell yourself as the best applicant for the job when you apply. The following are some ways to reach your job search goal.

- *Know yourself and your abilities.* Have a strong sense of who you are and be able to share that with others. Take stock of your assets and learn how to market them to employers.

- *Stay on top of job trends.* If necessary, learn new, cutting-edge skills that match changing employer requirements.

- *Increase your computer skills.* Knowing how to use technology increases your opportunities in the job market. Conduct online job searches. Visit employer Web site pages and key job sites, such as:

  - CareerPath^{SM}: **www.careerpath.com**
  - Monster Board: **www.monster.com**
  - CareerMosaic^{SM}: **www.careermosaic.com**
  - Yahoo! HotJobs: **http://hotjobs.yahoo.com**

- *Keep your résumé updated.* Customize your résumé to reflect the assets you bring to each job. Use key words that can be electronically scanned by potential employers to positions you want. Reflect continuous employment in your skill area. Summer employment should support your field of interest. Volunteer or obtain temporary jobs if you are unemployed. Select a résumé format that minimizes any gaps in employment.

- *Give job hunting your full attention.* Pay attention to the details in your résumés and applications. Errors will knock you out of the running. Get organized and stay focused on your goal.

- *Work on your network.* Keep in touch with your contacts and stay active in networking groups, in person and online.

- *Stay informed about job trends and companies.* Select targets of opportunity that match your skill areas. Request and study the annual reports of your target companies. Make good use of library and online resources. Read trade journals and business publications.

- *Stay positive.* A pleasant personality is necessary when contacting potential employers. Your eagerness to adapt and to be a team player is essential. Show that you are flexible. A sense of humor and positive attitude are pluses.

- *Prepare for the interview.* Learn everything you can about the job and the company. Dress for success, regardless of the type of job. Prepare answers to typical interview questions about your skills, your work history, and your work style. Have full confidence in what you bring to the employer, and show how your skills meet the company's specific hiring needs. Ask thoughtful questions about the job and the company. Never say anything negative about a former employer or co-worker. After the interview, follow up immediately with a thank-you letter or e-mail.

- *Go the extra mile.* Push yourself to pursue your goals; you will find the opportunity you are seeking.

Using an Employment Agency

Employment agencies, also known as recruiters, headhunters, or search firms, work for employers. A company asks the recruiter to find candidates for a certain position. If the recruiter is successful, he or she receives a fee from the employer. Because this fee often is a percentage of the new hire's salary, recruiters primarily fill high-paying jobs. Applicants do not pay any fees.

For many people, a different kind of agency may be more effective. A temporary agency or staffing agency sometimes helps firms fill permanent jobs. These may be "temp to perm" positions, which enable the company to try you out before offering a permanent job. Many clerical, factory, and telemarketing positions are filled by temporary or staffing agencies.

The important thing to remember with any agency is that the agency is paid by, and thus works for, the hiring employer — not for you. Register with as many agencies as you wish, but do not expect this method to be a magic ticket to your new job.

The Federal Trade Commission (FTC) advises that you may come across ads for agencies that misrepresent their services, promote fictitious job offerings, or charge high, up-front fees for services that may not even lead to a job for you. The FTC warns that even though the ad may list a toll-free 800-number, you may be switched a pay-per-call 900-number without your knowledge. If you run into this situation and need help, the FTC can sue businesses that fraudulently advertise employment openings and guarantee job placement.

The following advice is provided by the FTC in their publication "Help Wanted . . . Finding a Job," located on their Web site at **www.ftc.gov/bcp/edu/pubs/consumer/products/pro22.shtm**.

Types of Employment Service Firms

When you are unemployed, it may become tempting to turn to an employment service firm to help you find a new job. Before doing so, however, understand what these firms do and the differences among employment services. Often, you are required to pay a fee for a search firm's services. Investigate any employment service firm you are considering using to find out what services the firm provides, how much it will cost, and who is expected to pay. It is also important to find out what will happen if the firm fails to find a job for you, in particular whether you will still be expected to pay a fee.

There are employment services available to you that do not charge fees to either the job-seeker or the employer. Before you look at a fee-based service, visit your local Employment Security Commission office or JobLink site. (Resources are listed in Appendix C.) Also take a look at the job listings available through America's Job Bank (AJB) at **www.ajb.dni.us**. These listings are posted by the federally funded and state-operated Public Employment Service.

Other types of employment service firms, which charge a fee to either you or the employer, include:

- *Employment agencies or personnel placement services.* These agencies generally charge their fee to the employers, who have requested the agency's assistance in filling a specific position. Sometimes the fee will be shared by the job seeker and the employer. Employment agencies are usually licensed by the state.

- *Executive search firms or executive recruiters.* Sometimes recruiters are referred to as headhunters and are generally searching for executive-level personnel to fill specific positions within a company. Executive search firms generally charge their fees to the employer, who is usually looking for just the right person to fill a job within the management level of the company.

- *Temporary help services.* Businesses will contract with a temporary service to fill positions on short-term bases. Many times an employee is planning to be out for several weeks, for medical or personal leave, and the employer needs to find someone who can do the job while that person is gone. The employer pays the temporary service's fees.

- *Executive counseling services or career counseling services.* These agencies provide guidance on career directions and decisions, rather than specific job placement. You can get help with writing your résumé, developing interview skills, and learning more about the organizations that offer jobs in your area of interest. There will be an up-front fee to be paid for these services, and you, as the job seeker, will be fully responsible for that fee. The fee can be as high as $4,000.

- *Job listing services or advisory services.* These types of services often charge an upfront fee to the job seeker and provide information regarding job listings. However, they are not a placement firm. In addition, they often use a 900 number that you will have to pay for on a minute- or pay-per-call basis. Be aware that federal law prohibits the use of a toll-free number for calls for which you will actually be charged.

Protecting Yourself

Do not provide an upfront payment to any agency before doing your homework. The FTC advises that you follow some basic guidelines when considering work with any type of employment services agency:

- Verify that job listings are legitimate, particularly when provided through a fee-based service.

- Do not give your personal financial information, such as a credit card number or bank information, to anyone either in-person or over the phone without first verifying that the company is aboveboard. You might want to start with getting references from others who have used such services and become more familiar with all of the companies offering services to help you find a job.

- If at all possible, work with employment service funds that do not charge up-front fees. At the very least, review their refund policy to be sure you can get some money back if they do not provide leads or jobs.

- Review contracts and paperwork carefully. Be sure you fully understand the terms and conditions as written before paying any money to the firm.

- Be wary of a firm that promises to find you a job. Few things can be guaranteed in any employment environment.

- Review comments made by other job-finders, usually found on job boards, to see whether complaints or recommendations have been noted. Also check with your local Better Business Bureau office (**www.bbb.org**) to see if they have received any complaints about the employment service firm.

Before using an employment agency, investigate them thoroughly to ensure you are not paying too much up-front and that they will provide the services they promise.

Print and Internet Ads

Newspaper and Internet advertising are sources of potential job opportunities; however, newspaper ads are less popular today than they were in the past, and Internet recruitment is increasing. Through the Internet, you can find and often apply for positions and research companies that interest you. There are several places to look. One is the large job boards, such as

www.monster.com, **www.careerbuilder.com**, and **www.hotjobs.com**. At these sites, one can view thousands of job listings and post your résumé for employers to read.

There also are Web sites specific to a job type. Sites devoted to employment for bankers, journalists, technology experts, and many more are available. Perform a Google search of your job category to locate the types of sites you need. Many large employers have job listings on their own Web sites. Some allow or even require you to apply through their site.

Continue to check both print and Internet job listings as you search for your new job. Also read through your local newspaper each day to learn about opportunities to network, such as meetings of networking groups and upcoming job fairs.

Job Fairs

Job or career fairs are common in urban areas. These no-cost events involve many employers gathered at one location, such as a hotel, to meet job seekers. Career fairs can be a part of your search if you understand how they work.

Companies attend these events to build awareness and to stockpile a large pool of potential employees. They may have no openings on the day of the fair. But for large firms that often need many new workers, it is helpful to have information about potential candidates and to encourage people to apply for possible consideration in the future.

A fair is a good place for you to learn about local companies. You can pick up information and sometimes watch a video. You may be able to speak with a representative briefly, but do not necessarily expect an on-the-spot interview. Dress professionally and take résumés to distribute to employers who interest you.

Create Your Own Job

A growing trend among the newly unemployed is to create a job rather than hunt for another job, from which they may well be laid off again. With big business becoming more uncertain, the focus has turned to small businesses.

The American Recovery and Reinvestment Act (ARRA) was signed into law in February 2009. The Small Business Administration (SBA) provides an overview of the Act on their Web site, at **www.sba.gov/idc/groups/ public/documents/sba_homepage/recovery_act_overview_033009. pdf.** The SBA indicates that ARRA is an unprecedented effort to jump-start our economy, create or save millions of jobs, and ensure our nation can meet the challenges of the 21st century. The Recovery Act assigns a key role in this effort to the U.S. Small Business Administration, providing it with program tools that offer new economic incentives to small businesses and lenders alike, all aimed at growing our economy through job creation, re-starting lending, and investing in small businesses and the entrepreneurial spirit of Americans.

The Recovery Act takes a comprehensive approach to several problems facing small business today. The Act provides entrepreneurs and lenders financial relief from the current economic crisis that will help encourage borrowing and lending to all small businesses, including start-ups. The bill is divided into nine key components, including:

- Temporary Elimination of Loan Fees
- Temporary 90 Percent Guarantees
- Secondary Market Liquidity for Section 7(a) loans, SBA's largest

loan guarantee program, which serves a wide variety of small business borrowing needs

- America's Recovery Capital (ARC) Stabilization Loans
- Expanded Microloans
- Surety Bond Program Expansion
- Secondary Market for First Mortgages associated with Section 504 Certified Development Company loans, which support small business capital-asset and real-property investments
- Expanded Refinancing Project for Section 504 loans
- SBIC Program Expansion

The SBA is working to implement these elements with the goal of having the broadest impact on small businesses as rapidly and effectively as possible.

For guidance and advice on how to start your entrepreneurial effort and create your own job, consult with a small business counselor at your local community college. There is no cost for the one-on-one counseling sessions, and most seminars and classes are offered for free or at reduced costs. You can also get free business advice from the Service Corps of Retired Executives (SCORE).

CHAPTER 14
Résumés and Cover Letters

Finding another job involves more than just searching for the right position. The process requires you to present the best side of yourself in every aspect involved of the job search. The first way you will present yourself to a prospective employer is on paper (or an electronic document) through your résumé and cover letter. The purpose of these documents is to secure an interview. Approach your résumé and cover letter as though you were the employer, and consider what the hiring official wants to see.

He or she wants to see that you are the best fit for the job. Describe what you have done and how well you have done it; show clearly why you are well-qualified. This most often entails writing a basic résumé with your experience and education, and then modifying it when you apply for specific positions. If you are answering an ad, be certain that your résumé and cover letter address each requirement listed. You have only a few seconds to capture a recruiter's attention; improve your chances by loading your résumé with action words that are relevant to the job. If you have experience in several fields, you may wish to create separate résumés for each.

A great résumé is a simple demonstration of your skills and abilities. Follow these simple rules when writing your résumé:

1. Be clear and concise
2. Know the employer's contact information and proper business name
3. Know yourself
4. Include all skills and accomplishments relevant to the position
5. Use action words to describe your experience

Keep it simple and only include truthful information. Do not lie on a résumé, and do not change your employment dates. Recruiters and hiring managers will verify everything on your résumé. Discrediting yourself is the fastest way to lose your dream job.

The Biggest Mistakes of All

Here is a list of some of the major mistakes repeatedly seen by recruiters and hiring managers:

1. ***Not telling the truth on your résumé.*** You should not make up jobs on your résumé, and you should not say you have skills that you do not have. Do not put down that you were a manager if you were an assistant. Do not say you are experienced with Microsoft Excel if you can only input some figures once or twice. These points will be checked or tested, and your skills will fall short when you are on the job. The truth is the best answer.

2. ***Not checking for spelling and grammar errors.*** Do not send out a résumé full of spelling and grammar mistakes. Do not count on spell check to pick up errors. If you had wanted to type "form" but typed "from" instead, spell check will not know the difference. It

is the same for "was" and "saw;" both words are correctly spelled, depending on how they are used.

3. ***Not including contact information.*** This is the most common error, and it is particularly common on résumés submitted via the Internet.

4. ***Not providing an appropriate e-mail address.*** Just because your friends know to use the e-mail address iamstupid@hotmail.com does not mean it is the e-mail address to put down on your résumé. If you do not have an all-purpose, professional-sounding address, it is time to make one.

5. ***Not focusing on the job opportunity offered.*** It is important that your résumé focuses on the skills and accomplishments you can bring to the job of which you are applying. A generic résumé is great to have during the résumé-writing process, but it may not be appropriate for every job opportunity.

Résumé Styles

There are many styles of résumés, so it is important to choose the one that works best for you. The following information will outline some of the different résumé styles.

Chronological

A chronological résumé is one that follows a sequence of time. All your work experience is listed in reverse chronological order, with your current or most recent job first. This is often the preferred method for recruiters, hiring managers, and human resource specialists because it is easy to read and quickly shows your progressive work experience and growth. These people do not have and will not take the time to sort through information to find what they need to know — you have to make it easy for them.

Functional

A functional résumé focuses on your skills and experience rather than on your recent work history. This format highlights talents and accomplishments so managers and recruiters can quickly and easily spot what they are looking for. At the same time, it is a good choice for people who are changing careers or who have gaps in their employment history.

Targeted

A targeted résumé is one customized to highlight experiences that are relevant to the job for which you are applying. It takes more time and effort to write a targeted résumé, but it is worth it. The stakes are high when a perfect job comes along that seems just right for your qualifications and experience, so take the time to get it right — and get the job.

One of the easiest ways to target your résumé, instead of re-writing it entirely, is to include a career highlights section, also called a summary of qualifications. This information can be at the top of your résumé, serving as the first thing a recruiter or manager will see. After this section, carry on with your list of work experiences in chronological order, the same as in a chronological résumé.

Creative

This type of résumé is where you get to unleash your creativity to the point where almost anything goes. You need to include the required information; however, you get to package it in a fun way. This type of résumé format works if you are applying for a position in advertising or the arts. In these positions, creativity is a strong requirement for the job. But these résumés are not for every job sector; be cautious about diverting too far from the norm in most fields.

Web Résumés

With the extensive technological advancement of Web site development, creating your own Web site has become easy. With this step comes the opportunity to develop a Web site résumé. This type of résumé is not right for everyone. However, if you are in a field where it would be advantageous to display your talents, or in an artistic field where it would help to show your creativity, it might be appropriate to have. Anyone can have one, although it is not required, and it does show technological savvy. Web résumés also offer the advantage of being available 24 hours a day for reviewing. If you create a Web site résumé properly, you can provide an interactive experience that can help leave a recruiter feeling impressed and wanting more.

Some of the ways you can create a Web résumé are:

- Start a blog with **www.WordPress.com** or **www.Blogger.com** for free. You can input your résumé and clips here and simply provide your potential employer with the link.

- Create your own Web site. Some search engines like Google or Yahoo allow you to purchase a domain name for your own site (for example: **www.yournamehere.com**) and also provides templates if you do not want to pay for Web hosting. However, if you want to create a Web site from scratch, you can buy Web hosting from a site like **www.GoDaddy.com**.

Here are some real-life résumé samples:

Sample Chronological Résumé

Angela Pickles
Telephone: +55 51 4567 3295   **E-mail:** apickles@hotmail.com

PROFESSIONAL EXPERIENCE

March 2006-Present   *Buenos Aires, Argentina.*
Freelance Journalist
- Freelanced for different graphic and digital media.
- Published articles at: Il Riformista (Italy), CIO Magazine Latin America, Franchising Magazine, Mil Caracteres (Argentina). Topics ranging from Latin American Politics and Social Circumstances to Art & History.
- Provided articles in Spanish, Italian or English.

January 2005-March 2006   *Buenos Aires, Argentina.*
Marketing & Media Manager, *Modena Technologies Capital Partners*
- Managed company's internal and external communications.
- Marketed and e-marketed campaigns organization.
- Coordinated press policies and media contact.

December 2003 – January 2005   *Buenos Aires, Argentina.*
Media Manager, *Franchising Advisors*
- Edited franchising magazine.
- Franchised TV & Radio Show Executive Producer.
- Coordinated Press Policies and Media contact.

December 1997 – January 2003
Marketing Analyst, *Nevum Solutions Corp.*
- Served as Marketing Director's Executive Assistant.
- Coordinated clients and sales channel's interaction.

EDUCATION

January 2006 – December 2009   *Buenos Aires, Argentina.*
Art History.
Art history major, four years. National Museum of Art.

March 2006 – September 2006   *Buenos Aires, Argentina.*
Journalism & World Politics, 2006.
Four-month postgraduate course in American & Middle East Politics.

August 2003 – August 2005   *Buenos Aires, Argentina.*
Journalism
Instituto Taller Escuela Agencia (TEA).

COMPUTER SKILLS

- Microsoft Office (Access, Excel, Word, Publisher, PowerPoint), Internet, Outlook.
- Web & graphic design tools: Dreamweaver, FrontPage, Adobe Photoshop, Fireworks, Corel.

LANGUAGES

Spanish: Native.
Italian: Advanced oral and writing skills.
English: Advanced oral and writing skills.

Sample Functional Résumé

JOAN S. VOSS

1234 Dawes St. Libertyville, IL 60048 (123) 456-7890 professional_edge_literary@email.com

OBJECTIVE: To hold a position that incorporates my ability to produce compelling copy and meet tight deadlines.

PROFESSIONAL AND PERSONAL VALUE OFFERED
- Strong skills in writing persuasive, benefit-oriented, customer-focused copy
- Ability to tell a winning story in campaign or advertisements
- Ability to work on multiple projects and produce great copy under pressure
- Ability to react swiftly to copy requests without sacrificing quality
- Attention to detail and successful follow-through skills
- Knowledge of and ability to work efficiently in MS Office Suite for PC, especially Word, Outlook and Excel

PROFESSIONAL EXPERIENCE

Freelance Writer   **1996 - Present**
- Write original copy i.e. advertisements, marketing campaigns, print & web-based publications
- Review & evaluate notes regarding aspects of multi-media copy, isolating pertinent facts & details
- Write original item descriptions and item support copy, including headlines and emails
- Re-write/second-draft existing "live" item and item support copy
- Edit content coming from third parties, vendors, agencies, etc.
- Research as needed and dictated by writing tasks i.e. interviewing, fact-checking

ARGONAUT INSURANCE COMPANY, Chicago, IL   **1990 - 1996**
Executive Assistant to Senior V.P, Special Claims Department
- Composed a variety of printed ad campaigns regarding insurance-related news items as directed by Senior Vice President
- Wrote & applied graphics layout for corporate newsletter regarding medical malpractice & environmental issues
- Worked closely with staff members to gather facts on upcoming legal issues
- Transcribed daily reports

BRANHAM NEWSPAPER SALES, Chicago, IL   **1987 - 1990**
Editorial Assistant
- Coordinated staff meetings with major clients
- Edited sales materials for Executive V.P. & sales team
- Composed press releases for 85 newspapers nationwide
- Proofread promotional brochures prior to print release

PROFESSIONAL ASSOCIATIONS
1st Prize Winner – Iron Pyramid Publications Writing Contest – 2007
Who's Who in America, 2003 – 2007
Finalist, Writer's Digest Magazine Writing Contest – 2004
Finalist, Ella T. Grasso Literary Award, Unico National Convention – 2004
Editor's Choice Award, International Library of Poetry – 2002

PROFESSIONAL DEVELOPMENT
College of Lake County, Grayslake, IL – 1996 - 1998
Certified in software training sessions, P.C. Resources, Park Ridge, IL – 1991 - 1996
Fred Pryor Business Seminars 1991 – 1996
University of Illinois/Bachelor of Arts – 1986

Business & personal references provided upon request

Sample Targeted Résumé

Lynn Thorne
0000 Crescent Lane
La Plata, Maryland 00000
E-mail: Lynn@email.com
Phone: 555-123-4567   Fax: 555-654-3211

Specialties

Award-winning writer
- ✓ Serves as thorough researcher
- ✓ Maintains team player mentality
- ✓ Meets deadlines
- ✓ Generates imaginative ideas
- ✓ Communicates clearly

Writing Experience

Lollipop Copy, La Plata, MD
May 2004 – Present
Owner
Freelance work includes pitching ideas, creating concepts, and writing, proofing and editing copy for direct mail, brochures, newspaper articles, and Web sites. Clients include JCPenney Direct, *The Wall Street Journal, The Washington Post*, and *The Baltimore Sun,* Wireless Wave Magazine, and US News Ventures, among others. Wrote the book "Word of Mouth Advertising, Online and Off."

America's Promise, Alexandria, VA
May 2000 – October 2002
Director, Correspondence and Writing
Responsible for drafting, editing, and proofing correspondence for the President/CEO and the Chairman of the Board
Editorial Director
Responsible for creating, writing, editing, proofing, and disseminating marketing and communications materials

American Association for the Advancement of Science, Washington, DC
August 1999 – February 2000
Communications Specialist
In charge of writing press releases and media notices, editing a 300-page source book for media use, and organizing the press room (for 700+ media representatives) for the annual meeting

Related Experience

College of Southern Maryland, La Plata, MD
September 2003 – May 2005
Adjunct Faculty
Responsible for teaching Speech Communications and Developmental Reading classes. Created and wrote syllabi, lesson plans and classroom activities

WWBT-TV, Richmond, VA, **WAOW-TV**, Wausau, WI and **WVIR-TV**, Charlottesville, VA
February 1994 – January 1999
Producer, Reporter and Anchor
Generated ideas, gathered leads, and wrote news stories. Developed *Faith and Family* segment for 54th market TV station. Wrote and produced newscasts, and anchored both news and weather segments

Education

Virginia Commonwealth University, Richmond, VA
Graduated Magna Cum Laude 1993.
B.S. Degree Mass Communications

CASE STUDY: NINA VULTAGGIO

Owner, Vultaggio Communications
Web site: **www.vultaggio.com**

My company specializes in written communications of all types. When I assist clients with résumés, these are the points I keep in mind.

Keep it Short and Simple

One of the biggest problems with résumés is their dramatic length. People buy books based on the synopsis; they do not read the book in the bookstore. Human resources people are inundated with information from folks asking for a job. Unfortunately, most do not understand that the purpose of the résumé is to get permission for an interview. If you want to get to the interview phase, save the life story for when you are hired. Consider your résumé a short memo telling the reader why they want the longer memo. Use it to show them your value quickly. Show them what is in it for them if they call you in for an interview. If it takes you longer to read the statement than it does to ride from floor one to floor two in an elevator, it is too long.

The best way to do this is to write down everything, then begin to peel away the unnecessary words. Replace long explanations with bullets and statistics. Let them know that more information is available upon request.

What to Include and What to Omit

- Do include your contact information on every page of the résumé. Assume that your résumé will get shuffled and make sure that they can contact you from any page.
- Do follow a clean, clear pattern with your résumé. This shows clarity of thought.
- Do tell a story about your experience that leaves them wanting more. This connects them to who you are
- Do not tell them why you did not like your last boss. This shows that you focus on the negative and makes you appear argumentative.
- Do not tell them what type of schedule you expect. You need to show value before asking for favors.
- Do not include attachments if you are sending your résumé unsolicited. Most people will not open unsolicited attachments; paste it into the body of the e-mail.
- Do not include typographical errors. Make sure to proofread before sending; it shows you care.

CASE STUDY: NINA VULTAGGIO

How to Think Like a Decision Maker So You Can Answer His or Her Objections

To get into the hiring official's mind, you need to think about their objectives. Human resource professionals, business owners, and managers want to know if candidates will be reliable; if you can follow directions; if you are warm, friendly, and persistent; and if you will stay long enough for them to recoup the investment they make in you as a new hire. Show them with your résumé that you are that person with examples that illustrate times when you have proved your worth to a company.

Five Key Points That Must Be Covered to Maximize Your Chances of Success

1. A simple format. This shows you to be a clear thinker.
2. A clear summary that is no more than two sentences. This gives them an understanding of who you are and what you want to be.
3. Include your experience. Tell them what you have done that will help you to do their job well. Customize this to the position you want.
4. Provide references or testimonials. Include a statement or two from others who can attest to your character and professionalism. Make it easy for them to get a clear picture of you.
5. Let your personality show through. Connect with them with your words. Give them a reason to choose you over the other qualified candidates.

The Single-Biggest Mistake in Most Résumés and How to Avoid it

The single biggest mistake is the shotgun approach to getting a job. When you do not take the time to research the company and do not take the process seriously, it shows. Know something about the business and industry. Give information that shows that your experience matches their need. Use industry lingo and buzzwords. Show that you have done your homework and that you care.

CASE STUDY: SHEL HOROWITZ

Owner, Accurate Writing & More
Telephone: 413-586-2388; 800-683-WORD
Web site: **www.accuratewriting.com**

Writing résumés is a part of my writing and marketing business. I also do some career coaching and counseling.

In working with many people who have lost jobs, I have found that an important first step when faced with unemployment is to evaluate your options. If you have been unsatisfied in a previous position and always wanted to start your own business or shift fields, it may turn out to be a blessing. Many businesses can be started for little or no money and built gradually. Evaluate your skills and interests to see what sorts of jobs might be possible.

Start by listing your skills and interests, then think creatively about what kind of livelihood could fit those skills and interests. You do not have to find exactly the same kind of position you had; many skills are transferable. For example, knowledge of psychology is useful in teaching, human services, or sales. Residential or commercial construction experience can translate to carpentry, cabinet making, and odd-job repair.

Seek help in coping with unemployment. Find support from people who have been through it; from career counselors; and from human service professionals. Look in your local newspaper and online calendars to see if there are self-help support groups for the newly unemployed, and talk with reference librarians about resources.

To bridge the financial gap, find something you can do to make money, even if it is part-time and temporary. Cut non-essential expenses; most families can save a great deal by careful budgeting, combining multiple errands on car trips, seeking out free or low-cost entertainment, eating more carefully, making their own coffee, and not drinking alcohol when they go out to eat (you can get six or eight glasses of wine for the price of one drink in a bar if you buy your own bottle in a liquor store).

In this economy, people should plan ahead while still in the workforce. It is much easier to get through a period of unemployment if you have savings. If you do not, it is important not to be ashamed if you need a leg up, even public assistance, if you use it as a short-term bridge to give you the time you need to find something.

In writing résumés since 1977, I have learned that it is best to structure the résumé to highlight the strengths for a particular position. You may need more than one version.

CASE STUDY: SHEL HOROWITZ

Many formats can work better than the traditional chronological order, such as focusing on skills or accomplishments, or organizing several categories of work experience along different career paths. I urge you to get your résumé done professionally; it does not have to be expensive. Contact me if you cannot find anyone affordable in your own area.

On a résumé, I never bring up the reason for leaving. In an interview, it depends on why you were let go. If you were fired for just cause, I would explain how you have grown from that experience and built your skills and trustworthiness since the termination.

Pull out all the stops in your job search. Put out the word to everyone you know. Many jobs are not posted publicly. Read the book *Career Map* by Neil Yeager. Consider an online job search, for instance. Join Internet discussion groups in your field of interest. Attend trade shows, not just job fairs.

To help bulletproof your new job, do more than the minimum. Always seek out opportunities to learn more on the job and to make yourself helpful to others (in a non-pushy, non-patronizing way). Make it clear that you are happy to accept new tasks and challenges.

Writing the Cover Letter

Imagine yourself at a social event where there are dozens of guests mingling throughout the room. You spot a hiring manager for a company at which you would love to be employed. You work your way across the room and wait for a break in the conversation she is engaged in. Her head turns toward you; you greet her by name and extend your hand to introduce yourself. You have seconds to make an impression on her that will get you a business card or an invitation to e-mail your résumé.

The opening of your cover letter is like that handshake and brief introduction. Your reader is like that manager at a social event: busy, attention divided, not focused on you, and easily diverted.

Just like you will have to make a quick impression on that manager in the above example, your cover letter will quickly be dismissed if you do not make an immediate impact. A hiring executive may spend as little as 15-18 seconds reading your cover letter before he or she decides to continue reading — or put your cover letter down.

The most important part of your cover letter is your first couple of sentences. Hiring authorities may peruse dozens of applications a day. Your cover letter is necessary to distinguish yourself from the crowd, and it must do so quickly.

An opening paragraph with an impact will accomplish three tasks:

1. Start with a unique first sentence.
2. Introduce yourself to the reader.
3. Tell the reader why you are writing the letter.

Most cover letters will accomplish two of these three tasks with a generic opener, like:

I am responding to the advertisement for a B2B sales director on hotjobs.com. I have attached my résumé for your consideration.

While using that as your opening sentence may not get your cover letter tossed, it is important to consider that your reader may have read that exact same line 20 times already by the time he gets around to reading yours.

At the same time, it is best not to go overboard with an opening line like:

With ten years of experience in marketing, I am the answer to your company's needs! You can pull the advertisement for a marketing manager off Monster. com right now, because after you read my attached résumé, you will know you have found the right person for the job.

Like your handshake, your opening paragraph should be neither too weak, like the first example, nor overbearing, like the second. When you write your opening paragraph, you may want to pose a question that focuses on a high-need area for the employer, like:

Can you use a law enforcement officer with a case-closure rate of 90 percent to help decrease the crime rate in your city?

Just make sure the answer to whatever question you include in your opening paragraph is "yes." Do not let your first paragraph give the reader a chance to think "no." Remember, this is your commercial. Do not let them flip that channel on you and switch over to someone else's cover letter.

The opening paragraph of a cover letter is essential to grab the reader's attention, but the cover letter as a whole must have certain characteristics. Consider the following basic rules to help you write the best cover letter.

Rule 1: Cover letters should be to the point and make an impact.

There was a time when the general consensus for most résumés was that they be one sheet of paper. Because HR departments often had to sort, stack, and look over hundreds, if not thousands of résumés, multi-paged résumés were impractical at best. Today, résumés are often transmitted and stored electronically, and that old maxim has been discarded in favor of résumés with more detailed descriptions of job histories and skill sets.

Cover letters, on the other hand, should still be limited to a single page.

First off, the human resource personnel or hiring authority reading your cover letter will be using it to make a quick assessment. You have seconds, not minutes, to make an impression. If your readers have to flip a page or scroll down far on their computer screen, chances are good that they will stop reading. Your cover letter should be the summary notes, not the novel.

Another reason cover letters should be limited to one page is that they serve as a test of your abilities to an employer. Can you capture your reader's attention? How quickly can you do it? Can you briefly describe yourself, your skills, and show why you are right for the job — while being constrained to such a limited space? Your ability to do this may demonstrate your ability to sell to a customer, present information at a meeting, or give instructions to a team. The hiring authority is accessing more than what goes into your cover letter; they are accessing how well you wrote it. That is why it is important to do more than write a short cover letter. You must write one that makes an impact, as well.

Rule 2: Your cover letter and résumé should complement each other.

Though your cover letter will be tailored for the specific position you are applying to, it must be a reflection of your résumé each time you submit one. It should include several highlights from your résumé that you want to bring to the forefront and should also look like your résumé.

To ensure that your résumé and cover letter are unitary documents, you will want them to have visual similarities. Use the same font type, size, and header. When printing the documents, put them on matching high-quality paper. These details may seem small and inconsequential on the surface, but anything you can do to make your cover letter and résumé stand out positively is a good thing.

Conversely, your cover letter should not contain information that is not contained in your résumé. There are exceptions to this rule. There may come a time when a hobby (like photography or Web page design) can demonstrate skills needed for a position for which you have no workplace experience. In those instances, bringing up something that is not captured on your résumé can serve a vital function in your cover letter. However, most of the time you will want to take a few highlights from your résumé and delve deeper into them as you write your cover letter.

Rule 3: Show attention to detail.

Use a spelling and grammar checker. Read it. Re-read it. Read it again. Have someone else read your cover letter, if need be, but do not submit a cover letter with spelling or grammatical errors. No one is going to take your application seriously if you have not taken the time to make sure your one page cover letter is free of mistakes. This really cannot be emphasized enough.

Do research. Identify the person who might be reading your cover letter. Address your letter to them. Find out the address of the company; include this in your header. Make sure you have an appropriate salutation. Ensure that you meet all the requirements the job posting has requested. Just remember that details are crucial in writing a good cover letter.

If possible, find out some information about the company and the industry they are in. You will not want to spend a great deal of your one-page document revealing what you know of the company, but you want to at least convey that you have looked them up and are aware of what they do. A blurb or two will often suffice and will give the hiring authority the impression that you have an idea of what the company is about and want to be a part of it.

Make sure you include all important information in the cover letter. The components of a cover letter are:

- Contact information
- Date
- Address/Salutation
- Opening paragraph
- Content
- Closing paragraph
- Signature

Following these rules and including all the components of a cover letter will help ensure that your résumé is looked at by the hiring authority. Make sure you read your cover letter over before sending it, or have someone else read it. This way, you can catch all the mistakes.

Types of Cover Letters

Once you understand the basic guidelines to follow when writing cover letters, you must then decide what type of cover letter you are writing. Who is your audience? What do you intend for this cover letter to convey? Ultimately, in every cover letter, you are asking for an interview. But the details of that request — and the method by which it is delivered — may vary significantly.

Below is a brief description of some of the types of cover letters.

The Solicited Response

The first category of cover letters is the one that probably springs to mind immediately when you think of sending out your résumé — those sent out as a response to an advertised position.

In this type of letter, you will specifically highlight how your talents meet the requirements advertised in the job listing. You can think of this as the "best fit" cover letter. A company is looking for a certain individual with a certain skill set, and you will demonstrate to them that you are their "best fit."

Letters to a Recruitment Agency

The second type of cover letter you will likely produce is one to a job recruiter, an individual who finds qualified people for companies that are hiring. The purpose of this cover letter is to give the recruiter a fairly good summary of your skill set and what you are looking for in terms of employment so they, in turn, can sell you to one of their clients.

With any luck, the cover letter you prepare for a recruiter will be one that is following up on a contact they made to you. But, if that is not the case, you may still submit a cover letter to a recruiting agency, unsolicited or in response to an advertisement.

These letters are slightly more generic than the ones prepared in response to an advertised position, but there may be information you would include in these that would not go into the first type of cover letter. For example, you may include specific salary requirements or locations you prefer to work. The purpose of this type of cover letter is to give the recruiter an accurate accounting of your skills and abilities so they can present you in the best light to their audience: your prospective employers.

"Cold-Call" Letters

The third type of cover letter you may produce is that which will accompany an unsolicited résumé. Often referred to as "cold-call" letters, these may include:

- **Networking cover letters:** A networking letter is one where you are contacting professional and personal contacts, asking whether they know of any job openings in your area of expertise.

- **Referral cover letters:** A referral letter is one where you address your letter and résumé to someone who has been suggested to you by a friend or colleague.

- **Broadcast cover letters:** The broadcast cover letter is one where you seek to advertise to a company that you are on the job market, in hopes they will have a position that you would be qualified to fill.

Online Cover Letters

Another type of cover letter that you might compose is the one that will be attached to an online résumé. You may include this résumé on your blog or Web site, and **Monster.com**, **Yahoo! Hotjobs**, **CareerBuilder.com**, **Snagajob.com**, and many other sites allow you to upload and submit an online résumé for employers to review. They will ask if you would like to submit a cover letter along with that résumé. You do not have to include a cover letter with your online profile, but it is often a good idea. A cover letter will convey your personality to potential employers or recruiters who review those sites looking for résumés that fill their requirements.

These are probably the most generic cover letters you will write. Because you are not targeting a specific job posting or company, you will emphasize your skill sets in the hopes they catch an HR person's eye. These types of letters can often be the easiest, and, at the same time, the most challenging to write. It would be easy enough to write down what you can do and where you came from, but you need to take care that your cover letter does not become a simple laundry list of your skill sets and experience. Remember, the purpose of a cover letter is to inform and engage. These letters may be difficult to write because you do not know who will be reading. So you will need to be broad in your scope, but still captivating enough to capture the interest of a hiring director skimming through an online database.

Writing a Cover Letter After Being Fired or Laid Off

The currently shaky economic times we live in mean that people are being laid off in rather large numbers, thus the former stigma of losing one's job is quickly disappearing. When unemployment is high, this is not an uncommon situation. Employers realize this and are generally more sensitive to this fact. But *never* state negatives in a cover letter or during an interview.

If the hiring agent asks specific questions about reasons for job hunting, always be honest; always portray in the positive; and never become angry, stressed, or disrespectful to previous employers.

Another tip for dealing with periods of unemployment in the past is to simply put the years you were employed with a company on your résumé. The specific dates are no longer required. On the following pages, you will find sample cover letters. If you choose to mention your layoff in your cover letter, the first sample cover letter will demonstrate one way to approach that subject.

Sample Cover Letters:

JENNIFER LOHSL
111 Royal Court Circle
City, State 20291
(555) 555-5555

July 5, 2009
Mr. Jack Webb
Director of Procurement
Plaxo Inc.
111 Line Street
City, State 29108

Dear Mr. Webb:

As you are probably aware, Wagner and Bushnell announced a cutback in the size of its area workforce by over 2,000 employees. Unfortunately, my position was one of the ones eliminated by the company.

Should you be in the market for a proven energetic and productive procurement manager for either a corporate or division-led assignment, I would welcome the opportunity to speak with you. A brief summary of my qualifications are as follows:

- *B.S. Chemical Engineering — Pennsylvania State*

- *Five years of procurement experience, advancing from associate buyer to managing buyer*

- *Complete knowledge of all relevant computer software, including Microsoft Office*

The details of my career are laid out more completely in my attached résumé. After you review it, I am confident you will agree that I have a wide range of procurement experience over a varied range of products. While I am focused on the bottom line, as shown by the vast savings I secured for Wagner and Bushnell, I am also focused on quality. With shrewd negotiating skills, I never sacrifice one for the other.

I look forward to talking with you soon regarding my ability to make a similar impact on your company. I will call you later in the week to schedule an interview at your convenience.

Sincerely,

Jennifer Lohsl

Sample Solicited Response Cover Letter

Mr. Bernard Nobles
Publishing House 1
111 Tuku Drive
Jacksonville FL 34875

Dear Mr. Nobles:

It was with great interest that I read about your opening for a full-time reporter on your Web site. The position sounds perfect for someone who enjoys multi-tasking like I do, and I feeel confident in submitting my résumé and writing samples for your review.

My experience and skills make me an excellent candidate for this position. I have worked as a beat reporter for local government covering city and county commission meetings and as a feature reporter for the living section of my hometown newspaper with a circulation of 25,000 readers.

I enjoyed freelancing while I earned my BS in Journalism from the University of Florida and, thanks to an excellent photo journalism course, I have dabbled in photography and Photoshop editing ever since. I am an avid web browser and have my own Web site, which you can visit at www.mywebsite.com.

I believe that I am well-qualified for this position and think you will agree after you read the writing sample I have included. I hope we have an opportunity to meet in person to further discuss the details of this job opening.

Respectfully,

Keri Smith

Sample Cover Letter to a Recruiter

John Smith

3333 Winding Rd.

Thomas Town. FL 33333

Home (555) 555-5555 / Cell (222) 222-2222 / jsmith@email.com

January 1, 2009

Mr. Ben Anderson

Tech Placement Agency

111 Atlanta Blvd.

Jacksonville FL 34875

Dear Mr. Anderson,

Thank you for taking the time to look over this letter. I came across your recruiting agency in my efforts to find a new position. It appears that your company emphasizes placing people in technology firms, and that is exactly my background. I would love the opportunity to meet with you to see if you have any clients who would be interested in my skills.

I have been in the technology industry for more than 15 years. I have a bachelor's degree in Computer Information Systems, and have recently held a product manager position at XYZ Software. I have a strong background in web application development, with experiences in both Java and Visual Basic. Due to my CIS degree, my former employers chose to use my project management training to help initialize, guide, and complete several software development projects. My last project involved designing a subway kiosk system that passengers could enter information into regarding the best routes to their destination. I led a team of four programmers, one software architect, and two quality assurance engineers. Through our efforts, we were able to secure a 2.8 million dollar contract with the New York Transit

Authority to implement and maintain this subway system near the Manhattan section of the New York subway. In addition to my product management background, I also have experience in photography and graphics design. I currently hold several Photoshop certifications and am a contract photographer for one of my local newspapers. I have contributed some photo art to several recording artists' Web sites, most notably ABC Famous Band's current Web site logo. I love the ability to merge my creative passions with the digital medium, and feel I can offer a unique set of skills to many of your clients.

In conclusion, I hope I have given you a small glimpse of my abilities. I have attached my résumé, which gives a more detailed view of what my experiences are, and the skills I bring to the table. I feel that my mix of ability, creativity, and personality enhances any work environment that I am a part of and look forward to my next career opportunity. Please be advised that my target salary range is $60,000-$70,000. I am willing to travel, but cannot consider relocation at this time. Thank you again for looking over my résumé, and I hope that you will consider bringing me in for a more personal conversation. I relish the chance to discuss work opportunities with you, and I hope to hear from you soon.

Regards,

John Smith

Sample "Cold-call" Cover Letter

JANICE WILLIAMS
121 Blue Blvd.
Small Town WI 88888
(978) 555-5555
Jwilliams4638@email.com

September 7, 2009

Ms. Marsha Long
Vice President & General Counsel
Bradley, White, and Jones
111 Lincoln Ave.
Big Town, WI 83272

Dear Ms. Long:

Ashley Grant, one of my colleagues at Swanson Inc., suggested that I contact you. I understand that you and Ashley began your careers together at Cheese America and worked together for more than ten years. She speaks very highly of you.

Ms. Long, I am a corporate attorney and have worked in the legal division of Swanson Inc. for three years since my graduation from Yale Law School in 2006. My area of concentration has been Human Resource law, although I assisted colleagues in both patent and anti-trust cases.

I have attached a copy of my résumé for your reference.

My husband, Jack, and I have decided to relocate to Big Town. Jack has been offered a wonderful career opportunity there that we feel would be a mistake for him to turn down. Therefore, I find myself searching for a position that will be a positive career move for me as well. Ashley was confident you would be able to assist me in my search.

Even if you do not know of any specific openings for someone with my credentials, I would like to meet with you when I am in town the first week of October. Ashley thought you might be able to introduce me to some of your colleagues, as well to give me a jumpstart on my networking goals in your community. Thank you for your assistance in this matter.

Sincerely,

Janice Williams

Sample Online Cover Letter

Trisha Smith
111 Peach St.
Atlanta, GA 44444
(555) 555-5555

Dear Sir/Ma'am:

After working 12 years for a small, family-run insurance company, I find myself looking for new employment. The wonderful owner passed away and the family has decided not to continue the business he started. I worked as his bookkeeper and administrative assistant from the time I graduated with my bachelor's from the University of Georgia until now.

While his passing is a great loss for me, it is with excitement I embark on my quest for a new job. I am detail-oriented, keeping perfect books the entire time I worked at my current position (which held up to the close scru-

tiny of an IRS audit in 2002). I am an excellent multi-tasker, managing my duties as a mother of two boys and my employer's busy office schedule. I am a self-starter who does not need to be asked to fill a need — I simply get things done.

My résumé is listed to detail my skills and accomplishments, but I would enjoy speaking with any interested parties in greater length about how I can assist their office like I did for so many years for my former employer.

Regards,

Trisha Smith

CASE STUDY: DAN SCHAWBEL

Social media specialist
E-mail: dan.schawbel@gmail.com

My passion is in personal branding, which is how we market ourselves to others. I am employed as a social media specialist; my off-duty activities include blogging, publishing a magazine, and writing about personal branding. How can you work on forming your own personal brand? Establishing yourself online is one way. To do this:

1. Register a Web site domain name using your own name (JaneDoe.com) to protect your brand from others who share the same name.

2. Join and use your full name on the most popular social networks, such as LinkedIn℠, Facebook®, and Twitter℠. Why? Recruiters are using those databases to fill positions.

3. If you are 40 or older, you may consider youself to be an expert in your field or are passionate about something. Start a blog based around this topic on **www.WordPress.com** or **www.typepad.com**, which are both beginner blog services. I received a job offer through one of my blogs.

4. Network with other blog or Web site owners whom you have genuine interest in and exchange links or posts with them.

5. Post two to three times per week on your blog, and comment on other blogs.

CASE STUDY: DAN SCHAWBEL

The first step you should take following a job loss is to reach out to your strongest contacts. People locate jobs through people, so do not spend as much time submitting to "machines," such as large job Web sites, and more time facing people. You can do this online through blogging and social networks or offline at professional network gatherings.

A few tips for job searches:

- Do not use a résumé template you find online. Be creative and include your Web site information and some unique design to stand out from other applicants.

- Experience carries ten times more weight than your education or activities, so put that at the top of your résumé.

- Eye contact is critical to the success of your interview because it establishes how serious you are regarding both the position and the interviewer.

- Before you go to an interview, prepare and practice your personal brand statement. In a single sentence, you need to articulate who you are and what value you can contribute to the organization.

Typically, those who succeed at finding jobs after a layoff are the ones who have an open mind, are persistent, and are willing to learn new skills that they can apply to different job types.

CHAPTER 15
The Job Interview

With your résumé and applications submitted, get prepared for interviews. Ensure that employers can reach you by being available to answer the phone and checking your e-mail frequently. Whatever phone number you give, be sure that everyone who may answer it does so professionally and is prepared to take messages. Double-check your voice mail or answering machine to verify that it is working properly. If necessary, change your voice mail greeting to one that is simple and business-like.

Preparing for an Interview

When you are called for an interview, professionally but genuinely show your enthusiasm during the initial contact. Write down the information you are provided regarding the date, time, and location of the interview. Get the person's name who called you, as well as that of the person who will interview you. If they offer to provide directions, accept them and use them. If not, you can look up the address later on a map or online.

To prepare for the interview, whether you are scheduled for a phone or personal interview, learn all you can about the company. Study its Web site and conduct an Internet search for other information about the business. If you know someone employed there, ask about the firm's philosophy and preferences.

Be prepared for these types of questions:

- What are your greatest strengths and weaknesses?
- What has been your biggest challenge, and how did you solve it?
- How did you handle a particularly difficult situation with a co-worker?
- Where do you see yourself five years from now?
- Why do you want to work here?
- What would your last supervisor say about you?

When answering these questions, think of specific examples of accomplishments and goals. Think about your work history, and try to remember details about significant events. Rather than simply saying you are a team player, give an example of when you pitched in on a team effort, such as a group project that required everyone's involvement to succeed.

You should also ask questions to show your interest and knowledge of the company. Develop questions specific to the company based on your research. Local business newspapers can be a good source for current happenings. An expansion, a new product, a new headquarters, or current sales figures are examples of stories you may find about the company. Write your questions in a notebook that you can carry with you to the interview. Also use the notebook to jot notes about the employer's questions and any additional information that might be provided about the job or the company. A final question to ask the interviewer can be about the timing of the interview and hiring process.

In your initial interview, do not ask questions about the salary and benefits. Unless the interviewer volunteers the information, the only appropriate time to discuss this is when you have an actual job offer. Once you have received an offer and know that the employer is interested in hiring you, you will then have negotiating power.

The simple things are important when interviewing:

- Dress professionally and neatly, even if you know the standard attire is casual. You are selling yourself. Your clothes should be clean, pressed and in good condition.

- Do not wear overpowering perfume or cologne.

- Get foolproof directions well in advance. Do a test drive if possible.

- Arrive 10-15 minutes early.

- Do not eat, drink, or chew gum during the interview (unless it takes place over a meal).

- Be friendly to everyone you encounter. Greet the receptionist warmly. He or she may talk to the interviewer afterward about your demeanor.

- Greet the interviewer with a handshake, a confident smile, and a sincere "nice to meet you."

- Smile, listen carefully, and answer questions thoughtfully. Jot down questions or information in your notebook, but do not spend the entire interview writing, particularly when the interviewer is waiting for you to answer a question.

- Thank the interviewer as the meeting ends, and tell him or her you look forward to speaking again soon.

- Follow-up in writing within 24 hours.

- If you do not hear from the company during the specified time frame, give the interviewer a brief telephone call or send an e-mail to ask whether you may provide additional information.

Sample Thank-you/Follow-up Letter

Your Name
Your Address
Your City, State, Zip Code
Your Phone Number
Your E-mail

Date

Name
Title
Organization
Address
City, State, Zip Code

Dear Mr. /Ms. Last Name:

Thank you for taking the time yesterday to speak with me about the accounting position available with Acme Widgets. It was a pleasure to meet you and to learn more about your company.

After speaking with you, I believe that my skills and experience will be an asset to Acme Widget in the accounting position. In addition, I am a fast learner and have the adaptability needed for a diversified position. Aside from having the necessary computer skills for this position, I also offer an enthusiastic personality.

I am interested in working for your company and look forward to hearing from you once the final decisions are made regarding this position. Please feel free to contact me at (555) 123-1111 or via e-mail at your earliest convenience.

Thank you again for your time and consideration.

Sincerely,

Your Signature

Your Typed Name

Starting your letter with the words "thank you" immediately shows your appreciation. Follow-up with a reminder about your skills and qualifications and how they relate to the job. As with the cover letter, be brief, but point out that you are the best person for the job. Close with a strong statement that you are ready to go to work for the employer and are looking forward to getting their response. Remember to include your best contact information, whether that is a phone number or e-mail address.

How to Handle your Termination in an Interview

If you have been fired, your biggest worry may be how to handle this information with potential employers. The most important thing to remember in any interview situation is to be honest, but not to provide more information than requested.

When you are asked why you left your last position, be prepared with an honest answer that will present the situation in the best way possible. Practicing responses ahead of time will pay off when an interviewer pops the dreaded questions. Avoid dishonesty. The truth is certain to come to light and will bear serious consequences. If the company asks your former employer for a reference, learning that you are not eligible for rehire would cause concern — or worse. Some companies will terminate anyone who has been dishonest on an application or résumé.

CASE STUDY: STEPHANIE COUNCIL

MA Counseling Psychology and Counselor Education
Career Counselor

As a career counselor, I have worked with university students and alumni centers on job search strategies, interview skill attainment, and résumé creation. I also have volunteered with a local organization that assists homeless and displaced individuals in finding work, usually following a job loss or periods of unemployment. Beyond this, I consult with corporations on communications strategies to achieve business-directed goals.

The first thing recently laid off employees should do is to make sure that they respond with grace and dignity to the news, however difficult this may be. This can be highly impressive to co-workers and managers, who often have the power to hire down the line at other organizations. Check with human resources to be sure you are receiving a fair termination package. If you have a friend in human resources, ask for advice. Check with your state's unemployment office for available assistance, both financial and job search-related. This is an opportunity for change, but it is often difficult for people to recognize this because job loss can be scary. This is a time to think about how your skills and experiences can transfer to other areas and other careers that may be of more interest to you. And be sure you rely on your friends and family for emotional support.

As you begin to move on, remember that work is not just what we do to pay the bills. It is often a great source of joy or dissatisfaction in life. Often, employees who are uninterested in their work, are under-challenged, or are poorly suited for the job end up in risky situations. If you do not evaluate your long-term career goals and interests, you may end up repeating the same career mistakes over and over. Check with the county's unemployment office to see what workshops are available for career-life planning. If you attended college or a vocational school, see what services are available to alumni through the career center. Explore your interests, take inventory of your skills, and see how they may match to specific career paths.

CASE STUDY: STEPHANIE COUNCIL

To prepare for an interview, have a list of five skill statements available in your mind; the pressure of an interview is no time to rely on quick memory recall of experiences and skill statements. Remember that many interviews today are "behavioral," which means that rather than being asked what you would do in a certain situation, the interviewer may ask you what you actually did do in a certain  situation. When you have at least five skill statements ready to say, and as long as they cover five different areas of your experience or skill set, you should be able to throw out examples to these types of behavioral questions. Go prepared with a short "pitch" about yourself. One of the most common questions is "tell me about yourself." It might seem like an easy question, but it is better to have prepared in your mind the main points you want the interviewer to know about you.

Remember that you are in interview mode from the moment you pull into the parking lot; you never know whose office you parked in front of. It is not unusual for a hiring manager to ask the receptionist how you treated him or her at check in. Be courteous and respectful to everyone you meet as a good habit. If the subject of job termination comes up, you need to address it honestly. But make this a way to show how you turned a weakness or negative experience into a positive or strength. Never lie during an interview, and never bad-mouth former employers.

CONCLUSION

Moving On: What Losing a Job Taught Me

"I think the biggest lesson I have gained is about the importance of maintaining positive relationships with those around you, no matter what the circumstances around the job loss. A graceful exit pays back in multiple ways. Twenty years ago, when I lost my first job, I was angry and pushed back by deleting a file that created an inconvenience for those who had to carry the work forward. Now I would never do something like that; I understand that the relationships are more valuable than the job. Former bosses, colleagues, and employees are now some of my best references and sources of business."

Alice Brink, public relations professional and owner of A Brink & Company

"From losing a job, I recognized that I should have taken independence more seriously. I always knew it was an important issue, but I should have made it an extreme priority."

David Varn, former manager in the financial industry

"I learned that no company will have loyalty to you just because you were a good employee and had loyalty to them. You need to be on the ready and know what is out there in your field and keep up with trends, networking, and your résumé, even if you are not currently looking for a new job by choice. That way, you will be able to hit the ground running if it happens to you again (and for me, it did). You have to look out for you."
Kristen Hirsch, marketing communications manager

"Address any concerns that you have on the job and document them where necessary. If a supervisor is giving you a hard time and refuses to let you get a word in edgewise, send an e-mail addressing your grievances."
Liz Kupcha, marketing professional

"I will survive this. You can't keep crusty and rugged (people) down."
Sheila White, advertising account manager

Using the information provided in this book, you now have the knowledge and the resources available to you to survive a layoff or termination. You know your rights and your employer's obligations, how to challenge a termination if necessary, and where to turn for assistance. Although it may not seem like it at the time, often a layoff or termination propels a person into making the next move — whether that is a new job, a new career, or a new business venture. It may take some time, and you may need to do some work to get there, but you *can* survive unemployment.

APPENDIX A
Glossary

The Americans with Disabilities Act: A portion of this law applies to employment and bans discrimination based on disabling conditions.

Bumping rights: Employees' seniority plays a role in who is laid off; most often applies to union workers.

The Civil Rights Act: Bans discriminating against workers because of their race, color, religion, gender, genetic information, or national origin (sexual harassment and pregnancy discrimination are banned as gender discrimination).

The Civil Service Reform Act: Prevents discrimination.

The Consolidated Omnibus Budget Reconciliation Act (COBRA): This law requires all employers with 20 or more workers to offer ongoing health insurance when jobs are lost for any reason. Your coverage can be extended for up to 18 months at the group rate of the company.

Collective bargaining: Union and company officials arrange the contract and conditions of employment for all union members.

Complaint: A statement of a claim or case submitted to a court.

Contingency: An arrangement in which a lawyer is paid out of any settlement awarded.

Corporate restructuring: Employees are dismissed due to reduced workload or business slowdown.

Defamation: An employer says or writes something about an employee that causes that employee to lose money, such as losing a job or not getting a promotion.

Demand letter: A letter from a lawyer explaining why a person is working with a lawyer and the facts supporting a claim. It will also state that unless the employer offers an acceptable settlement, client will file a lawsuit.

Depositions: Oral statements from witnesses taken by lawyers before going to court.

Discovery requests: The process in which an attorney and a former employer's attorney ask for documents relating to the case.

Downsizing: Employees are dismissed due to reduced workload or business slowdown.

Employee Retirement Income Security Act (ERISA): This law bans employers from interfering with workers' rights to receive retirement benefits. This prevents a company from discharging a worker who is likely to claim benefits in the near future.

Employment at-will: A work arrangement in which the employee may leave the job at any time and the employer may terminate the employee at any time, for any reason. Most workers are employed at-will.

Federal Age Discrimination in Employment Act: This law prohibits discrimination against workers aged 40 to 64.

Firing with cause: Some action on the part of the employee led to the termination.

Firing without cause: Terminating an employee for a reason not related to work or conduct. It is legal to fire workers for any reason or no reason in many cases.

Front-pay: The difference between what someone expects to earn after a wrongful discharge case is closed until a future date and what would have been earned if the former job had been retained.

Genetic Information Nondiscrimination Act: Bans health insurance companies from using genetic information to set premiums or determine enrollment eligibility. Employers cannot use genetic information in hiring, firing, or promotion decisions.

The Health Insurance Portability and Accountability Act (HIPPA): This law includes provisions to protect workers covered by a group health plan. It helps workers retain or receive coverage for pre-existing conditions and bans discrimination based on the health of a worker. It gives employees the right to purchase individual health policies if their COBRA coverage has ended and they are not eligible for a new group plan. This is important for those who have pre-existing or current conditions; HIPPA says one cannot be denied coverage because of health status.

Illegal discrimination: Unfair treatment, including termination, of an employee who is part of a protected group. Protected groups include race, gender, age, and others.

Layoff: Temporary or permanent loss of a job due to reduced workload or business slowdown.

Non-compete agreement: A document that says that one cannot work for a similar business or competitor for a specified time.

Nondisclosure agreement: A document that states you will not reveal company secrets or speak negatively of a firm in public.

The Older Workers Benefit Protection Act: An employee's age cannot be used as the reason for discrimination in benefits; older workers cannot be singled out during a staff reduction process.

Pre-filing stage: The process of gathering all documentation possible for a court case.

Rapid Response: A U.S. Department of Labor program that aids workers who are laid off in securing new employment.

Reasonable accommodation: A change in the job, facility, and/or equipment to adapt for workers' needs; for example, providing a wheelchair ramp to allow a disabled worker to be employed or adjusting work schedules to permit a worker to attend religious services.

Reduction in force: Employees are dismissed due to reduced workload or business slowdown.

The Rehabilitation Act: Prohibits discrimination against disabled persons who work for the federal government.

Remedy: Action that is court-ordered to repair the damage done to the worker. This may be a return to work, financial compensation, or other "cures."

Retaliation: Firing an employee for bringing a charge against the company or for filing a workers' compensation claim.

Service letters: Written statements providing certain details of employment, which may include the reason for termination.

Summary judgment: A former employer, or any defendant in a court case, will have his or her attorney state that the accusing employee's case is so weak that it should not go to a jury, and will ask the judge to dismiss it.

Summons: Order to appear in court.

Whistleblowers: Workers who report practices on the job that are illegal or harmful to the public.

Worker Adjustment and Retraining Notification (WARN) Act: Requires that workers in certain situations be given 60 days' notice of the job loss.

Wrongful discharge: An illegal termination. Examples include breaking an employment contract or firing someone who has a legal contract spelling out terms of employment; breaking a union contract; firing a "whistleblower;" letting someone go because of personal or political activities outside of work hours; firing someone who refuses to break a law or public policy when asked to by the employer; and illegal discrimination.

APPENDIX B
Federal Whistleblower Protection Laws

Workers who report practices on the job that are illegal or harmful to the public cannot be fired for that reason. If you believe you have been discriminated against or that your employer has retaliated against you for reporting safety or health concerns, you may file a complaint with the Occupational Safety and Health Administration (OSHA). The following details the federal laws protecting whistleblowers:

Section 11(c) of the Occupational Safety and Health Act of 1970 (OSH Act) — Provides protection against retaliation based on employee's exercising a variety of rights guaranteed under the OSH Act, such as filing a safety and health complaint with OSHA or participating in an inspection.

29 CFR Part 1977 – Discrimination Against Employees Exercising Rights under the Williams-Steiger OSH Act — These are regulations implementing federal statutes designed to regulate employment conditions related to occupational safety and health.

Surface Transportation Assistance Act of 1982 (STAA) — Provides specific safety and health discrimination protections for truck drivers and other employees relating to the safety of commercial motor vehicles. Coverage includes private-sector workers whose work affects the safety of vehicles with a gross vehicle weight rating (or a gross vehicle weight) of 10,001 pounds or more; vehicles designed to transport more than ten passengers, including the driver; and vehicles transporting materials determined by the U.S. Department of Transportation to be hazardous.

29 CFR Part 1978 – Rules for Implementing Section 405 of the Surface Transportation Assistance Act of 1982 — Provides regulatory information on employee protection from discrimination when the employee has engaged in a protected activity pertaining to commercial motor vehicle safety and health matters.

Asbestos Hazard Emergency Response Act of 1986 (AHERA) — Provides employee protection against retaliation for reporting violations of environmental laws relating to asbestos in elementary and secondary school systems, whether public or non-profit private.

International Safety Container Act of 1977 (ISCA) — Provides specific protection for employees against retaliation for reporting the existence of unsafe shipping containers.

Energy Reorganization Act of 1978 (ERA) — Provides occupational safety and health discrimination protections for employees of operators, applicants, contractors, and subcontractors of nuclear power plants licensed by the Nuclear Regulatory Commission, and for employees of contractors working under contract with the U.S. Department of Energy (so-called GOCO sites).

Clean Air Act of 1977 (CAA) — Provides discrimination protection and provides for the development and enforcement of standards regarding air quality and air pollution. Employees are protected from retaliation for reporting violations, or alleged violations, of the standards.

Safe Drinking Water Act of 1974 (SDWA) — Requires that all drinking water systems in public buildings and new construction of all types be lead free. Employees are protected from retaliation for reporting violations, or alleged violations, of the law.

Federal Water Pollution Control Act of 1972 (FWPCA) — Also called the "Clean Water Act," which basically prohibits any and all hazardous pollution of waters that provide a natural habitat for living things. Persons reporting such pollution, or alleged pollution, are protected from discrimination.

Toxic Substances Control Act (TSCA), 15 USC § 2622 — Regulates the manufacture, distribution, and use of certain toxic substances. Employees are protected from retaliation for reporting violations, or alleged violations, of the Act.

Solid Waste Disposal Act of 1976 (SWDA) — Also called the Resource Conservation and Recovery Act (RCRA), provides technical and financial assistance for the development of facilities for the recovery of energy and other resources from discarded materials, and to regulate the management of hazardous waste. Employees are protected from discrimination for exercising certain rights under the Acts.

Comprehensive Environmental Response, Compensation, and Liability Act of 1980 (CERCLA) — Provides for liability, compensation, cleanup, and emergency response for hazardous substances released into the environment and for the cleanup of inactive hazardous waste disposal sites. Employees are protected from discrimination for exercising certain rights under the Acts.

Wendell H. Ford Aviation Investment and Reform Act for the 21st Century (AIR21) — Provides anti-discrimination coverage to employees of air carriers, contractors, or subcontractors of air carriers who raise safety concerns.

29 CFR 1979 – Procedures for the Handling of Discrimination Complaints under Section 519 of the Wendell H. Ford Aviation Investment and Reform Act for the 21st Century — Provides information on employee protection from discrimination by air carriers, contractors, or subcontractors of air carriers because the employee has engaged in protected activity pertaining to a violation or alleged violation of any order, regulation, or standard of the Federal Aviation Administration or any other provision of federal law relating to air carrier safety.

Corporate and Criminal Fraud Accountability Act of 2002 (CCFA) (Sarbanes-Oxley Act) — Provides anti-discrimination protection to employees of publicly traded corporations who report violations of the Securities Exchange Act or any other federal law relating to fraud against shareholders.

29 CFR Part 1980 – Procedures for the Handling of Discrimination Complaints under Section 806 of the Corporate and Criminal Fraud Accountability Act of 2002 — Provides information on employee protection from discrimination by companies and representatives of companies because the employee has engaged in protected activity pertaining to a violation or alleged violation of any rule or regulation of the Securities and Exchange Commission, or any provision of federal law relating to fraud against shareholders.

Pipeline Safety Improvement Act (PSIA), 49 USC § 60129 — Provides discrimination protection for employees who report violations, or alleged violations, of federal law regarding pipeline safety and security or who refuse to violate such provisions.

29 CFR 1981 – Procedures for the Handling of Discrimination Complaints under Section 6 of the Pipeline Safety Improvement Act of 2002 — Provides procedures and time frames for the handling of discrimination complaints under the Pipeline Safety Act, including procedures and time frames for employee complaints to the Occupational Safety and Health Administration (OSHA), investigations by OSHA, appeals of OSHA determinations to an administrative law judge (ALJ) for a hearing de novo, hearings by ALJs, review of ALJ decisions by the Administrative Review Board (acting on behalf of the Secretary), and judicial review of the Secretary's final decision.

29 CFR Part 24 – Procedures for the Handling of Discrimination Complaints under Federal Employee Protection Statutes — Implements employee protection provisions under the Safe Drinking Water Act, Water Pollution Control Act, Toxic Substances Control Act, Solid Waste Disposal Act, Clean Air Act, Energy Reorganization Act, and Comprehensive Environmental Response, Compensation, and Liability Act.

APPENDIX C

Resources by State

Breakdown of State Discrimination Laws

The following provides the key points of job-related discrimination laws, broken down by state, to supplement the information on being fired illegally, discussed in Chapter 6.

Alabama

Private employers with 20 or more employees may not make employment decisions based on:

- Age (40 and older)

Alaska

Private employers with one or more employees may not make employment decisions based on:

- Age (40 and older)
- Ancestry or national origin
- Physical and mental disability
- AIDS/HIV diagnosis
- Gender
- Race or color

- Marital status
- Pregnancy and/or parenthood
- Religion or creed
- Mental illness

Arizona

Private employers with 15 or more employees may not make employment decisions based on:

- Age (40 and older)
- Ancestry or national origin
- Physical and mental disability
- AIDS/HIV diagnosis
- Gender
- Race or color
- Religion or creed
- Genetic testing results

Arkansas

Private employers with nine or more employees may not make employment decisions based on:

- Ancestry or national origin
- Physical and mental disability
- Gender
- Pregnancy
- Race or color
- Religion or creed
- Genetic testing results

California

Private employers with five or more employees may not make employment decisions based on:

- Age (40 and older)
- Ancestry or national origin
- Physical and mental disability
- AIDS/HIV diagnosis
- Gender
- Pregnancy
- Race or color
- Religion or creed
- Sexual orientation
- Genetic testing results

- Marital status
- Medical condition
- Gender identity
- Political affiliations

Colorado

Private employers with one or more employees may not make employment decisions based on:

- Age (40 to 70)
- Ancestry or national origin
- Physical, learning, and mental disability
- AIDS/HIV diagnosis
- Gender
- Pregnancy
- Race or color
- Religion or creed
- Lawful conduct off the job
- Mental illness

Connecticut

Private employers with three or more employees may not make employment decisions based on:

- Age (40 and older)
- Ancestry or national origin
- Past/present physical, learning, and mental disability, including mental retardation
- AIDS/HIV diagnosis
- Gender
- Marital status
- Pregnancy
- Race or color
- Religion or creed
- Sexual orientation
- Genetic testing results

Delaware

Private employers with four or more employees may not make employment decisions based on:

- Age (40 and older)
- Ancestry or national origin
- Physical and mental disability
- AIDS/HIV diagnosis
- Gender
- Marital status

- Pregnancy
- Race or color
- Religion or creed
- Genetic testing results

District of Columbia

Private employers with one or more employees may not make employment decisions based on:

- Age (18 and older)
- Ancestry or national origin
- Physical and mental disability
- AIDS/HIV diagnosis
- Gender
- Marital status, including domestic partnership
- Pregnancy and/or parenthood
- Race or color
- Religion or creed
- Sexual orientation
- Genetic testing results
- Gender identity
- Political affiliations
- School enrollment
- Family duties
- Source of income
- Place of residence or business
- Personal appearance
- Smoking
- Any reason except individual merit

Florida

Private employers with 15 or more employees may not make employment decisions based on:

- Age
- Ancestry or national origin
- Handicap
- AIDS/HIV diagnosis
- Gender
- Marital status
- Race or color
- Religion or creed
- Sickle cell trait

Georgia

Private employers with 15 or more employees regarding disability and 10 or more regarding gender may not make employment decisions based on:

- Physical and mental disability
- Gender

Hawaii

Private employers with one or more employees may not make employment decisions based on:

- Age
- Ancestry or national origin
- Physical and mental disability
- AIDS/HIV diagnosis
- Gender
- Marital status
- Pregnancy
- Race or color
- Religion or creed
- Sexual orientation
- Genetic testing results
- Arrest and/or court records, unless there is a conviction closely related to the job

Idaho

Private employers with five or more employees may not make employment decisions based on:

- Age (40 and older)
- Ancestry or national origin
- Physical and mental disability
- Gender
- Pregnancy
- Race or color
- Religion or creed
- Genetic testing results

Illinois

Private employers with 15 or more employees (one or more as relates to disability) may not make employment decisions based on:

- Age (40 and older)
- Ancestry or national origin
- Physical and mental disability
- AIDS/HIV diagnosis
- Gender
- Marital status
- Pregnancy
- Race or color
- Religion or creed
- Sexual orientation
- Genetic testing results
- Gender identity
- Citizenship status
- Military status
- Unfavorable military discharge
- Arrest record

Indiana

Private employers with six or more employees (one or more as relates to age and 15 or more as relates to disability) may not make employment decisions based on:

- Age (40 to 70)
- Ancestry or national origin
- Physical and mental disability
- Gender
- Race or color
- Religion or creed

Iowa

Private employers with four or more employees may not make employment decisions based on:

- Age (18 and older)
- Ancestry or national origin
- Physical and mental disability
- AIDS/HIV diagnosis
- Gender
- Pregnancy
- Race or color
- Religion or creed
- Sexual orientation
- Genetic testing results

Kansas

Private employers with four or more employees may not make employment decisions based on:

- Age (18 and older)
- Ancestry or national origin
- Physical and mental disability
- AIDS/HIV diagnosis

- Gender
- Race or color
- Religion or creed
- Genetic testing results
- Military status

Kentucky

Private employers with eight or more employees may not make employment decisions based on:

- Age (40 and older)
- Ancestry or national origin
- Physical and mental disability
- AIDS/HIV diagnosis
- Gender
- Race or color

- Religion or creed
- Smoking or non-smoking preference
- Occupational Pneumoconiosis with no respiratory impairment as the result of exposure to coal dust

Louisiana

Private employers with 20 or more employees, or 25 or more as relates to pregnancy, may not make employment decisions based on:

- Age (40 and older)
- Ancestry or national origin
- Physical and mental disability
- Gender

- Pregnancy
- Race or color
- Religion or creed
- Genetic testing results
- Sickle cell trait

Maine

Private employers with one or more employees may not make employment decisions based on:

- Age
- Ancestry or national origin
- Physical and mental disability
- Gender
- Pregnancy
- Race or color

- Religion or creed
- Sexual orientation
- Genetic testing results
- Gender identity
- Prior workers' compensation claims
- Prior whistleblowing

Maryland

Private employers with 15 or more employees may not make employment decisions based on:

- Age (40 and older)
- Ancestry or national origin
- Physical and mental disability
- Gender
- Marital status

- Pregnancy
- Race or color
- Religion or creed
- Sexual orientation
- Genetic testing results

Massachusetts

Private employers with six or more employees may not make employment decisions based on:

- Age (40 and older)
- Ancestry or national origin
- Physical and mental disability
- AIDS/HIV diagnosis
- Gender
- Marital status

- Race or color
- Religion or creed
- Sexual orientation
- Genetic testing results
- Military service
- Arrest record

Michigan

Private employers with one or more employees may not make employment decisions based on:

- Age
- Ancestry or national origin
- Physical and mental disability
- AIDS/HIV diagnosis
- Gender
- Marital status
- Pregnancy
- Race or color
- Religion or creed
- Genetic testing results
- Height or weight
- Arrest record

Minnesota

Private employers with one or more employees may not make employment decisions based on:

- Age (18 to 70)
- Ancestry or national origin
- Physical and mental disability
- AIDS/HIV diagnosis
- Gender
- Sexual orientation or perceived sexual orientation
- Genetic testing results
- Gender identity
- Marital status
- Pregnancy
- Race or color
- Religion or creed
- Membership in local commission
- Public assistance recipient status

Mississippi

All employers may not make employment decisions based on military status. No other groups are protected unless the employer receives public funding.

Missouri

Private employers with six or more employees may not make employment decisions based on:

- Age (40-70)
- Ancestry or national origin
- Physical and mental disability
- AIDS/HIV diagnosis
- Gender
- Pregnancy
- Race or color
- Religion or creed
- Genetic testing results

Montana

Private employers with one or more employees may not make employment decisions based on:

- Age
- Ancestry or national origin
- Physical and mental disability
- Gender
- Marital status
- Pregnancy
- Race or color
- Religion or creed

Nebraska

Private employers with 15 or more employees (25 or more as relates to age, and no employers may consider genetic testing results) may not make employment decisions based on:

- Age (40 to 70)
- Ancestry or national origin
- Physical and mental disability
- AIDS/HIV diagnosis
- Gender
- Marital status
- Pregnancy
- Race or color
- Religion or creed
- Genetic testing results

Nevada

Private employers with 15 or more employees may not make employment decisions based on:

- Age (40 and older)
- Ancestry or national origin
- Physical and mental disability
- Gender
- Pregnancy
- Religion or creed
- Religion or creed
- Sexual orientation
- Genetic testing results
- Lawful use of any product off the job
- Use of service animal

Private employers with five or more employees may not make employment decisions based on:

- Age (40 and older)
- Ancestry or national origin
- Physical and mental disability
- AIDS/HIV diagnosis
- Gender
- Marital status
- Pregnancy
- Race or color
- Religion or creed
- Sexual orientation
- Genetic testing results
- Gender identity
- Medical condition

New Hampshire

Private employers with six or more employees may not make employment decisions based on:

- Age
- Ancestry or national origin
- Physical and mental disability
- Gender
- Marital status
- Pregnancy
- Race or color
- Religion or creed
- Sexual orientation
- Genetic testing results

New Jersey

Private employers with one or more employees may not make employment decisions based on:

- Age (18 to 70)
- Ancestry or national origin
- Past and/or present physical and mental disability
- AIDS/HIV diagnosis
- Gender
- Marital status, including domestic partnership
- Pregnancy
- Race or color
- Religion or creed
- Sexual orientation
- Genetic testing results and/or any genetic predispositions
- Gender identity
- Military service or status
- Smoking or non-smoking preference
- Use of guide or service dog

New Mexico

Private employers with four or more employees (20 or more as relates to age, 15 or more as relates to gender identity, and 50 or more as relates to marital status) may not make employment decisions based on:

- Age (40 and older)
- Ancestry or national origin
- Marital status
- Pregnancy
- Race or color
- Religion or creed
- Sexual orientation
- Genetic testing results
- Gender identity
- Serious medical condition

New York

Private employers with four or more employees may not make employment decisions based on:

- Age (18 and older)
- Physical and mental disability
- Ancestry or national origin
- Genetic testing results

- AIDS/HIV diagnosis
- Gender
- Marital status
- Pregnancy
- Race or color
- Religion or creed
- Sexual orientation

- Lawful use of any product off the job
- Military status
- Observance of Sabbath
- Political activities
- Use of service dog

North Carolina

Private employers with 15 or more employees may not make employment decisions based on:

- Age
- Ancestry or national origin
- Physical and mental disability
- AIDS/HIV diagnosis
- Gender
- Race or color

- Religion or creed
- Genetic testing results
- Lawful use of any product off the job
- Military service
- Sickle cell trait

North Dakota

Private employers with one or more employees may not make employment decisions based on:

- Age (40 and older)
- Ancestry or national origin
- Physical and mental disability
- Gender
- Marital status

- Pregnancy
- Race or color
- Religion or creed
- Lawful conduct off the job
- Public assistance recipient status

Ohio

Private employers with four or more employees may not make employment decisions based on:

- Age (40 and older)
- Ancestry or national origin
- Physical, learning, and mental disability
- Gender
- Pregnancy
- Race or color
- Religion or creed

Oklahoma

Private employers with 15 or more employees may not make employment decisions based on:

- Age (40 and older)
- Ancestry or national origin
- Physical and mental disability
- Gender
- Race or color
- Religion or creed
- Genetic testing results
- Military service
- Smoking or non-smoking preference

Oregon

Private employers with four or more employees (six or more as relates to disability) may not make employment decisions based on:

- Age (18 and older)
- Ancestry or national origin
- Physical and mental disability
- Gender
- Marital status
- Pregnancy
- Race or color
- Religion or creed
- Genetic testing results

Pennsylvania

Private employers with four or more employees may not make employment decisions based on:

- Age (40 to 70)
- Ancestry or national origin
- Physical and mental disability
- Gender
- Pregnancy
- Race or color
- Religion or creed
- Familial status
- Having a GED rather than a high-school diploma
- Use of guide or service animal

Rhode Island

Private employers with four or more employees (one or more as relates to gender-based wage discrimination) may not make employment decisions based on:

- Age (40 and older)
- Ancestry or national origin
- Physical and mental disability
- AIDS/HIV diagnosis
- Gender
- Pregnancy
- Race or color
- Religion or creed
- Sexual orientation
- Genetic testing results
- Gender identity
- Domestic abuse victim status

South Carolina

Private employers with 15 or more employees may not make employment decisions based on:

- Age (40 and older)
- Ancestry or national origin
- Physical and mental disability
- Gender
- Pregnancy
- Race or color
- Religion or creed

South Dakota

Private employers with one or more employees may not make employment decisions based on:

- Ancestry or national origin
- Physical, learning, and mental disability
- Gender

- Race or color
- Religion or creed
- Genetic testing results
- Pre-existing injury

Tennessee

Private employers with eight or more employees (one or more as relates to gender-based wage discrimination) may not make employment decisions based on:

- Age (40 and older)
- Ancestry or national origin
- Physical and mental disability

- Gender
- Race or color
- Religion or creed

Texas

Private employers with 15 or more employees may not make employment decisions based on:

- Age (40 and older)
- Ancestry or national origin
- Physical and mental disability
- Pregnancy
- Race or color

- Gender
- Pregnancy
- Race or color
- Religion or creed
- Genetic testing results

Utah

Private employers with 15 or more employees may not make employment decisions based on:

- Age (40 and older)
- Ancestry or national origin
- Disability as outlined in federal law
- AIDS/HIV diagnosis

- Gender
- Pregnancy
- Race or color
- Religion or creed
- Genetic testing results

Vermont

Private employers with one or more employees may not make employment decisions based on:

- Age (18 and older)
- Ancestry or national origin
- Physical and mental disability
- AIDS/HIV diagnosis
- Gender

- Race or color
- Religion or creed
- Sexual orientation
- Genetic testing results
- Place of birth

Virginia

All employers may not make employment decisions based on:

- Age
- Ancestry or national origin
- Physical and mental disability
- Gender
- Marital status

- Pregnancy
- Race or color
- Religion or creed
- Genetic testing results
- Use of service animal

Washington

Private employers with eight or more employees (one or more as relates to gender-based wage discrimination) may not make employment decisions based on:

- Age (40 and older)
- Ancestry or national origin
- Physical, sensory, and mental disability
- AIDS/HIV diagnosis
- Gender
- Marital status
- Pregnancy
- Race or color
- Religion or creed
- Sexual orientation
- Genetic testing results
- Gender identity
- Hepatitis C diagnosis
- Membership in state militia
- Use of a guide dog

West Virginia

Private employers with 12 or more employees may not make employment decisions based on:

- Age (40 and older)
- Ancestry or national origin
- Physical and mental disability
- AIDS/HIV diagnosis
- Gender
- Race or color
- Religion or creed
- Smoking off the job

Wisconsin

Private employers with one or more employees may not make employment decisions based on:

- Age (40 and older)
- Ancestry or national origin
- Physical and mental disability
- AIDS/HIV diagnosis
- Gender
- Marital status
- Pregnancy
- Race or color
- Religion or creed
- Sexual orientation

- Genetic testing results
- Arrest or conviction
- Lawful use of any product off the job

- Military service or status
- Honesty testing

Wyoming

Private employers with two or more employees may not make employment decisions based on:

- Age (40 and older)
- Ancestry or national origin
- Gender
- Race or color

- Religion or creed
- Military service or status
- Smoking off the job

Dislocated Worker Assistance Centers by State

Alabama
Workforce Development Division
Alabama Department of
Economic and Community Affairs
401 Adams Avenue
P.O. Box 5690
Montgomery, AL 36103-5690
334-242-5300
Fax: 334-242-5855

Alaska
Department of Labor and
Workforce Development
P.O. Box 11149
Juneau, AK 99811
907-465-1882

Arizona
Dislocated Workers Unit
Arizona Workforce
1789 West Jefferson
Site Code 920Z
Phoenix, AZ 85007
602-542-2494
Fax: 602-542-2491

Arkansas
Dislocated Worker Services
Arkansas Employment
Security Department
P.O. Box 2981
Little Rock, AR 72203
501-682-1818

California

CA Employment Development
Department
Workforce Services Division
P.O. Box 826880 (MIC 50)
Sacramento, CA 94280-0001
916-654-6206
Fax: 916-654-7921

Colorado

Colorado Department of
Labor and Employment
633 17th Street, Suite #700
Denver, CO 80202-3660
303-318-8840
Fax: 303-318-8930

Connecticut

CT Department of Labor
200 Folly Brook Blvd.
Weathersfield, CT 06109
860-263-6588
Fax: 860-263-6039

Delaware

Division of Unemployment
and Training
P.O. Box 9828
4425 North Market Street
Wilmington, DE 19809
302-761-8114

District of Columbia

Department of Employment
Services
602 H Street NE
Washington, DC 20002
202-698-3495
Fax: 202-673-8630

Florida

REACT Program
107 E. Madison Street
Tallahassee, FL 32399-4137
850-921-3326

Georgia

Georgia Department of Labor
Suite 440
148 Andrew Young International
Blvd., NE
Atlanta, GA 30303
404-232-3505
Fax: 404-232-3503

Hawaii

830 Punchbowl Street Room #329
Honolulu, HI 96813
808-586-8825
Fax: 808-586-8822

Idaho

Idaho Commerce and Labor
317 W. Main
Boise, ID 83735-0790

208-332-3570 ext. 3316
Fax: 208-332-7417

Illinois
Bureau of Workforce Development
Illinois Department of
Commerce & Economic
Opportunity
620 East Adams, 5th Floor
Springfield, IL 62701
217-558-2435
Fax: 217-557-5506

Indiana
Indiana Dept. of
Workforce Development
Indiana Government Center South
10 North Senate
Indianapolis, IN 46204
317-233-4010
Fax: 317-233-6081

Iowa
Iowa Workforce Development
1000 East Grand Avenue
Des Moines, IA 50319-0209
Telephone: (515) 281-5387 or
(800) JOB-IOWA

Kansas
1000 SW Jackson Street, Suite 100
Topeka, KS 66612-1354
Phone: (785) 296-3481

Fax: (785) 296-5055
TTY Service: (785) 296-3487

Kentucky
Rapid Response Team
Office of Employment
and Training
Division of Workforce Services
275 East Main Street
Mailstop 2WA
Frankfort, KY 40601
502-564-7456
Fax: 502-564-7459

Louisiana
Louisiana Department of Labor
Labor Market Information
Research and Statistics Division,
LMI Unit
1001 North 23rd Street
Post Office Box 94094
Baton Rouge, LA 70804-9094
Fax: (225) 342-9192
oois@lwc.la.gov

Maine
Maine Department of Labor
Bureau of Employment Services
55 State House Station
Augusta, ME 04333-0055
Phone: (207) 623-7981

Maryland
Dislocated Workers Unit
Department of Labor, Licensing
and Regulations
Office of Employment
and Training
1100 North Eutaw Street
Room 601
Baltimore, MD 21201
410-767-2833
Fax: 410-333-5162

Massachusetts
Massachusetts Division of
Career Services
340 Main Street
Suite 650 A
Worcester, MA 01608
508-890-3218
Fax: 508-792-7327

Michigan
Michigan Department of
Labor and Economic Growth
Michigan Department of Labor &
Economic Growth
611 West Ottawa, 4th Floor,
PO Box 30004
Lansing, MI 48909
517-335-1943
Cell: 517-242-4452
Fax: 517-373-4648

Minnesota
Economic Development
Minnesota Department of Employ-
ment and Economic Development
(DEED)
Main Office
1st National Bank Building
332 Minnesota Street, Suite E200
Saint Paul, MN 55101-1351

Mississippi
Mississippi Department of
Employment Security
1235 Echelon Parkway
Jackson, MS 39213
601-321-6554
Fax: 601-321-6598

Missouri
Division of Workforce
Development
P.O. Box 1087
Jefferson City, MO 65102
573-751-3349
Fax: 573-751-8162

Montana
Dislocated Worker/Rapid
Response Unit
Statewide Workforce
Programs Bureau
Workforce Services Division

Montana Department of Labor
and Industry
P.O. Box 1728
Helena, MT 59624
406-444-4513
Fax: 406-444-3037

Nebraska
Nebraska Workforce Development
Dept. of Labor
550 S. 16th Street
PO Box 94600
Lincoln, NE 68509
402-471-8574
Fax: 402-471-3050

Nevada
Department of Employment,
Training, and Rehabilitation
500 E. Third Street
Carson City, NV 89713
775-684-0320
Fax: 775-687-1073

New Hampshire
Dept. of Resources &
Economic Development
P.O. Box 1856
Concord, NH 03302-1856
603-271-2341
Fax: 603-271-6784

New Jersey
New Jersey Dept. of Labor and
Workforce Development
Office of Workforce Initiatives
John Fitch Plaza, P.O. Box 933
Trenton, NJ 08625-0933
609-984-3519
Fax: 609-777-3202

New Mexico
New Mexico Department of
Workforce Solutions
1596 Pacheco Street, Suite 201
Santa Fe, NM 87505
505-827-6895
Fax: 505-827-6812

New York
New York Department of Labor
State Campus Office Building #12
Albany, NY 12240
518-457-0380
Fax: 518-457-9526

North Carolina
North Carolina Department of
Commerce/Employment and
Training
313 Chapanoke Road Suite 120
Raleigh, NC 27603
919-329-5248
Fax: 919-662-4770

North Dakota
Dislocated Worker Office
Job Service North Dakota
1000 E Divide Avenue
P.O. Box 5507
Bismarck, ND 58506-5507
701-328-3066

Ohio
Ohio Department of Job and
Family Services
4020 E. 5th Avenue
Columbus, OH 43219
614-644-0564

Oklahoma
Oklahoma Employment Security
Commission
2401 N. Lincoln
Oklahoma City, OK 73152
405-557-5395
Fax: 405-557-1478

Oregon
Community Colleges and
Workforce Development
255 Capitol Street NE
Salem, OR 97310
503-378-8648, ext. 226
Fax: 503-378-3365

Pennsylvania
Bureau of Workforce Investment
12th Floor, Labor & Industry
Building
7th and Forster Streets
Harrisburg, PA 17120
717-783-1951
Fax: 717-772-5478

Puerto Rico
Yolanda Rivera Ortiz
Directora Auxiliar, UETDP
Edificio Compañía Fomento
Industrial, Piso 2 Avenida F.D.
Roosevelt #355, Hato Rey,
P.R. 00918
P.O. Box 192159, San Juan PR
00919-2159
(787) 754-5504 ext. 339
Fax: (787)754-7052
Email: yrivera@cdorh.org

Rhode Island
Rhode Island Department of
Labor and Training
1511 Pontiac Avenue,
Building 73, 3rd Floor
Cranston, RI 02920
401-462-8804
Fax: 401-462-8798

South Carolina
South Carolina Department of
Commerce
1201 Main Street, Suite 1600
Columbia, SC 29201-3200
866-721-7867 or 803-737-2601
Fax: 803-737-2119

South Dakota
700 Governors Drive
Pierre, SD 57501-2291
605-773-5017
Fax: 605-773-3216

Tennessee
Dislocated Worker Unit/Rapid
Response Team
Tennessee Workforce Development
Davy Crocker Tower, 12th Floor
500 James Robertson Parkway
Nashville, TN 37245-0658
818-253-5868
Fax: 615-741-3003

Texas
Texas Workforce Commission
101 E. 15t Street, Room 506T
Austin, TX 78778
512-936-0406
Fax: 512-936-0331

Utah
Utah Department of Workforce
Services
140 East 300 South, Suite 500
Salt Lake City, UT 84111
801-526-4312
Fax: 801-526-9662

Vermont
Vermont Department of Labor
5 Green Mountain Drive
P.O. Box 488
Montpelier, VT 05602
802-828-4177
Fax: 802-828-4374

U.S. Virgin Islands
Virgin Islands Department
of Labor
2203 Church Street, Christiansen
St. Croix, VI 00820
340-773-1994
Fax: 340-773-0094

Virginia
State Dislocated Worker Unit
Governor's Office for
Workforce Development
1001 East Broad Street
Old City Hall Office Building,
Suite 222
Richmond, VA 23219
Phone: 804-225-3050
Fax: 804-225-2631

Washington
Washington State Employment
Security Department
P.O. Box 9046
Olympia, WA 98507-9046
360-438-4627
Fax: 360-438-4666

West Virginia
Workforce West Virginia
Dislocated Worker Services Unit
112 California Avenue, Room 409
Charleston, WV 25305-0112
Phone: 304-558-8415
Fax: 304-558-7029

Wisconsin
Division of Workforce Excellence
Wisconsin Department of
Workforce Development
201 E. Washington Avenue
Madison, WI 53707-1784
608-266-7406
Fax: 608-267-0330

Wyoming
Department of Workforce Services
Wyoming Department of
Employment
P.O. Box 2760
Casper, WY 82602
307-235-3270
Fax: 307-235-3293

State Living Assistance Programs

To apply for living assistance, contact your state's program, found in the following list.

Alabama Family Assistance
Web site: **www.dhr.state.al.us/counties.asp**
Telephone: 334-242-1310

Alaska Temporary Assistance Program
Web site: **http://health.hss.state.ak.us/dpa/programs/atap**
Telephone: 907-465-3347

Arizona Cash Assistance Program
Web site: **www.azdes.gov**
Telephone: 602-542-9935

California CalWORKs
Web site: **www.dss.cahwnet.gov/foodstamps/PG839.htm**
Telephone: 866 - 262-9881

Colorado Works
Web site: **www.colorado.gov/cs/Satellite/CDHS-ColoradoWorks/**
CCW/1194261855486
Telephone: 303-866-5700

Connecticut Temporary Assistance for Needy Families
Web site: **www.dss.state.ct.us/svcs/tanf.htm**
Telephone: 800-842-1508

Delaware Temporary Assistance for Needy Families
Web site: **www.state.de.us/dhss/dss/tanf.html**
Telephone: 302-255-9500

District of Columbia Temporary Assistance for Needy Families
Web site: **www.dhs.dc.gov/dhs/cwp/view,a,3,q,568277,dhsNav,**
|30980|.asp
Telephone: 202-279-6002

Florida Temporary Assistance for Needy Families
Web site: **www.dcf.state.fl.us/ess/tanf.shtml**
Telephone: 850-487-1111

Georgia Temporary Assistance for Needy Families
Web site: **http://dfcs.dhr.georgia.gov**
Telephone: 800-869-1150

Hawaii Financial Assistance
Web site: **www.realchoices.org**
Telephone: 808-643-1643

Idaho Temporary Assistance for Families
Web site: **www.healthandwelfare.idaho.gov**
Telephone: 208-334-5500

Illinois Temporary Assistance for Needy Families
Web site: **www.dhs.state.il.us**
Telephone: 800-843-6154

Indiana Temporary Assistance for Needy Families
Web site: **www.in.gov**
Telephone: 800-622-4932

Iowa Family Investment Program
Web site: **www.dhs.state.ia.us**
Telephone: 800-972-2017

Kansas Successful Families Program
Web site: **www.srskansas.org/ISD/ees/taf-ga.htm**
Telephone: 888-369-4777

Kentucky Transitional Assistance Program
Web site: **https://apps.chfs.ky.gov/Office_Phone/index.aspx**
Telephone: 502-564-7050

Louisiana Family Independence Temporary Assistance Program
Web site: **www.dss.state.la.us/index.cfm?md=pagebuilder&tmp=home &pid=139**
Telephone: 888-524-3578

Maine Temporary Assistance for Needy Families
Web site: **www.maine.gov/dhs/bfi/Office%20Locations.htm**
Telephone: 207-287-6897

Maryland Temporary Cash Assistance
Web site: **www.dhr.state.md.us/how/cashfood/tca.htm**
Telephone: 800-332-6347

Massachusetts Transitional Aid to Families with Dependent Children
 Web site: **www.mass.gov/dta**
Telephone: 800-249-2007

Michigan Family Independence Program
Web site: **www.michigan.gov/fia**
Telephone: 517-373-2035

Minnesota Family Investment Program
Web site: **www.dhs.state.mn.us/main/idcplg?IdcService=GET_DY-NAMIC_CONVERSION&dDocName=id_004112&RevisionSelectionMethod=LatestReleased**
Telephone: 651-431-4000

Mississippi Temporary Assistance for Needy Families
Web site: **www.mdhs.state.ms.us/ea_tanf.html**
Telephone: 800-948-4060

Missouri Temporary Assistance for Needy Families
Web site: **http://dss.missouri.gov/fsd/tempa.htm**
Telephone: 573-751-4815

Montana Temporary Assistance for Needy Families
Web site: **www.dphhs.mt.gov**
Telephone: 406-444-1788

Nebraska Aid to Dependent Children
Web site: **www.hhs.state.ne.us/fia/adc.htm**
Telephone: 800-254-4202

Nevada Temporary Assistance for Needy Families
Web site: **http://dwss.nv.gov**
Telephone: 775-684-0500

New Hampshire Temporary Assistance to Needy Families
Web site: **www.dhhs.nh.gov/DHHS/TANF/default.htm**
Telephone: 800-852-3345 ext. x4238

New Jersey Work First
Web site: **www.state.nj.us/humanservices/dfd**
Telephone: 609-288-2400

New Mexico Temporary Assistance for Needy Families
Web site: **www.hsd.state.nm.us/isd/fieldoffices.html**
Telephone: 888-473-3676

New York Temporary Assistance for Needy Families
Web site: **www.otda.state.ny.us**
Telephone: 800-342-3009

North Carolina Work First
Web site: **www.ncdhhs.gov**
Telephone: 800-662-7030

North Dakota Temporary Assistance for Needy Families
Web site: **http://lnotes.state.nd.us/dhs**
Telephone: 800-472-2622

Ohio Works First
Web site: **www.ohioworkforce411.gov/jobseekers/
onestopmap.stm**
Telephone: 614-466-6282

Oklahoma Temporary Assistance for Needy Families
Web site: **www.okdhs.org/programsandservices/tanf**
Telephone: 866-411-1877

Oregon Temporary Assistance for Needy Families
Web site: **www.oregonhelps.org**
Telephone: 503-945-5651

Pennsylvania Temporary Assistance for Needy Families
Web site: **www.dpw.state.pa.us/About/OIM/003670281.htm**
Telephone: 800-692-7462

Rhode Island Family Independence Program
Web site: **www.dhs.state.ri.us/dhs/dfipref.htm**
Telephone: 401-462-5300

South Carolina Family Independence
Web site: **www.state.sc.us/dss/contact.html**
Telephone: 800-768-5700

South Dakota Temporary Assistance for Needy Families
Web site: **www.state.sd.us/social/TANF/index.htm**
Telephone: 605-773-4678

Tennessee Families First
Web site: **www.tnjustice.org/family/default.htm**
Telephone: 888-863-6178

Texas Temporary Assistance for Needy Families
Web site: **www.yourtexasbenefits.com/wps/portal**
Telephone: 800-448-3927

Utah Family Employment Program
Web site: **www.utah.gov**
Telephone: 801-526-9675

Vermont Reach Up
Web site: **www.dsw.state.vt.us/Programs_pages/Reach_Up/ Reach_Up.htm**
Telephone: 800-287-0589

Virginia Temporary Assistance for Needy Families
Web site: **www.dss.state.va.us/localagency/index.html**
Telephone: 800-552-3431

Washington WorkFirst
Web site: **www.workfirst.wa.gov/resources/parents.asp**
Telephone: 360-902-0627

West Virginia WORKS
Web site: **www.wvdhhr.org/bcf/family_assistance/wvworks.asp**
Telephone: 800-642-8589

Wisconsin Works
Web site: **http://dcf.wi.gov/w2/wisworks.htm**
Telephone: 608-266-0327

Wyoming Temporary Assistance for Needy Families
Web site: **http://dfsweb.state.wy.us/districts/base2.htm**
Telephone: 307-777-5846

State Departments of Labor

Alabama Department of Labor
P.O. Box 303500
Montgomery, AL 36130-3500
334-242-3460
www.alalabor.state.al.us

Alaska Department of
Labor and Workforce Development
P.O. Box 11149
Juneau, AK 99822-2249
907-465-2700
www.labor.state.AK.us

Arizona Industrial Commission
800 West Washington Street
Phoenix, AZ 85007
602-542-4515
www.ica.state.AZ.us
Arkansas Department of Labor
10421 West Markham
Little Rock, AR 72205
501-682-4500
www.Arkansas.gov/labor

California Labor and
Workforce Development Agency
801 K Street, Suite 2101
Sacramento, CA 95814

916-327-9064
www.dir.CA.gov/dlse
www.labor.CA.gov

Colorado Department of
Labor and Employment
633 17th St., Suite 201
Denver, CO 80202-3660
303-318-8000
www.COworkforce.com

Connecticut Department of Labor
200 Folly Brook Blvd.
Wethersfield, CT 06109-1114
860-263-6000
www.CT.gov/dol

Delaware Secretary of Labor
4425 N. Market St., 4th FL
Wilmington, DE 19802
302-761-8000
www.Delawareworks.com

District of Columbia
Employment Services Department
64 New York Ave., NE, Suite 3000
Washington, DC 20002
202-724-7000
www.DOES.DC.gov

Florida Agency for Workforce
Innovation
The Caldwell Building
107 East Madison St. Suite 100
Tallahassee, FL 32399-4120
850-245-7105
www.Floridajobs.org

Georgia Department of Labor
Sussex Place, Room 600
148 Andrew Young International
Blvd., NE
Atlanta, GA 30303
404-656-3011
commissioner@dol.state.GA.us
www.dol.state.GA.us

Hawaii Department of
Labor & Industrial Relations
830 Punchbowl Street
Honolulu, HI 96813
808-586-8842
www.Hawaii.gov/labor

Idaho Department of Labor
317 W. Main St.
Boise, ID 83735-0001
208-332-3570
800-843-3193
www.labor.Idaho.gov

Illinois Department of Labor
160 N. LaSalle Street
13th Fl, Suite C-1300
Chicago, IL 60601
312-793-2800
www.state.IL.us/agency/idol

Indiana Department of Labor
Indiana Government Center South
402 W. Washington Street
Room W195
Indianapolis, IN 46204
317-232-2655
www.IN.gov/labor

Iowa Workforce Development
1000 East Grand Avenue
Des Moines, IA 50319-0209
515-281-5387
www.Iowaworkforce.org/labor

Kansas Department of Labor
401 S.W. Topeka Blvd.
Topeka, KS 66603-3182
785-296-5000
www.dol.KS.gov

Kentucky Department of Labor
1047 U.S. Hwy 127 South, Suite 4
Frankfort, KY 40601-4381
502-564-3070
www.labor.KY.gov

Louisiana Workforce Commission
1001 N. 23rd Street
Baton Rouge, LA 70802
225-342-3111
www.LAworks.net

Maine Department of Labor
45 Commerce Drive
Augusta, ME 04330
207-623-7900
www.state.ME.us/labor

Maryland Department of
Labor and Industry
500 N. Calvert Street, Suite 401
Baltimore, MD 21202
410-230-6001
www.dllr.state.MD.us

Massachusetts Department of
Labor & Work Force Development
One Ashburton Place, Rm 2112
Boston, MA 02108
617-626-7100
www.Mass.gov/eolwd
www.state.ma.us

Michigan Department of
Labor & Economic Growth
P.O. Box 30004
Lansing, MI 48909

517-373-1820
www.Michigan.gov/cis

Minnesota Department of
Labor and Industry
443 Lafayette Road North
St. Paul, MN 55155
651-284-5005
www.doli.state.MN.us

Mississippi Department of
Employment Security
1235 Echelon Parkway
P.O. Box 1699
Jackson, MS 39215-1699
601-321-6000
www.mdes.MS.gov

Missouri Labor and
Industrial Relations
P.O. Box 599
3315 W. Truman Boulevard
Jefferson City, MO 65102-0599
573-751-2461
www.dolir.MO.gov/lirc

Montana Department of
Labor and Industry
P.O. Box 1728
Helena, MT 59624-1728
406-444-2840
www.dli.MT.gov

Nebraska Department of Labor
550 South 16th Street
Box 94600
Lincoln, NE 68509-4600
402-471-9000
www.dol.nebraska.gov

Nevada Department of
Business and Industry
555 E. Washington Ave.,
Suite 4100
Las Vegas, NV 89101-1050
702-486-2650
www.laborcommissioner.com
www.NV.gov

New Hampshire Department
of Labor
State Office Park South
95 Pleasant Street
Concord, NH 03301
603-271-3176
www.labor.state.NH.us

New Jersey Department of Labor
1 John Fitch Plaza
P.O. Box 110
Trenton, NJ 08625-0110
609-777-3200
lwd.dol.state.nj.us/labor/
index.shtml

New Mexico Department of Labor
P.O. Box 1928
401 Broadway, N.E.
Albuquerque, NM 87103-1928
505-841-8450
www.dol.state.NM.us

New York Department of Labor
W. Averell Harriman State Office
Campus
Building 12
Albany, NY 12240
518-457-9000
www.labor.state.NY.us

North Carolina Department
of Labor
4 West Edenton Street
Raleigh, NC 27601-1092
919-733-7166
www.nclabor.com

North Dakota Department
of Labor
State Capitol Building
600 East Boulevard, Dept 406
Bismarck, ND 58505-0340
701-328-2660
www.nd.gov/labor

Ohio Department of Commerce
77 South High Street, 22nd Floor
Columbus, OH 43215
614-644-2239
www.com.state.OH.us

Oklahoma Department of Labor
4001 N. Lincoln Blvd.
Oklahoma City, OK 73105-5212
405-528-1500
www.state.OK.us/~okdol

Oregon Bureau of Labor and
Industries
800 NE Oregon St., Suite 1045
Portland, OR 97232
971-673-0761
www.Oregon.gov/boli

Pennsylvania Department of
Labor and Industry
1700 Labor and Industry Bldg
7th and Forster Streets
Harrisburg, PA 17120
717-787-5279
www.dli.state.PA.us

Rhode Island Department of
Labor and Training
1511 Pontiac Avenue
Cranston, RI 02920

401-462-8000
www.dlt.state.RI.us

South Carolina Department of
Labor, Licensing, & Regulations
P.O. Box 11329
Columbia, SC 29211-1329
803-896-4300
www.llr.state.SC.us

South Dakota Department
of Labor
700 Governors Drive
Pierre, SD 57501-2291
605-773-3101
www.dol.sd.gov

Tennessee Department of
Labor & Workforce Development
220 French Landing Drive
Nashville, TN 37243
615-741-6642
www.state.TN.us/labor-wfd

Texas Workforce Commission
101 East 15th St.
Austin, TX 78778
512-475-2670
www.twc.state.TX.us

Utah Labor Commission
160 E. 300 S. Ste. 300

Salt Lake City, UT 84111
801-530-6800
www.Laborcommission.Utah.gov

Vermont Department of Labor
5 Green Mountain Drive
P.O. Box 488
Montpelier, VT 05601-0488
802-828-4000
www.labor.vermont.gov

Virginia Department of
Labor and Industry
Powers-Taylor Building
13 S. 13th Street
Richmond, VA 23219
804-371-2327
www.doli.Virginia.gov

Washington Department of
Labor and Industries
7273 Linderson Way SW
Tumwater, WA 98501-5414
360-902-5800
www.lni.WA.gov

West Virginia Division of Labor
749 B Building, Capitol Complex
Charleston, WV 25305
304-558-7890

www.wvlabor.org/
newwebsite/pages/index.html

Wisconsin Department of
Workforce Development
201 E. Washington Ave., #A400
P.O. Box 7946
Madison, WI 53707-7946
608-266-3131
www.dwd.state.WI.us

Wyoming Department of
Employment
1510 East Pershing Blvd.
Cheyenne, WY 82002
307-777-7261
http://wydoe.state.wy.us

American Samoa
Uunai Legal Services Clinic
P.O. Box 6341
Pago Pago, AS 96799
684-633-2892

Legal Services Corporation State Offices

Alabama

Legal Services Alabama Inc.
207 Montgomery St.
Suite 1200 Bell Building
Montgomery, AL 36104-3534
866-456-6353
www.LegalServicesAlabama.org

Alaska

Alaska Legal Services
Corporation
1648 Cushman Street,
Suite 300
Fairbanks, AK 99701-6202
800-478-5401
www.alsc-law.org

Arizona

Community Legal Services Inc.
305 South 2nd Avenue
P.O. Box 21538
Phoenix, AZ 85036-1538
800-852-9075

Southern Arizona Legal Aid, Inc.
2343 East Broadway Boulevard,
Ste. 200
Tucson, AZ 85719
520-623-9465
www.sazlegalaid.org

DNA-People's Legal Services Inc.
P.O. Box 306
Window Rock, AZ 86515
928-871-4151
www.nativelegalnet.org

Arkansas

Legal Aid of Arkansas, Inc.
714 South Main Street
Jonesboro, AR 72401
870-972-9224

Center for Arkansas Legal Services
303 West Capitol Avenue,
Suite 200
Little Rock, AR 72201
501-376-3423

California

Greater Bakersfield Legal
Assistance Inc.
615 California Avenue
Bakersfield, CA 93304
661-325-5943
www.gbla.org

Central California Legal Services
1401 Fulton Street, Suite 700
Fresno, CA 93721
559-570-1200
www.centralcallegal.org

Neighborhood Legal Services of Los
Angeles County
1102 E. Chevy Chase Drive
Glendale, CA 91205
818-291-1760
www.nls-la.org

Inland Counties Legal Services Inc.
1040 Iowa Avenue, Suite 109
Riverside, CA 92507
909-368-2555
www.inlandlegal.org

Legal Services of Northern
California Inc.
517 12th Street

Sacramento, CA 95814
916-551-2150
www.lsnc.net

Legal Aid Society of Orange
County Inc.
2101 N. Tustin Ave.
Santa Ana, CA 92705
800-834-5001
www.legal-aid.com

California Indian Legal
Services Inc.
609 S. Escondido Blvd.
Escondido, CA 92025
760-746-8941
www.calindian.org

Bay Area Legal Aid
1735 Telegraph Avenue
Oakland, CA 94612
510-663-4755
www.baylegal.org

Legal Aid Foundation of
Los Angeles
1102 South Crenshaw Boulevard
Los Angeles, CA 90019-3111
323-801-7991
www.lafla.org

Legal Aid Society of San Diego Inc.
110 South Euclid Avenue
San Diego, CA 92114
877-534-2524
www.lassd.org

California Rural Legal
Assistance Inc.
631 Howard Street Suite 300
San Francisco, CA 94105-3907
415-777-2752
www.crla.org

Colorado

Colorado Legal Services
1905 Sherman Street
Suite 400
Denver, CO 80203
303-837-1313
www.coloradolegalservices.org

Connecticut

Statewide Legal Services of
Connecticut Inc.
425 Main Street 4th Floor
Middletown, CT 06457
800-453-3320
www.slsct.org

Delaware

Legal Services Corporation
of Delaware Inc.
100 West 10th Street Suite 203
Wilmington, DE 19801
302-575-0408
www.lscd.com

District of Columbia

Neighborhood Legal Services Program of the District of Columbia
680 Rhode Island Avenue, N.E.
Washington, DC 20002
202-269-5100
www.nlsp.org

Florida

Community Legal Services of Mid-Florida Inc.
128-A Orange Avenue #100
Daytona Beach, FL 32114-4310
800-363-2357
www.clsmf.org

Florida Rural Legal Services
3210 Cleveland Ave.
P.O. Box 219
Fort Meyers, FL 33902
239-334-4554
www.frls.org

Legal Services of Greater
Miami Inc.
3000 Biscayne Boulevard
Suite 500
Miami, FL 33137-4129
305-576-0080
www.lsgmi.org

Legal Services of North Florida Inc.
2119 Delta Boulevard
Tallahassee, FL 32303-4209
850-385-9007
www.lsnf.org

Bay Area Legal Services, Inc.
Riverbrook Center, 2nd Floor
829 W. Martin Luther
King Jr. Blvd.
Tampa, FL 33603
813-232-1343
www.bals.org

Three Rivers Legal Services Inc.
901 NW 8th Avenue, Suite D5
Gainesville, FL 32601
352-372-0519
www.trls.org

Coast to Coast Legal Aid of South
Florida Inc.
491 North State Road 7

Plantation, FL 33317
954-736-2400
www.legalaid.org/index.html

Georgia

Georgia Legal Services Program
104 Marietta Street, Suite 250
Atlanta, GA 30303
404-206-5175
www.glsp.org

Atlanta Legal Aid Society Inc.
151 Spring Street N.W.
Atlanta, GA 30303-2097
404-524-5811
www.atlantalegalaid.org

Guam

Guam Legal Services Corporation
113 Bradley Place
Hagatna, GU 96910
671-477-9811

Hawaii

Legal Aid Society of Hawaii
924 Bethel Street
Honolulu, HI 96813
808-536-4302
www.legalaidhawaii.org

Native Hawaiian Legal
Corporation
1164 Bishop Street, Suite 1205
Honolulu, HI 96813-2826
808-521-2302
http://nhlchi.org

Idaho

Idaho Legal Aid Services Inc.
310 North Fifth Street
P.O. Box 913
Boise, ID 83701-0913
208-345-0106
www.idaholegalaid.org

Illinois

Legal Assistance Foundation of
Metropolitan Chicago
111 W. Jackson Blvd. 3rd Floor
Chicago, IL 60604-3502
312-341-1070
www.lafchicago.org

Land of Lincoln Legal Assistance
Foundation
8787 State St., Suite 201
East St. Louis, IL 62203-2026
618-398-0958
www.lollaf.org

Prairie State Legal Services Inc.
975 North Main Street
Rockford, IL 61103-7064
815-965-2134
www.pslegal.org

Indiana

Indiana Legal Services, Inc.
Market Square Ctr. Suite 1800
151 North Delaware Street
Indianapolis, IN 46204-2523
800-869-0212
www.indianajustice.org

Iowa

Iowa Legal Aid
1111 Ninth Street Suite 230
Des Moines, IA 50314-2527
800-532-1275
www.iowalegalaid.org

Kansas

Kansas Legal Services Inc.
712 South Kansas Ave. Suite 200
Topeka, KS 66603-3808
800-723-6953
www.kansaslegalservices.org

Kentucky

Legal Aid of the Bluegrass
104 East 7th Street
Covington, KY 41011
859-431-8200
www.lablaw.org

Legal Aid Society
416 West Muhammad Ali Blvd
Louisville, KY 40202-2353
800-292-1862
www.laslou.org

Appalachian Research and Defense
Fund of Kentucky
120 North Front Avenue
Prestonsburg, KY 41653-1221
800-556-3876
www.ardfky.org

Kentucky Legal Aid
1700 Destiny Lane
Bowling Green, KY 42104
866-452-9243
www.klaid.org

Louisiana

Capital Area Legal Services
Corporation
200 Third Street
Baton Rouge, LA 70801
225-387-5173
www.calscla.org

Legal Services of North
Louisiana, Inc.
720 Travis Street
Shreveport, LA 71101
800-826-9265
www.cp-tel.net/klsc

Acadiana Legal Service
Corporation
1020 Surrey Street
P.O. Box 4823
Lafayette, LA 70502-4823
800-256-1175
www.la-law.org

Southeast Louisiana Legal Services
Corporation
1200 Derek Drive Suite 100
P.O. Drawer 2867
Hammond, LA 70404-2867
800-349-0886
www.slls.org

Maine

Pine Tree Legal Assistance Inc.
88 Federal Street

P.O. Box 547
Portland, ME 04112-0547
207-774-8211
www.ptla.org

Maryland

Legal Aid Bureau Inc.
500 East Lexington Street
Baltimore, MD 21202
800-999-8904
www.mdlab.org

Massachusetts

Volunteer Lawyers Project of the
Boston Bar Association
99 Chauncy Street, Suite 400
Boston, MA 02111
617-423-0648
www.vlpnet.org

New Center for Legal
Advocacy, Inc.
257 Union Street
New Bedford, MA 02740
800-244-9023
www.ncla.net

Merrimack Valley Legal
Services Inc.
35 John Street Suite 302

Lowell, MA 01852-1101
978-458-1465
www.mvlegal.org

Massachusetts Justice Project
57 Suffolk Street
Suite 401
Holyoke, MA 01040-5028
800-639-1209

Michigan

Legal Services of South Central
Michigan Inc.
420 North Fourth Avenue
Ann Arbor, MI 48104-1197
734-665-6181
www.lsscm.org

Legal Services of Eastern Michigan
436 South Saginaw Street
Flint, MI 48502
800-322-4512
www.lsem-mi.org

Legal Services of Northern
Michigan Inc.
Parkside Mini Mall
1349 S Otsego Avenue Unit 7B
Gaylord, MI 49735
888-645-9993
www.lsnm.org

Western Michigan Legal Services
Cornerstone Building Suite 400
89 Ionia Avenue N.W.
Grand Rapids, MI 49503
616-774-0672
www.legalaidwestmich.org

Legal Aid and Defender
Association, Inc.
613 Abbott Street
Detroit, MI 48226
313-967-5555
www.ladadetroit.org

Michigan Indian Legal
Services Inc.
814 South Garfield Avenue
Suite A
Traverse City, MI 49686-3430
800-968-6877
www.mils.org

Micronesia

Micronesian Legal Services, Inc.
Chalon Kanoa Village, District #2
P.O. Box 500269
Saipan, MP 96950-0269
670-234-6243

Minnesota

Legal Aid Service of
Northeastern Minnesota
302 Ordean Building
424 West Superior Street
Duluth, MN 55802
800-622-7266
www.lasnem.org

Central Minnesota Legal
Services Inc.
430 First Ave. North, Suite 359
Minneapolis, MN 55401-1780
612-334-5970
www.centralmnlegal.org

Legal Services of Northwest
Minnesota Corporation
1015 7th Ave. N.
P.O. Box 838
Moorhead, MN 56560-0838
800-450-8585
www.lsnmlaw.org

Southern Minnesota Regional Legal
Services
166 E. Fourth Street, Suite 200
St. Paul, MN 55101-1448
651-228-9823
www.smrls.org

Anishinabe Legal Services Inc.
411 First Street N.W.
P.O. Box 157
Cass Lake, MN 56633-0157
800-422-1335

Mississippi

North Mississippi Rural Legal
Services Inc.
5 County Road 1014
P.O. Box 767
Oxford, MS 38655
800-898-8731
www.nmrls.com

Mississippi Center for Legal
Services
111 East Front Street·
P.O. Drawer 1728
Hattiesburg, MS 39403-1728
601-545-2950

Missouri

Legal Services of Eastern
Missouri Inc.
4232 Forest Park Avenue
St. Louis, MO 63108
800-444-0514
www.lsem.org

Mid-Missouri Legal Services
Corporation
205 East Forest Avenue
Columbia, MO 65203
800-568-4931

Legal Services of Southern
Missouri
2872 South Meadowbrook
Springfield, MO 65807
800-444-4863

Legal Aid of Western Missouri
1125 Grand Blvd., #1900
Kansas City, MO 64106
816-474-6750
www.lawmo.org

Montana

Montana Legal Services Association
616 Helena Avenue, Suite 100
Helena, MT 59601
406-442-9830
www.mtlsa.org

Nebraska

Legal Aid of Nebraska
1904 Farnam Street
Suite 500

Omaha, NE 68102-1969
888-991-9921
www.nebls.com

Nevada

Nevada Legal Services
530 South 6th Street
Las Vegas, NV 89101
702-386-0404
www.nlslaw.net

New Hampshire

Legal Advice & Referral
Center, Inc.
48 South Main Street
Concord, NH 03301
800-639-5290
www.larcnh.org

New Jersey

Legal Services of Northwest Jersey
34 West Main Street, Suite 301
Somerville, NJ 08876-2218
908-231-0840
www.lsnj.org/lsnwj

South Jersey Legal Services
745 Market Street
Camden, NJ 08102-1117
856-964-2010

Northeast New Jersey Legal
Services Corporation
574 Summit Avenue
Jersey City, NJ 07306-2797
201-792-6363

Essex-Newark Legal Services
Project, Inc.
5 Commerce Street, 2nd Floor
Newark, NJ 07102
973-624-4500

Ocean-Monmouth Legal Services
303 West Main Street
Freehold, NJ 07728
732-866-0020

Central Jersey Legal Services
317 George Street, Ste. 201
New Brunswick, NJ 08901-2006
732-249-7600

New Mexico

New Mexico Legal Aid
301 Gold SW
First Floor (zip 87102)
P.O. Box 25486
Albuquerque, NM 87125-5486
505-243-7871
www.nmlegalaid.org

New York

Legal Aid Society of Northeastern
New York
55 Colvin Avenue
Albany, NY 12206
800-462-2922
www.lasnny.org

Neighborhood Legal Services Inc.
Main Seneca Building
237 Main Street
4th Floor
Buffalo, NY 14203
716-847-0650
www.nls.org

Nassau/Suffolk Law Services
Committee Inc.
One Helen Keller Way 5th Floor
Hempstead, NY 11550
516-292-8100
www.nslawservices.org

Legal Services NYC
350 Broadway 6th Floor
New York, NY 10013-9998
646-442-3310
www.legalservicesnyc.org

Legal Assistance of Western
New York
One West Main Street
Rochester, NY 14614
585-325-2520
www.lawny.org

Legal Aid Society of Mid-New York
Inc.
255 Genesee Street, 2nd Floor
Utica, NY 13501-3405
315-793-7000
www.lasmny.org

Legal Services of the Hudson Valley
4 Cromwell Place
White Plains, NY 10601
914-949-1305
www.lshv.org

North Carolina

Legal Aid of North Carolina Inc.
224 South Dawson Street
P.O. Box 26087
Raleigh, NC 27601-6087
919-856-2564
www.legalaidnc.org

North Dakota

Legal Services of
North Dakota, Inc.
1025 Third Street North
P.O. Box 1893
Bismarck, ND 58502-1893
800-634-5263
**www.legalassist.org/tree/lsnd_
tree.html**

Ohio

Community Legal Aid
Services, Inc.
50 South Main Street, Suite 800
Akron, OH 44308
800-998-9454
www.communitylegalaid.org

Legal Aid Society of
Greater Cincinnati
215 East Ninth Street
Suite 200
Cincinnati, OH 45202
800-582-2682
www.lascinti.org

The Legal Aid Society of Cleveland
1223 West Sixth St. 4th Floor
Cleveland, OH 44113-1354

216-687-1900
www.lasclev.org

The Legal Aid Society
of Columbus
1108 City Park Avenue
Columbus, OH 43206
614-224-8374
www.columbuslegalaid.org

Ohio State Legal Services
Association
555 Buttles Avenue
Columbus, OH 43215-1137
614-221-7201
www.ohiolegalservices.org

Legal Aid of Western Ohio
525 Jefferson Ave., Ste. 400
Suite 640
Toledo, OH 43604
877-894-4599
www.lawolaw.org

Oklahoma

Oklahoma Indian Legal
Services Inc.
4200 Perimeter Center Drive,
Suite 222
Oklahoma City, OK 73112

800-658-1497
www.oilsonline.org

Legal Aid Services of Oklahoma
2915 North Classen Boulevard
Suite 500
Oklahoma City, OK 73106
405-557-0020
www.legalaidok.org

Oregon

Legal Aid Services of Oregon
921 SW Washington, Suite 500
Portland, OR 97205
503-224-4086
www.lasoregon.org

Pennsylvania

Philadelphia Legal
Assistance Center
42 South 15th Street
Suite 500
Philadelphia, PA 19102
215-981-3800
www.philalegal.org

MidPenn Legal Services
213-A North Front Street
Harrisburg, PA 17101-2240

717-232-0581
www.midpenn.org

Neighborhood Legal
Services Association
928 Penn Avenue
Pittsburgh, PA 15222-3799
866-761-6572
www.nlsa.us

North Penn Legal Services
65 E. Elizabeth Avenue
Suite 800
Bethlehem, PA 18018
610-317-8757
www.northpennlegal.org

Southwestern Pennsylvania Legal
Services Inc.
10 West Cherry Avenue
Washington, PA 15301
800-846-0871
www.swplsconsortium.org

Northwestern Legal Services
Renaissance Centre, Suite 700
1001 State Street
Erie, PA 16501
800-753-5704
www.nwls.org

Legal Aid of Southeastern
Pennsylvania
625 Swede Street
Norristown, PA 19401
610-275-5400
www.lasp.org

Laurel Legal Services Inc.
306 South Pennsylvania Avenue
Greensburg, PA 15601-3066
800-253-9558
http://wpalaw.org

Puerto Rico

Puerto Rico Legal Services, Inc.
1859 Ave. Ponce de Len-Pda 26
Apartado 9134
San Juan, PR 00908-9134
800-981-5342
www.servicioslegales.org

Community Law Office Inc.
170 Calle Federico Costa
Box 194735
San Juan, PR 00919-4735
787-751-1600
www.servicioslegales.org

Rhode Island

Rhode Island Legal Services Inc.
56 Pine Street 4th Floor
Providence, RI 02903
800-662-5034
www.rils.org

South Carolina

South Carolina Legal Services
701 South Main Street,
Greenville, SC 29601
800-763-4825
www.sclegal.org

South Dakota

East River Legal Services
335 North Main Ave. Suite 300
Sioux Falls, SD 57104
800-952-3015

Dakota Plains Legal Services Inc.
P.O. Box 727
Mission, SD 57555-0727
800-658-2297
www.dpls.org

Tennessee

Legal Aid of East Tennessee
502 South Gay Street Suite 404

Knoxville, TN 37902-1502
865-637-0484
www.laet.org

Memphis Area Legal Services Inc. /
Claridge House Bldg., Suite 200
109 North Main Street
Memphis, TN 38103-5013
901-523-8822
www.malsi.org

Legal Aid Society of Middle Tennessee and the Cumberlands
300 Deaderick Street
Nashville, TN 37201-1103
615-244-6610
www.las.org

West Tennessee Legal Services Inc.
210 West Main Street
P.O. Box 2066
Jackson, TN 38302-2066
731-423-0616
www.wtls.org

Texas

Legal Aid of Northwest Texas
600 E. Weatherford
2nd Floor
Fort Worth, TX 76102

800-955-3959
www.lanwt.org

Texas RioGrande Legal Aid
300 South Texas Boulevard
Weslaco, TX 78596
800-369-0574
www.trla.org

Lone Star Legal Aid
414 East Pillar Street
Nacogdoches, TX 75961-5511
800-354-1889
www.lonestarlegal.org

Utah

Utah Legal Services Inc.
205 North 400 West,
Salt Lake City, UT 84103-1125
801-924-3183
www.andjusticeforall.org

Vermont

Legal Services Law Line of
Vermont Inc.
30 Elmwood Avenue
Burlington, VT 05401
800-639-8857
www.lawlinevt.org

Virginia

Potomac Legal Aid Society, Inc.
6400 Arlington Blvd. Suite 600
Falls Church, VA 22042
866-534-5243
www.potomaclegalaid.org

Southwest Virginia Legal Aid
Society Inc.
227 West Cherry Street
Marion, VA 24354
800-277-6754
www.svlas.org

Central Virginia Legal Aid
Society Inc.
101 West Broad St., Suite 101
Richmond, VA 23220
800-868-1012
www.cvlas.org

Legal Aid Society of
Eastern Virginia
125 St. Paul's Blvd.
Suite 400
Norfolk, VA 23510
888-868-1072
www.laseva.org

Virginia Legal Aid Society Inc.
513 Church Street
P.O. Box 6200
Lynchburg, VA 24505
434-528-4722
www.vlas.org

Blue Ridge Legal Services Inc.
204 North High Street
P.O. Box 551
Harrisonburg, VA 22803
800-237-0141
www.brls.org

Virgin Islands

Legal Services of the Virgin Islands
3017 Estate Orange Grove
Christiansted, St. Croix
U.S. Virgin Islands 00820-4375
340-773-2626
www.legalservicesvi.org

Washington

Northwest Justice Project
401 Second Ave. South Suite 407
Seattle, WA 98104
888-201-1012
www.nwjustice.org

West Virginia

Legal Aid of West Virginia, Inc.
922 Quarrier Street, 4th Floor
Charleston, WV 25301
800-642-8279
www.lawv.net

Wisconsin

Legal Action of Wisconsin Inc.
230 West Wells Street Room 800
Milwaukee, WI 53203-1866
414-278-7722
www.legalaction.org

Wisconsin Judicare Inc.
300 Third Street Suite 210
Wausau, WI 54403
800-472-1638
www.judicare.org

Wyoming

Legal Aid of Wyoming Inc.
211 West 19th Street, Suite 201
Cheyenne, WY 82001
1-877-432-9955
www.wyominglegalservices.com

Equal Employment Opportunity Commission (EEOC)
Contacts for Each State

Note: The appropriate office for your area may be in another state.

Alabama

Birmingham District Office
1900 3rd Avenue, North
Suite 101
Birmingham, AL 35203-2397
Phone: 205-731-1359
TDD: 205-731-0095

Alaska

Seattle District Office
Federal Office Building
909 First Avenue, Suite 400
Seattle, WA 98104-1061
Phone: 206-220-6883
TDD: 206-220-6882

Arkansas

Little Rock Area Office
425 West Capitol Avenue
Suite 625

Little Rock, AR 72201
Phone: 501-324-5060
TDD: 501-324-5481

Arizona

Phoenix District Office
3300 N. Central Avenue
Phoenix, AZ 85012-1848
Phone: 602-640-5000
TDD: 602-640-5072

California

Fresno Local Office
1265 West Shaw Avenue, Suite 103
Fresno, CA 93711
Phone: 209-487-5793
TDD: 209-487-5837

Los Angeles District Office
255 E. Temple
4th Floor
Los Angeles, CA 90012
Phone: 213-894-1000
TDD: 213-894-1121

Oakland Local Office
1301 Clay Street
Suite 1170-N
Oakland, CA 94612-5217
Phone: 510-637-3230

TDD: 510-637-3234

San Diego Area Office
401 B Street
Suite 1550
San Diego, CA 92101
Phone: 619-557-7235
TDD: 619-557-7232

San Francisco District Office
901 Market Street
Suite 500
San Francisco, CA 94103
Phone: 415-356-5100
TDD: 415-356-5098

San Jose Local Office
96 North 3rd Street
Suite 200
San Jose, CA 95112
Phone: 408-291-7352
TDD: 408-291-7374

Colorado

Denver District Office
303 E. 17th Avenue
Suite 510
Denver, CO 80203
Phone: 303-866-1300
TDD: 303-866-1950

Connecticut

Boston Area Office
John F. Kennedy Federal Building
Government Center
4th Floor, Room 475
Boston, MA 02203
Phone: (617) 565-3200
TTY: (617) 565-3204

Delaware

Philadelphia Area Office
21 South 5th Street
4th Floor
Philadelphia, PA 19106
Phone: 215-451-5800
TTY: 215-451-5814

District of Columbia

Washington Field Office
1400 L Street, NW, Suite 200
Washington, DC 20005
Phone: 202-275-7377
TDD: 202-275-7518

Florida

Miami District Office
One Biscayne Tower
2 South Biscayne Boulevard

Suite 2700
Miami, FL 33131
Phone: 305-536-4491
TDD: 305-536-5721

Tampa Area Office
501 East Polk Street, 10th Floor
Tampa, FL 33602
Phone: 813-228-2310
TDD: 813-228-2003

Georgia

Atlanta District Office
100 Alabama Street
Suite 4R30
Atlanta, GA 30303
Phone: 404-562-6800
TDD: 404-562-6801

Savannah Local Office
410 Mall Boulevard
Suite G
Savannah, GA 31406-4821
Phone: 912-652-4234
TDD: 912-652-4439

Hawaii

Honolulu Local Office
300 Ala Moana Boulevard,

Room 7123-A
PO Box 50082
Honolulu, HI 96850-0051
Phone: 808-541-3120
TDD: 808-541-3131

Idaho

Seattle District Office
Federal Office Building
909 First Avenue, Suite 400
Seattle, WA 98104-1061
Phone: 206-220-6883
TDD: 206-220-6882

Illinois

Chicago District Office
500 West Madison Street
Suite 2800
Chicago, IL 60661
Phone: 312-353-2713
TDD: 312-353-2421

Indiana

Indianapolis District Office
101 W. Ohio Street
Suite 1900
Indianapolis, IN 46204-4203
Phone: 317-226-7212
TDD: 317-226-5162

Iowa

Milwaukee District Office
310 West Wisconsin Avenue
Suite 800
Milwaukee, WI 53203-2292
Phone: 414-297-1111
TDD: 414-297-1115

Kansas

Kansas City Area Office
400 State Avenue
Suite 905
Kansas City, KS 66101
Phone: 913-551-5655
TDD: 913-551-5657

Kentucky

Louisville Area Office
600 Dr. Martin Luther
King, Jr. Place
Suite 268
Louisville, KY 40202
Phone: 502-582-6082
TDD: 502-582-6285

Louisiana

New Orleans District Office
701 Loyola Avenue

Suite 600
New Orleans, LA 70113-9936
Phone: 504-589-2329
TDD: 504-589-2958

Maine

Maine Human Rights Commission
51 State House Station
Augusta, ME 04333-0051
Phone: 207-624-6050
TDD: 207-624-6063

Maryland

Baltimore District Office
City Crescent Building
10 South Howard Street
3rd Floor
Baltimore, MD 21201
Phone: 410-962-3932
TDD: 410-962-6065

Massachusetts

Boston Area Office
John F. Kennedy Federal Building
Government Center
4th Floor, Room 475
Boston, MA 02203
Phone: (617) 565-3200
TTY: (617) 565-3204

Michigan

Detroit District Office
477 Michigan Avenue
Room 865
Detroit, MI 48226-9704
Phone: 313-226-7636
TDD: 313-226-7599

Minnesota

Minneapolis Area Office
330 South Second Avenue
Suite 430
Minneapolis, MN 55401-2224
Phone: 612-335-4040
TDD: 612-335-4045

Mississippi

Jackson Area Office
207 West Amite Street
Jackson, MS 39201
Phone: 601-965-4537
TDD: 601-965-4915

Missouri

St. Louis District Office
Robert A. Young Building
122 Spruce Street
Room 8.100

St. Louis, MO 63103
Phone: 314-539-7800
TDD: 314-539-7803

Montana

Seattle District Office
Federal Office Building
909 First Avenue, Suite 400
Seattle, WA 98104-1061
Phone: 206-220-6883
TDD: 206-220-6882

Nevada

Las Vegas Area Office
333 Las Vegas Blvd South
Suite 8112
Las Vegas, NV 89101
Phone: 800-669-4000
TTY: 800-669-6820

San Francisco District Office
901 Market Street
Suite 500
San Francisco, CA 94103
Phone: 415-356-5100
TDD: 415-356-5098

New Hampshire

Boston Area Office

John F. Kennedy Federal Building
Government Center
4th Floor, Room 475
Boston, MA 02203
Phone: (617) 565-3200
TTY: (617) 565-3204

New Jersey

Newark Area Office
1 Newark Center, 21st Floor
Newark, NJ 07102-5233
Phone: 201-645-6383
TDD: 201-645-3004

New Mexico

Albuquerque District Office
505 Marquette Street, NW
Suite 900
Albuquerque, NM 87102
Phone: 505-248-5201
TDD: 505-248-5240

New York

Buffalo Local Office
6 Fountain Plaza
Suite 350
Buffalo, NY 14202
Phone: 716-846-4441
TDD: 716-846-5923

New York District Office
33 Whitehall St
New York, NY 10004-2112
Phone: 804-441-3470
TDD: 804-441-3578

North Carolina

Charlotte District Office
129 West Trade Street
Suite 400
Charlotte, NC 28202
Phone: 704-344-6682
TDD: 704-344-6684

Greensboro Local Office
801 Summit Avenue
Greensboro, NC 27405-7813
Phone: 910-333-5174
TDD: 910-333-5542

Raleigh Area Office
1309 Annapolis Drive
Raleigh, NC 27608-2129
Phone: 919-856-4064
TDD: 919-856-4296

North Dakota

Minneapolis Area Office
330 South Second Avenue

Suite 430
Minneapolis, MN 55401-2224
Phone: 612-335-4040
TDD: 612-335-4045

Ohio

Cincinnati Area Office
525 Vine Street
Suite 810
Cincinnati, OH 45202-3122
Phone: 513-684-2851
TDD: 513-684-2074

Cleveland District Office
1660 West Second Street
Suite 850
Cleveland, OH 44113-1454
Phone: 216-522-2001
TDD: 216-522-8441

Oklahoma

Oklahoma Area Office
210 Park Avenue
Oklahoma City, OK 73102
Phone: 405-231-4911
TDD: 405-231-5745

Oregon

Seattle District Office

Federal Office Building
909 First Avenue, Suite 400
Seattle, WA 98104-1061
Phone: 206-220-6883
TDD: 206-220-6882

Pennsylvania

Philadelphia District Office
21 South 5th Street
4th Floor
Philadelphia, PA 19106
Phone: 215-451-5800
TDD: 215-451-5814

Pittsburgh Area Office
1001 Liberty Avenue
Suite 300
Pittsburgh, PA 15222-4187
Phone: 412-644-3444
TDD: 412-644-2720

Puerto Rico

San Juan Local Office
525 F.D. Roosevelt Ave.
Plaza Las Americas, Suite 1202
San Juan, Puerto Rico 00918-8001
Phone: 800-669-4000
TTY: 800-669-6820

Rhode Island

Boston Area Office
John F. Kennedy Federal Building
Government Center
4th Floor, Room 475
Boston, MA 02203
Phone: (617) 565-3200
TTY: (617) 565-3204

South Carolina

Greenville Local Office
Wachovia Building, Suite 530
15 South Main Street
Greenville, SC 29601
Phone: 803-241-4400
TDD: 803-241-4403

South Dakota

Minneapolis Area Office
330 South Second Avenue
Suite 430
Minneapolis, MN 55401-2224
Phone: 612-335-4040
TDD: 612-335-4045

Tennessee

Memphis District Office
1407 Union Avenue
Suite 521

Memphis, TN 38104

Phone: 901-544-0115

TDD: 901-544-0112

Nashville Area Office

50 Vantage Way

Suite 202

Nashville, TN 37228

Phone: 615-736-5820

TDD: 615-736-5870

Texas

Dallas District Office

207 S. Houston Street

3rd Floor

Dallas, TX 75202-4726

Phone: 214-655-3355

TDD: 214-655-3363

El Paso Area Office

The Commons, Building C,

Suite 100

4171 N. Mesa Street

El Paso, TX 79902

Phone: 915-534-6550

TDD: 915-534-6545

Houston District Office

1919 Smith Street, 7th Floor

Houston, TX 77002

Phone: 713-209-3320

TDD: 713-209-3367

San Antonio District Office

5410 Fredericksburg Road

Suite 200

San Antonio, TX 78229-3555

Phone: 210-229-4810

TDD: 210-229-4858

Utah

Phoenix District Office

3300 N. Central Avenue

Phoenix, AZ 85012-1848

Phone: 602-640-5000

TDD: 602-640-5072

U.S. Virgin Islands

San Juan Local Office

525 F.D. Roosevelt Ave.

Plaza Las Americas, Suite 1202

San Juan, Puerto Rico 00918-8001

Phone: 800-669-4000

TTY: 800-669-6820

Vermont

Boston Area Office

John F. Kennedy Federal Building

Government Center

4th Floor, Room 475
Boston, MA 02203
Phone: (617) 565-3200
TTY: (617) 565-3204

Virginia

Norfolk Area Office
World Trade Center
101 West Main Street
Suite 4300
Norfolk, VA 23510
Phone: 804-441-3470
TDD: 804-441-3578

Richmond Area Office
3600 West Broad Street
Room 229
Richmond, VA 23230
Phone: 804-278-4651
TDD: 804-278-4654

Washington

Seattle District Office
Federal Office Building
909 First Avenue, Suite 400
Seattle, WA 98104-1061
Phone: 206-220-6883
TDD: 206-220-6882

West Virginia

Philadelphia District Office
21 South 5th Street
4th Floor
Philadephia, PA 19106
Phone: (215) 440-2600
TTY: (215) 440-2610

Wisconsin

Milwaukee District Office
310 West Wisconsin Avenue
Suite 800
Milwaukee, WI 53203-2292
Phone: 414-297-1111
TDD: 414-297-1115

Wyoming

Denver District Office
303 E. 17th Avenue
Suite 510
Denver, CO 80203
Phone: 303-866-1300
TDD: 303-866-1950

State Civil Rights Offices

If you suffered a form of discrimination not enforced by EEOC, contact your civil rights office. This applies to cases of discrimination based on sexual orientation, status as a parent, marital status, and political affiliation. Although these cases are not enforced by EEOC, many federal agencies, states, and local governments do enforce them. Your nearest civil rights office can assist you in taking the proper steps.

Note: Not all states have such offices.

Alaska

Alaska State Commission on
Human Rights
800A Suite 204
Anchorage, AK 99501-3669
907-274-4692
http://gov.state.ak.us/aschr

Arizona

Arizona State Attorney General
Phoenix Office
1275 West Washington St.
Phoenix, AZ 85007

602-542-5025
**www.attorney-general.state.az.us
/civil_rights**

California

Department of Justice Civil Rights
Enforcement Section
Public Inquiry Unit
P.O. Box 944255
Sacramento, CA 94244-2550
916-322-3360
http://ag.ca.gov/civil.php

California Dept. of Fair Employment and Housing
2218 Kausen Drive
Suite 100
Elk Grove, CA 95758
916-478-7230
www.dfeh.ca.gov

Colorado

Colorado Civil Rights Division
1560 Broadway, Suite 1050
Denver, CO 80202
303-894-2997
800-262-4845 in state
www.dora.state.co.us/civil-rights

Connecticut

Connecticut Commission on Human Rights and Opportunities
21 Grand St.
Hartford, CT 06106
860-541-3400
800-477-5737
www.state.ct.us/chro

Delaware

Delaware Human Relations Division
820 North French St. 4th Floor
Wilmington, DE 19801
302-577-5050
www.state.de.us/sos/hr

District of Columbia

District of Columbia, Office of Human Rights
441 4th St., NW, Suite 570N
Washington, DC 20001
202-727-4559
202-724-9589
www.ohr.dc.gov

Florida

Florida Commission on Human Relations
2009 Apalachee Parkway, Suite 200
Tallahassee, FL 32301
850-488-7082
800-342-8170
http://fchr.state.fl.us

Georgia

Georgia Human Relations Commission
2 Martin Luther King Jr # 1102
Atlanta, GA 30334
404-463-2500
http://www.dol.state.ga.us/wp/

Hawaii

Hawaii Civil Rights Commission
830 Punchbowl St. Room 411
Honolulu, HI 96813
808-586-8636
http://hawaii.gov/hcrc/

Idaho

Idaho Human Rights Commission
1109 Main St. Ste. 450
P.O. Box 83720
Boise, ID 83702
208-334-2873
www.state.id.us/ihrc

Illinois

Illinois Dept. of Human Rights
100 W Randolph St. Suite 10-100
Chicago, IL 60601
312-814-6200
www.state.il.us/dhr

Indiana

Indiana Civil Rights Commission
100 N Senate Ave. Room N103
Indianapolis, IN 46204
317-232-2600
800-628-2909
www.state.in.us/icrc

Iowa

Iowa Civil Rights Commission
400 E. 14th Street
Grimes State Office Bldg.
Des Moines, IA 50319-1004
515-281-4121
800-457-4416
www.state.ia.us/government/crc

Kansas

Kansas Human Rights
Commission
900 SW Jackson, Suite 568-S
Topeka, KS 66612-1258
785-296-3206
www.ink.org/public/khrc

Kentucky

The Office of Equal Employment
Opportunity and Contract Com-
pliance
Capitol Annex, Room 395
Frankfort, KY 40601
Telephone: 502-564-2874
Facsimile: 502-564-1055
http://finance.ky.gov

Louisiana

Louisiana Commission on
Human Rights
1001 N. 23rd St., Suite 262
Baton Rouge, Louisiana 70802
Phone: 225-342-6969
Fax: 225-342-2063
TDD: 1-888-248-0859
www.gov.state.la.us

Maine

Maine Human Rights Commission
51 State House Station
Augusta, ME 04330
207-624-6050
www.state.me.us/mhrc

Maryland

Maryland Human Rights
Commission
6 St. Paul St.
Baltimore, MD 21202
410-767-8600
800-637-6247 in state
www.mchr.state.md.us

Massachusetts

Massachusetts Commission Against
Discrimination
1 Ashburton Pl., Room 601
Boston, MA 02108
617-994-6000
www.state.ma.us/mcad

Michigan

Michigan Department of
Civil Rights
Capital Tower Building
Capitol Tower Building, Ste. 800
Lansing, MI 48933
(517) 335-3165
www.michigan.gov

Missouri

Missouri Commission
Human Rights

Department of Labor and
Industrial Relations
P.O. Box 1129
3315 W Truman Blvd.
Jefferson City, MO 65102-1129
573-751-3325
www.workplacefairness.org/agencies_MO

Montana

Dept. of Labor and Industry, Human Rights Commission
Walt Sullivan Building
1327 Lockey Avenue
P.O. Box 1728
Helena, MT 596204-1728
406-444-4344
800-542-0807 in state
http://erd.dli.mt.gov/

Nebraska

Nebraska Equal Opportunity
Commission
301 Centennial Mall South,
5th Floor
P.O. Box 94934
Lincoln, NE 68509-4934
402-471-2024
800-642-6112
www.nol.org/home/NEOC

Nevada

Department of Employment Training and Rehabilitation
Nevada Equal Rights Commission
555 E. Washington Avenue
Suite 4000
Las Vegas, NV 89101
702-486-7161
http://detr.state.nv.us

New Hampshire

New Hampshire Human Rights Commission
2 Chenell Dr. #2
Concord, NH 03301-8501
603-271-2767
www.state.nh.us/hrc

New Jersey

New Jersey Department of Law and Public Safety
Division on Civil Rights
140 E Front St., 6th Floor
P.O. Box 090
Trenton, NJ 08625-0090
609-292-4605
www.nj.gov/oag/dcr/index.html

New Mexico

New Mexico Human Rights Division
Department of Labor
501 Mountain Road NE
Albuquerque, NM 87102
505-843-1900
www.state.nm.us/dol

New York

New York State Division of Human Rights
One Fordham Plaza, 4th Floor
Bronx, New York 10458
718-741-8400
www.dhr.state.ny.us/

North Carolina

North Carolina Human Relations Commission
217 W Jones St. 4th Floor
Raleigh, NC 27603
919-733-7996
www.doa.state.nc.us

North Dakota

North Dakota Department of Labor, Division of Human Rights

State Capital
600 East Boulevard Avenue,
Dept 406
Bismarck, ND 58505-0340
701-328-2660
800-582-8032
www.nd.gov/labor/

Ohio

Ohio Civil Rights Commission
30 E Broad St. Suite, 5th Floor
Columbus, OH 43215-3414
614-466-5928
www.state.oh.us/crc

Oklahoma

Oklahoma Civil Rights
Commission
2101 N Lincoln Blvd.
Oklahoma City, OK 73105
405-521-2360
www.ok.gov/oesc_web/

Oregon

Oregon Civil Rights Division
Bureau of Labor and Industry
800 NE Oregon St. #32
Suite 1070
Portland, OR 97232

971-673-0761
www.boli.state.or.us/

Pennsylvania

Pennsylvania Human Relations
Commission
1101-1125 A. Front Street,
5th Floor
Harrisburg, PA 17104-2515
Voice: 717-787-9784
Text Telephone: 717-787-7279
www.phrc.state.pa.us

Rhode Island

Rhode Island Commission for
Human Rights
180 Westminster St., 3rd Floor
Providence, RI 02903
401-222-2661
www.richr.ri.gov/frames.html

South Carolina

South Carolina Human Affairs
Commission
P.O. Box 4490
2611 Forest Dr. Suite 200
Columbia, SC 29204
803-737-7800
www.state.sc.us/schac

South Dakota

South Dakota Department of Commerce & Regulation,
Division of Human Rights
700 Governors Drive
Pierre, SD 57501
605-773-4493
www.state.sd.us/dcr/hr

Tennessee

Tennessee Human Rights
Commission
710 James Robertson Parkway
Suite 100
Corner of Rosa Parks Blvd.
Nashville, TN 37243-1219
Phone: 615-741-5825
www.state.tn.us/humanrights

Texas

Texas Workforce Commission Civil
Rights Division
P.O. Box 13493
6830 Highway 290 East, Suite 250
Austin, TX 78711
512-437-3450
www.state.tx.us

Utah

Utah Anti-Discrimination Division
160 E. 300 S. Ste. 300
Salt Lake City, UT 84111
801-530-6800
http://laborcommission.utah.gov

Vermont

Vermont Human Rights
Commission
14-16 Baldwin Street
Montpelier, VT 05633-6301
802-828-2480
www.hrc.state.vt.us

Virginia

Virginia Council on Human Rights
1220 Bank Street Jefferson Building, 3rd Floor
Richmond, VA 23219
804-225-2292
www.chr.state.va.us

Washington

Washington State Human Rights
Commission
P.O. Box 42490
711 S Capital Way #402
Olympia, WA 98504-2490

360-753-6770

800-233-3247

www.hum.wa.gov

West Virginia

West Virginia Human Rights
Commission
1321 Plaza East Room 108A
Charleston, WV 25301-1400
304-558-2616
888-676-5546
www.wvf.state.wv.us/wvhrc

Wisconsin

Wisconsin Equal Rights Division
Dept. of Workforce Development
P.O. Box 8928
201 E Washington Ave. Room
A300
Madison, WI 53708-8928
608-266-6860
www.dwd.state.wi.us/er

Wyoming

Wyoming Department of Employment Labor Standards
Fair Employment Program
1510 E. Pershing, West Wing
Cheyenne, WY 82002
wydoe.state.wy.us/doe.asp?ID=3

State Workforce Investment Act Offices

Alabama

Alabama Department of Economic
and Community Affairs
Post Office Box 5690
Montgomery, Alabama
36103-5690
Phone: 334-242-5100
Fax: 334-242-5099
**www.adeca.alabama.gov/default.
aspx**

Alaska

Division of Business Partnerships
Dept. of Labor &
Workforce Development
1016 W. 6th Avenue, Suite 205
Anchorage, Alaska 99501
Phone: 907-465-4890
Fax: 907-465-3212
http://labor.state.ak.us/

American Samoa

American Samoa
Department of Human Resources
Employee Development and
Training Division
American Samoa Government

Pago Pago, American Samoa 96799
Phone: 684-633-4485
Fax: 684-633-5667

Arizona

Arizona Department of Economic
Security
Employment Administration
1789 West Jefferson Street
Site Code 920-Z
Post Office Box 6123
Phoenix, Arizona 85005-6123
Phone: 602-542-3667
Fax: 602-542-3690

Arkansas

Arkansas Workforce
Investment Board.
Two Capital Mall
Little Rock, Arkansas 72201
Phone: 501-371-1020
Fax: 501-371-1030

California

Labor and Workforce Development
Agency
801 K Street, Suite 2101
Sacramento, California 95814
Phone: 916-327-9064
Fax: 916-327-9158

Colorado

Workforce Development Programs
Colorado Dept. of Labor & Employment
633 17th Street, Suite 201
Denver, Colorado 80202-3660
Phone: 303-318-8000
Fax: 303-318-4157

Connecticut

Connecticut Labor Department
200 Folly Brook Boulevard
Wethersfield, Connecticut 06109
Phone: 860-263-6000
Fax: 860-263-6529

Delaware

Delaware Department of Labor
4425 North Market Street
Wilmington, Delaware 19801
Phone: 302-761-8001
Fax: 302-761-6617

District of Columbia

DC Department of
Employment Services
64 New York Avenue, N.E.,
Suite 3000
Washington, D.C. 20002

Phone: 202-724-7000
Fax: 202-673-6993

Fax: 671-475-7045
E-mail: connent@ite.net

Florida

Agency for Workforce Innovation
The Caldwell Building
107 East Madison Street,
MSC 110
Tallahassee, Florida 32399-4128
Phone: 850-245-7105
Fax: 850-921-3223

Georgia

Governor's Office of Workforce Development
270 Washington Street, SW,
Suite 5191
Atlanta, Georgia 30334
Phone: 404-463-5030
Fax: 404-463-5043

Guam

Guam Department of Labor
Agency for Human Resources
Suite 400, GCIC Building
414 W. Soledad Avenue
Hagatna, Guam 96932
Phone: 671-475-7043

Hawaii

Department of Labor and Industrial
Relations
830 Punchbowl St.
Honolulu, Hawaii 96831
Phone: 808-586-8842
Fax: 808-586-9099

Idaho

Idaho Department of Labor
317 Main Street
Boise, Idaho 83735
Phone: 208-332-3570
Fax: 208-334-6430

Illinois

Department of Commerce & Economic Opportunity
100 W. Randolph, 3rd Floor
Chicago, Illinois 60601
Phone: 312-814-7179
Fax: 312-814-1400

Indiana

IN Department of
Workforce Development

Indiana Government Center, South
10 North Senate Avenue, SE 211
Indianapolis, Indiana 46204-2277
Phone: 317-232-1920
Fax: 317-233-8480

Iowa

Iowa Workforce Development
1000 East Grand Avenue
Des Moines, Iowa 50319-0209
Phone: 515-281-5387

Kansas

Kansas Department of Commerce
1000 S.W. Jackson Street,
Suite 100
Topeka, Kansas 66612-1354
Phone: 785-296-3481
Fax: 785-296-5055

Kentucky

Office of Employment and Training
Department for Workforce
Investment
Education Cabinet
275 East Main Street, 2nd Floor
Frankfort, Kentucky 40601
Phone: 502-564-7456
Fax: 502-564-7459

Louisiana

Louisiana Department of Labor
1001 North 23rd Street
Post Office Box 94094
Baton Rouge, Louisiana
70802
Phone: 225-342-3111

Maine

Maine Department of Labor
54 State House Station
Augusta, Maine 04333-0054
Phone: 207-623-7900

Maryland

Department of Labor, Licensing &
Regulation
500 North Calvert Street #401
Baltimore, Maryland 21202
Phone: 410-230-6001

Massachusetts

Department of Workforce
Development
19 Staniford Street, First Floor
Boston, Massachusetts 02114
Phone: 617-626-5300

Michigan

Workforce Programs
Department of Labor &
Economic Growth
201 N. Washington Square
Victor Office Center, 5th Floor
Lansing, Michigan 48913
Phone: 517-335-5875
Fax: 517-335-5945

Minnesota

Workforce Services Division
Department of Employment and
Economic Development
1st National Bank Building
332 Minnesota Street, Suite E200
St. Paul, Minnesota 55101-1351
Phone: 651-259-7114

Mississippi

Mississippi Department of Employ-
ment Security
1235 Echelon Parkway
Post Office Box 1699
Jackson, Mississippi 39215-1699
Phone: 601-321-6000

Missouri

Division of Workforce
Development
421 East Dunklin Street
Post Office Box 1087
Jefferson City, Missouri
65102-1087
Phone: 573-751-3349
Fax: 573-751-8162

Montana

Department of Labor and Industry
Post Office Box 1728
Helena, Montana 59624-1728
Phone: 406-444-2840
Fax: 406-444-1394

Nebraska

Office of Workforce Services
Nebraska Department of Labor
Post Office Box 94600
550 South 16th Street
Lincoln, Nebraska 68509-4600
Phone: 402-471-3405
Fax: 402-471-2318

Nevada

Nevada Department of
Employment, Training and Rehabilitation
500 East Third Street, Suite 200
Carson City, Nevada 89713

Phone: 775-684-3849
Fax: 775-684-3850

New Hampshire

Workforce Opportunity
Council, Inc.
64 Old Suncook Road
Concord, New Hampshire 03301
Phone: 603-228-9500

New Jersey

New Jersey Department of Labor &
Workforce Development
John Fitch Plaza - Labor Building
Post Office Box 110
Trenton, New Jersey 08625-0110
Phone: 609-292-2975
Fax: 609-984-9681

New Mexico

New Mexico Department of Work-
force Solutions
401 Broadway, NE
Albuquerque, New Mexico 87102
Phone: 505-841-4000
Fax: 505-841-8491

New York

New York State Department
of Labor
W.Averell Harriman State Office
Campus
Building 12
Albany, New York 12240
Phone: 518-457-9000
Fax: 518-457-6908

North Carolina

NC Commission on
Workforce Development
NC Department of Commerce
4301 Mail Service Center
Raleigh, North Carolina
27699-4301
Phone: 919-733-4151

North Dakota

Job Service North Dakota
PO Box 5507
Bismarck, North Dakota
58506-5507
Phone: 701-328-2825
Fax: 701-328-4000

Northern Mariana Islands

CNMI Workforce Investment
Agency
Caller Box 10007
Saipan, CM 96950
Phone: 670-664-1758
Fax: 670-322-7333

Ohio

Office of Workforce Development
Ohio Dept. of Job and
Family Services
30 E. Broad Street, 32nd Floor
Post Office Box 1618
Columbus, Ohio 43215
Phone: 614-466-2100

Oklahoma

State Employment Security
Commission
Will Rogers Memorial Office
Building
2401 N. Lincoln Blvd.
Oklahoma City, Oklahoma 73105
Phone: 405-557-7100

Oregon

Department of Community Colleges and Workforce Development

255 Capitol Street, NE,
Third Floor
Salem, Oregon 97310-1600
Phone: 503-378-8648 ext. 0
Fax: 503-378-3365

Pennsylvania

Workforce Development
Pennsylvania Department of Labor
and Industry
Labor and Industry Building,
Room 1200
Seventh & Forrester Streets
Harrisburg, Pennsylvania 17120
Phone: 717-787-3354
Fax: 717-787-8826

Puerto Rico

Puerto Rico Dept. of Labor &
Human Resources
Prudencio Rivera-Martinez
Building
Post Office Box 195540
San Juan, Puerto Rico 00918
Phone: 787-754-5824
Fax: 787-753-9550

Rhode Island

Dept. of Labor & Training

Center General Complex
1511 Pontiac Ave., Building #73-3
Cranston, Rhode Island
02920-4407
Phone: 401-462-8000
Fax: 401-462-8872

South Carolina

Workforce Development
South Carolina Department of
Commerce
1201 Main Street, Suite 1600
Columbia, South Carolina 29201
Phone: 803-737-0400
Fax: 803-806-3533

South Dakota

South Dakota Department of Labor
Kneip Building
700 Governors Drive
Pierre, South Dakota 57501-2291
Phone: 605-773-3101 voice/TTY
Fax: 605-773-6184

Tennessee

Tennessee Department of Labor &
Workforce Development
220 French Landing Dr.
Nashville, Tennessee 37243

Phone: 615-741-6642
Fax: 615-741-5078

Texas

Texas Workforce Commission
101 East 15th St., Room 618
Austin, Texas 78778-0001
Phone: 512-463-0735
Fax: 512-475-2321

Utah

Department of Workforce Services
P.O. Box 45249
Salt Lake City, Utah 84145-0249
Phone: 801-526-9675
Fax: 801-526-9211

Vermont

Department of Employment
and Training
5 Green Mountain Drive
Post Office Box 488
Montpelier, Vermont 05601-0488
Phone: 802-828-4000
Fax: 802-828-4022

Virgin Islands

Virgin Islands Department
of Labor

2203 Church Street
Christiansted
St. Croix, USVI 00820-4612
Phone: 340-773-1994
Fax: 340-773-0094

Virginia

Workforce Investment System
Governor's Office For Workforce
Development
Old City Hall, Suite 135
101 N. 14th Street, 15th Floor
Richmond, Virginia 23219
Phone: 804-819-4901
Fax: 804-819-4760

Washington

Washington State Employment Security Department
Post Office Box 9046
Olympia, Washington 98507-9046
Phone: 360-902-9500
Fax: 360-438-3224

West Virginia

WORKFORCE West Virginia
1321 Plaza East
Charleston, West Virginia 25325
Phone: 304-558-0342

Wisconsin

Wisconsin Department of Workforce Development
Division of Employment
and Training
201 East Washington Avenue
Post Office Box 7946
Madison, Wisconsin 53707-7946
Phone: 608-266-3131
Fax: 608-266-1784

Wyoming

Department of Workforce Services
122 West 25th Street
Herschler Building, Suite 2-E
Cheyenne, Wyoming 82002
Phone: 307-777-8650
Fax: 307-777-5857

State Health Insurance Continuation Laws

The Federal Consolidated Omnibus Budget Reconciliation Act (COBRA) applies only to companies with 20 or more employees. Most states have enacted their own laws regarding the continuation of health insurance for companies with less than 20 employees. The following are state regulations that apply to those not covered by COBRA.

Alabama

Coverage: 18 months for subjects of domestic abuse who have lost coverage they had under abuser's insurance and who do not qualify for COBRA.

Arizona

Employers affected: All employers who offer group disability insurance.

Length of coverage for dependents: Insurer must either continue coverage for dependents or convert to individual policy upon death of covered employee, divorce, or legal separation. Coverage must be the same unless the insured chooses a lesser plan.

Time employer has to notify employee of continuation rights: No provisions for employer.

Insurance policy must include notice of conversion privilege. Clerk of court must provide notice to anyone filing for divorce that dependent spouse is entitled to convert health insurance coverage.

Time employee has to apply: 31 days after termination of existing coverage.

Arkansas

Employers affected: All employers who offer group health insurance.

Eligible employees: Continuously insured for previous three months.

Length of coverage for employee: 120 days.

Length of coverage for dependents: 120 days.

Time employee has to apply: 10 days.

California

Employers affected: Employers who offer group health insurance and have two to 19 employees.

Eligible employees: Continuously insured for previous three months.

Qualifying event: Termination of employment; reduction in hours.

Length of coverage for employee: 36 months.

Length of coverage for dependents: 36 months.

Time employer has to notify employee of continuation rights: 15 days.

Time employee has to apply: 31 days after group plan ends; 30 days after COBRA or Cal-COBRA ends (63 days if converting to an individual plan).

Special situations: Employee who is at least 60 years old and has worked for employer for previous 5 years may continue benefits for self and spouse beyond COBRA or Cal-COBRA limits (also applies to COBRA employers). Employee who began receiving COBRA coverage on or after January 1, 2003, and whose COBRA coverage is for less than 36 months, may use Cal-COBRA to bring total coverage up to 36 months.

Colorado

Employers affected: All employers who offer group health insurance.

Eligible employees: Employees continuously insured for previous six months.

Length of coverage for employee: 18 months.

Length of coverage for dependents: 18 months.

Time employer has to notify employee of continuation rights: Within ten days of termination.

Time employee has to apply: 30 days after termination; 60 days if employer fails to give notice.

Connecticut

Employers affected: All employers who offer group health insurance.

Eligible employees: Continuously insured for previous three months.

Length of coverage for employee: 18 months, or until eligible for Social Security benefits.

Length of coverage for dependents: 18 months, or until eligible for Social Security benefits; 36 months in case of employee's death or divorce.

Time employer has to notify employee of continuation rights: 14 days.

Time employee has to apply: 60 days.

Special situations: When facility closes or relocates, employer must pay for insurance for employee and dependents for 120 days or until employee is eligible for other group coverage, whichever comes first. This does not affect employee's right to conventional continuation coverage, which begins when 120-day period ends.

District of Columbia

Employers affected: Employers with fewer than 20 employees.

Eligible employees: All covered employees are eligible.

Length of coverage for employee: Three months.

Length of coverage for dependents: Three months.

Time employer has to notify employee of continuation rights: Within 15 days of termination of coverage.

Time employee has to apply: 45 days after termination of coverage.

Florida

Employers affected: Employers with fewer than 20 employees.

Eligible employees: Full-time (25 or more hours per week) employees covered by employer's health insurance plan.

Length of coverage for employee: 18 months.

Length of coverage for dependents: 18 months.

Time employer has to notify employee of continuation rights: Carrier notifies within 14 days of learning of qualifying event (employer is responsible for notifying carrier).

Time employee has to apply: 30 days from receipt of carrier's notice.

Georgia

Employers affected: All employers who offer group health insurance.

Eligible employees: Employees continuously insured for previous six months.

Length of coverage for employee: Three months plus any part of the month remaining at termination.

Length of coverage for dependents: Three months plus any part of the month remaining at termination.

Special situations: Employee, spouse, or former spouse who is 60 years old and who has been covered for previous six months may continue coverage until eligible for Medicare. (Applies to companies with more than 20 employees; does not apply when employee quits for reasons other than health.)

Hawaii

Employers affected: All employers required to offer health insurance (those paying a regular employee a monthly wage at least 86.67 times state hourly minimum — about $542 per month).

Length of coverage for employee: If employee is hospitalized or prevented from working by sickness, employer must pay insurance premiums for three months or for as long employer continues to pay wages, whichever is longer.

Illinois

Employers affected: All employers who offer group health insurance.

Eligible employees: Employees continuously insured for previous three months.

Length of coverage for employee: Nine months.

Length of coverage for dependents: Nine months (but see below).

Time employee has to apply: Ten days after termination or reduction in hours or receiving notice from employer, whichever is later, but not more than 60 days from termination or reduction in hours. Special situations: Upon death or divorce, two years' coverage for spouse under 55 and eligible dependents who were on employee's plan; until eligible for Medicare or other group coverage for spouse over 55 and eligible dependents who were on employee's plan. As of July 1, 2004, dependent child who has reached plan age limit or who was not already covered by plan is also entitled to two years' continuation coverage.

Indiana

Employers affected: Employers with at least three employees.

Eligible employees: Employed by same employer for at least one year and continuously insured for previous 90 days.

Length of coverage for employee: 12 months.

Length of coverage for dependents: 12 months.

Time employer has to notify employee of continuation rights: Ten days after employee becomes eligible for continuation coverage.

Time employee has to apply: Must apply directly to insurer within 30 days after becoming eligible for continuation coverage.

Iowa

Employers affected: All employers who offer group health insurance.

Eligible employees: Employees continuously insured for previous three months.

Length of coverage for employee: Nine months.

Length of coverage for dependents: Nine months.

Time employer has to notify employee of continuation rights: Ten days after termination of coverage.

Time employee has to apply: Ten days after termination of coverage or receiving notice from employer, whichever is later, but no more than 31 days from termination of coverage.

Kansas

Employers affected: All employers who offer group health insurance.

Eligible employees: Employees continuously insured for previous three months.

Length of coverage for employee: Six months.

Length of coverage for dependents: Six months.

Time employee has to apply: 31 days from termination of coverage.

Kentucky

Employers affected: All employers who offer group health insurance.

Eligible employees: Employees continuously insured for previous three months.

Length of coverage for employee: 18 months.

Length of coverage for dependents: 18 months.

Time employer has to notify employee of continuation rights: Employer must notify insurer as soon as employee's coverage ends; insurer then notifies employee.

Time employee has to apply: 31 days from receipt of insurer's notice, but no more than 90 days after termination of group coverage.

Louisiana

Employers affected: All employers who offer group health insurance and have fewer than 20 employees.

Eligible employees: Employees continuously insured for previous three months.

292 What to Do When You Are Fired or Laid Off

Length of coverage for employee: 12 months.

Length of coverage for dependents: 12 months.

Time employee has to apply: Must apply and submit payment before group coverage ends.

Special situations: Surviving spouse who is 50 or older may have coverage until remarriage or eligibility for Medicare or other insurance.

Maine

Employers affected: All employers who offer group health insurance.

Eligible employees: Employees continuously insured for previous three months.

Length of coverage for employee: One year (either group or individual coverage at discretion of insurer).

Length of coverage for dependents: One year (either group or individual coverage at discretion of insurer). Upon death of insured, coverage continued for depends only if original plan provided for coverage. Time employee has to apply: 90 days from termination of group coverage.

Special situations: Temporary layoff or work-related injury or disease: Employee and employee's dependents entitled to one year group or individual continuation coverage. (Must have been continuously insured for previous six months; must apply within 31 days from termination of coverage.)

Maryland

Employers affected: All employers who offer group health insurance.

Eligible employees: Employees continuously insured for previous three months.

Length of coverage for employee: 18 months.

Length of coverage for dependents: 18 months upon death of employee; upon change in marital status, 18 months or until spouse remarries or becomes eligible for other coverage.

Time employer has to notify employee of continuation rights: Must notify insurer within 14 days of receiving employee's continuation request.

Time employee has to apply: 45 days from termination of coverage. Employee begins application process by requesting an election of continuation notification form from employer.

Massachusetts

Employers affected: All employers who offer group health insurance and have fewer than 20 employees.

Eligible employees: All covered employees are eligible.

Length of coverage for employee: 18 months; 29 months if disabled.

Length of coverage for dependents: 18 months upon termination or reduction in hours; 29 months if disabled; 36 months on divorce, death of employee, employee's eligibility for Medicare, or employer's bankruptcy.

Time employer has to notify employee of continuation rights: When employee becomes eligible for continuation benefits.

Time employee has to apply: 60 days.

Special situations: Termination due to plant closing: 90 days of coverage for employee and dependents, at the same payment terms as before closing.

Minnesota

Employers affected: All employers who offer group health insurance and have two or more employees.

Eligible employees: All covered employees are eligible.

Length of coverage for employee: 18 months; indefinitely if employee becomes totally disabled while employed.

Length of coverage for dependents: 18 months for current spouse; divorced or widowed spouse can continue until eligible for Medicare or other group health insurance. Upon divorce, dependent children can continue until they no longer qualify as dependents under plan. Upon death of employee, spouse and/or dependent children can continue for 36 months.

Time employer has to notify employee of continuation rights: Within ten days of termination of coverage.

Time employee has to apply: 60 days from termination of coverage or receipt of employer's notice, whichever is later.

Missouri

Employers affected: All employers who offer group health insurance.

Eligible employees: Employees continuously insured for previous three months.

Length of coverage for employee: Nine months.

Length of coverage for dependents: Nine months.

Time employer has to notify employee of continuation rights: No later than date group coverage would end.

Time employee has to apply: 31 days from date group coverage would end.

Montana

Employers affected: All employers who offer group disability insurance.

Eligible employees: All employees.

Length of coverage for employee: One year (with employer's consent).

Time employee has to apply: 31 days from date group coverage would end.

Special situations: Insurer may not discontinue benefits to child with disabilities after child exceeds age limit for dependent status.

Nebraska

Employers affected: Employers not subject to federal COBRA laws.

Eligible employees: All covered employees.

Length of coverage for employee: Six months.

Length of coverage for dependents: One year upon death of insured employee. Subjects of domestic abuse who have lost coverage under abuser's plan and who do not qualify for COBRA may have 18 months' coverage (applies to all employers).

Time employer has to notify employee of continuation rights: Within ten days of termination of employment, employer must send notice by certified mail.

Time employee has to apply: Ten days from receipt of employer's notice.

Nevada

Employers affected: Employers with fewer than 20 employees.

Eligible employees: Employees continuously insured for previous 12 months.

Length of coverage for employee: 18 months.

Length of coverage for dependents: 36 months; insurer cannot terminate coverage for a disabled, dependent child who is too old to qualify as a dependent under the plan.

Time employer has to notify employee of continuation rights: 14 days after receiving notice of employee's eligibility.

Time employee has to apply: Must notify employer within 60 days of becoming eligible for continuation coverage; must apply within 60 days after receiving employer's notice. Special situations: While employee is on leave without pay due to disability, 12 months for employee and dependents (applies to all employers).

New Hampshire

Employers affected: Employers with two to nineteen employees.

Eligible employees: All insured employees are eligible.

Length of coverage for employee: 18 months; 29 months if disabled at termination or during first 60 days of continuation coverage.

Length of coverage for dependents: 18 months; 29 months if disabled at termination or during first 60 days of continuation coverage; 36 months upon death of employee, divorce or legal separation, loss of dependent status, or employee's eligibility for Medicare. Time employer has to notify employee of continuation rights: Within 15 days of termination of coverage.

Time employee has to apply: Within 31 days of termination of coverage.

Special situations: Layoff or termination due to strike: Six months' coverage with option to extend for an additional 12 months. Surviving, divorced, or legally separated spouse who is 55 or older may continue benefits available until eligible for Medicare or other employer-based group insurance.

New Jersey

Employers affected: Employers with two to fifty employees.

Eligible employees: Employed full time (25 or more hours).

Length of coverage for employee: 18 months; 29 months if disabled at termination or during first 60 days of continuation coverage.

Length of coverage for dependents: 18 months; 29 months if disabled at termination or during first 60 days of continuation coverage; 36 months upon death of employee, divorce or legal separation, loss of dependent status, or employee's eligibility for Medicare.

Time employer has to notify employee of continuation rights: At time of qualifying event, employer or carrier notifies employee.

Time employee has to apply: Within 30 days of qualifying event.

Special benefits: Coverage must be identical to that offered to current employees.

Special situations: Total disability: Employee who has been insured for previous three months and employee's dependents are entitled to continuation coverage that includes all benefits offered by group policy (applies to all employers).

New Mexico

Employers affected: All employers who offer group health insurance.

Eligible employees: All insured employees are eligible.

Length of coverage for employee: Six months.

Length of coverage for dependents: May continue group coverage or convert to individual policies upon death of covered employee or divorce or legal separation.

Time employer has to notify employee of continuation rights: Insurer or employer gives written notice at time of termination.

Time employee has to apply: 30 days after receiving notice.

New York

Employers affected: All employers who offer group health insurance and have fewer than 20 employees.

Eligible employees: All covered employees are eligible.

Length of coverage for employee: 18 months; 29 months if disabled at termination or during first 60 days of continuation coverage.

Length of coverage for dependents: 18 months; 29 months if disabled at termination or during first 60 days of continuation; 36 months upon death of employee, divorce or legal separation, loss of dependent status, or employee's eligibility for Medicare.

Time employee has to apply: 60 days after termination or receipt of notice, whichever is later.

North Carolina

Employers affected: All employers who offer group health insurance.

Eligible employees: Employees continuously insured for previous three months.

Length of coverage for employee: 18 months.

Length of coverage for dependents: 18 months.

Time employer has to notify employee of continuation rights: Employer has option of notifying employee as part of the exit process.

Time employee has to apply: 60 days.

North Dakota

Employers affected: All employers who offer group health insurance.

Eligible employees: Employees continuously insured for previous three months.

Length of coverage for employee: 39 weeks.

Length of coverage for dependents: 39 weeks; 36 months if required by divorce or annulment decree.

Time employee has to apply: Within ten days of termination or of receiving notice of continuation rights, whichever is later, but no more than 31 days from termination.

Ohio

Employers affected: All employers who offer group health insurance.

Eligible employees: Employees continuously insured for previous three months who are entitled to unemployment benefits.

Length of coverage for employee: Six months.

Length of coverage for dependents: Six months.

Time employer has to notify employee of continuation rights: At termination of employment.

Time employee has to apply: Whichever is earlier: 31 days after coverage terminates; ten days after coverage terminates if employer notified employee of continuation rights prior to termination; ten days after employer notified employee of continuation rights, if notice was given after coverage terminated.

Oklahoma

Employers affected: All employers who offer group health insurance.

Eligible employees: Employees insured for at least six months. (All other employees and their dependents entitled to 30 days' continuation coverage.)

Length of coverage for employee: Only for losses or conditions that began while group policy was in effect: three months for basic coverage; six months for major medical at the same premium rate prior to termination of coverage.

Length of coverage for dependents: Only for losses or conditions that began while group policy was in effect: three months for basic coverage; six months for major medical at the same premium rate prior to termination of coverage.

Special benefits: Includes maternity care for pregnancy begun while group policy was in effect.

Oregon

Employers affected: Employers not subject to federal COBRA laws.

Eligible employees: Employees continuously insured for previous three months.

Length of coverage for employee: Six months.

Length of coverage for dependents: Six months.

Time employee has to apply: Ten days after termination or after receiving notice of continuation rights, whichever is later, but not more than 31 days.

Special situations: Surviving, divorced, or legally separated spouse who is 55 or older and dependent children entitled to continuation coverage until spouse remarries or is eligible for other coverage. Must include dental, vision, or prescription drug benefits if they were offered in original plan (applies to employers with 20 or more employees).

Rhode Island

Employers affected: All employers who offer group health insurance.

Eligible employees: All insured employees are eligible.

Length of coverage for employee: 18 months (but not longer than continuous employment). Cannot be required to pay more than one month's premium at a time.

Length of coverage for dependents: 18 months (but not longer than continuous employment). Cannot be required to pay more than one month's premium at a time.

Time employer has to notify employee of continuation rights: Employers must post a conspicuous notice of employee continuation rights.

Time employee has to apply: 30 days from termination of coverage.

Special situations: If right to receiving continuing health insurance is stated in the divorce judgment, divorced spouse has right to continue coverage as long as employee remains covered or until divorced spouse remarries or becomes eligible for other group insurance. If covered employee remarries, divorced spouse must be given right to purchase an individual policy from same insurer.

South Carolina

Employers affected: All employers who offer group health insurance.

Eligible employees: Employees continuously insured for previous six months.

Length of coverage for employee: Six months (in addition to part of month remaining at termination).

Length of coverage for dependents: Six months (in addition to part of month remaining at termination).

Time employer has to notify employee of continuation rights: At time of termination must clearly and meaningfully advise employee of continuation rights.

South Dakota

Employers affected: All employers who offer group health insurance.

Eligible employees: All covered employees.

Length of coverage for employee: 18 months; 29 months if disabled at termination or during first 60 days of continuation coverage.

Length of coverage for dependents: 18 months; 29 months if disabled at termination or during first 60 days of continuation coverage; 36 months upon death of employee, divorce or legal separation, loss of dependent status, or employee's eligibility for Medicare.

Special situations: When employer goes out of business: 12 months' continuation coverage available to all employees. Employer must notify employees within ten days of termination of benefits; employees must apply within 60 days of receipt of employer's notice or within 90 days of termination of benefits if no notice given.

Tennessee

Employers affected: All employers who offer group health insurance.

Eligible employees: Employees continuously insured for previous three months.

Length of coverage for employee: Three months (in addition to part of month remaining at termination).

Length of coverage for dependents: Three months (in addition to part of month remaining at termination); 15 months upon death of employee or divorce.

Special situations: Employee or dependent who is pregnant at time of termination entitled to continuation benefits for six months following the end of pregnancy.

Texas

Employers affected: All employers who offer group health insurance.

Eligible employees: Employees continuously insured for previous three months.

Length of coverage for employee: Six months.

Length of coverage for dependents: Six months.

Time employee has to apply: 31 days from termination of coverage or receiving notice of continuation rights from employer or insurer, whichever is later.

Special situations: Layoff due to a labor dispute: Employee entitled to continuation benefits for duration of dispute, but no longer than six months.

Utah

Employers affected: All employers who offer group health insurance.

Eligible employees: Employees continuously insured for previous six months.

Length of coverage for employee: Six months.

Length of coverage for dependents: Six months.

Time employer has to notify employee of continuation rights: In writing within 30 days of termination of coverage.

Time employee has to apply: Within 30 days of receiving employer's notice of continuation rights.

Vermont

Employers affected: All employers who offer group health insurance and have fewer than 20 employees.

Eligible employees: Employees continuously insured for previous three months.

Length of coverage for employee: Six months.

Length of coverage for dependents: Six months.

Time employee has to apply: Within 60 days (upon death of employee or group member); within 30 days (upon termination, change of marital status, or loss of dependent status) of the date that group coverage terminates, or the date of being notified of continuation rights, whichever is sooner.

Virginia

Employers affected: All employers who offer group health insurance.

Eligible employees: Employees continuously insured for previous three months.

Length of coverage for employee: 90 days.

Length of coverage for dependents: 90 days.

Time employer has to notify employee of continuation rights: 15 days from termination of coverage.

Time employee has to apply: Must apply for continuation and pay entire 90-day premium before termination of coverage.

Special situations: Employee may convert to an individual policy instead of applying for continuation coverage (must apply within 31 days of termination of coverage).

Washington

Employers affected: All employers who offer and pay for group health insurance.

Eligible employees: Insured employees on strike.

Length of coverage for employee: Six months if employee goes on strike.

Length of coverage for dependents: Six months if employee goes on strike.

Special situations: Former employees may continue benefits for a period of time agreed upon with the employer. At the end of that time, the employee may then convert to an individual policy unless terminated for misconduct; in that case, employee's spouse and dependents may convert, but not employee.

West Virginia

Employers affected: Employers providing insurance for at least ten employees.

Eligible employees: All covered employees are eligible.

Length of coverage for employee: 18 months in case of involuntary layoff.

Wisconsin

Employers affected: All employers who offer group health insurance.

Eligible employees: Employees continuously insured for previous three months.

Length of coverage for employee: 18 months (or longer at insurer's option).

Length of coverage for dependents: 18 months (or longer at insurer's option).

Time employer has to notify employee of continuation rights: Five days from termination of coverage.

Time employee has to apply: 30 days after receiving employer's notice.

Wyoming

Employers affected: Employers not subject to federal COBRA laws.

Eligible employees: Employees continuously insured for previous three months.

Length of coverage for employee: 12 months.

Length of coverage for dependents: 12 months.

Time employee has to apply: 31 days from termination of coverage.

LIHEAP State Grantees

The Low Income Home Energy Assistance Program (LIHEAP) does not provide assistance directly to individuals but allows state agencies to help low income families with paying their utility bills. To inquire about LI-HEAP assistance, the general public should use the public inquiry telephone number if available for their State. That number may provide the public with information about the State's program much quicker than the LIHEAP agency number. Further information about a State's LIHEAP program can be obtained from State LIHEAP Web sites where available.

REGION 1

Ms. Carlene Taylor
Manager
Energy & Refugee Services
Department of Social Services
25 Sigourney Street, 10th Floor
Hartford, CT 06106
TEL: 860-424-5889
FAX: 860-424-4952
E-MAIL: carlene.taylor@ct.gov
WEB SITE: **www.ct.gov/dss/cwp/view.asp?a=2353&q=305194**
PUBLIC INQUIRIES: 1-800-842-1132

Ms. Jo-Ann Choate
LIHEAP Coordinator
Energy and Housing Services
Maine State Housing Authority
353 Water Street
Augusta, ME 04330

TEL: 207-624-5708
FAX: 207-624-5780
E-MAIL: jchoate@mainehousing.org
WEB SITE: **www.mainehousing.org/ENERGYPrograms.
aspx?oProgramCategory=4**
PUBLIC INQUIRIES: 1-800-452-4668

Mr. Gerald Bell
Director
Community Services Programs
Division of Community Services
Department of Housing and Community Development
100 Cambridge Street, Suite 300
Boston, MA 02114-2524
TEL: 617-573-1438
FAX: 617-573-1460
E-MAIL: gerald.bell@state.ma.us
WEB SITE: **www.mass.gov/dhcd/components/cs/Fuel/default.htm**
WINTER HEATING HELPLINE WEB SITE: **www.mass.gov/?pageID
=ocaconstituent&L=2&L0=Home&L1=Consumer&sid=Eoca**
PUBLIC INQUIRIES: 1-800-632-8175

Ms. Celeste Lovett
Fuel Assistance Program Manager
Governor's Office of Energy
and Community Services
57 Regional Drive
Concord, NH 03301-8519
TEL: 603-271-2155
FAX: 603-271-2615
E-MAIL: CLOVETT@GOV.State.NH.US
WEB SITE: **www.nh.gov/oep/programs/fuelassistance/index.htm**

Mr. Matteo Guglielmetti
Project Manager
Rhode Island Office of Energy Resources
One Capitol Hill
Providence, RI 02908-5850
TEL: 401-574-9112
FAX: 401-574-9125
E-MAIL: matteog@energy.ri.gov
WEB SITE: **www.energy.ri.gov**
PUBLIC INQUIRIES: 401-574-9100

Mr. Richard Moffi
LIHEAP Coordinator
Office of Home Heating Fuel Assistance
Department for Children and Families
103 South Main Street
Waterbury, VT 05676
TEL: 802-241-1097
FAX: 802-241-4327
E-MAIL: richard.moffi@ahs.state.vt.us
WEB SITE: **http://dcf.vermont.gov/esd/fuel_assistance**
PUBLIC INQUIRIES: 1-800-479-6151 or 1-802-241-1165

REGION 2

Mr. Jose Sanchez
Supervisor
Department of Community Affairs
Division of Community Resources
Office of Low-Income Energy Conservation
101 South Broad Street

P.O. Box 811
Trenton, NJ 08625-08111
TEL: 609-984-6670
FAX: 609-292-9798
E-MAIL: JSanchez@DCA.state.nj.us
WEB SITE: **www.energyassistance.nj.gov**
PUBLIC INQUIRIES: 1-800-510-3102

Ms. Phyllis Morris
LIHEAP Coordinator
Division of Employment and Transitional Supports
New York State Office of Temporary and Disability Assistance
40 North Pearl Street
Albany, NY 12243-0001
TEL: 518-473-0332
FAX: 518-474-9347
E-MAIL: NYSHEAP@dfa.state.ny.us
WEB SITE: **www.otda.state.ny.us/main/heap**
PUBLIC INQUIRIES: 1-800-342-3009

REGION 3

Ms. Leslie Lee
Management Analyst
Department of Health and Social Services
Division of State Service Centers
1901 N. Dupont Hwy.
New Castle, DE 19720
TEL: 302-255-9681
FAX: 302-255-4463
E-MAIL: leslie.lee@state.de.us

1-800-464-HELP (4357)
NEW CASTLE COUNTY: 654-9295
KENT COUNTY: 674-1782
SUSSEX COUNTY: 856-6310
WEB SITE: **www.dhss.delaware.gov/dssc/liheap.html**
PUBLIC INQUIRIES: 1-800-464-HELP (4357)

Mr. Keith Anderson
LIHEAP Director
District of Columbia Energy Office
Reeves Center, Suite 300
2000 14th St. N.W.
Washington, D.C. 20001
TEL: 202-478-1417
FAX: 202-673-6725
E-MAIL: keith.anderson@dc.gov
WEB SITE: **http://dceo.dc.gov/dceo/cwp/view,a,3,q,601877.asp**
PUBLIC INQUIRIES: 202-673-6750 or 6700

Mr. Ralph Markus
Director
Office of Home Energy Programs
Department of Human Resources
311 West Saratoga Street
Baltimore, MD 21202
TEL: 410-767-7415
FAX: 410-333-0079
E-MAIL: rmarkus@dhr.state.md.us
WEB SITE: **www.dhr.state.md.us/meap**
PUBLIC INQUIRIES: 1-800-352-1446

Ms. Donna Roe
Director
Division of Federal Programs
Department of Public Welfare
P.O. Box 2675
Harrisburg, PA 17105
TEL: 717-772-7906
FAX: 717-772-6451
E-MAIL: LIHEAPMAIL@state.pa.us
WEB SITE: **www.dpw.state.pa.us/ServicesPrograms/LIHEAP**
PUBLIC INQUIRIES: 1-866-857-7095

Ms. Andrea Gregg
Program Manager
Energy & Emergency Assistance Unit
Division of Benefit Programs
Virginia Department of Social Services
7 N. 8th Street
Richmond, VA 23219
TEL: 804-726-7368
FAX: 804-726-7358
E-MAIL: andrea.gregg@dss.virginia.gov
WEB SITE: **www.dss.virginia.gov/benefit/ea/index.html**
PUBLIC INQUIRIES: 1-800-230-6977

Ms. Danita Jones
LIHEAP Director
Division of Family Assistance
West Virginia Department of Health and Human Resources
350 Capitol Street, Rm B-18
Charleston, WV 25301-3704

TEL: 304-558-8290

FAX: 304-558-2059

E-Mail: danita.d.jones@wv.gov

WEB SITE: **www.wvdhhr.org/bcf/family_assistance/utility.asp**

PUBLIC INQUIRIES: 1-800-642-8589

REGION 4

Mr. Gareth D. Whitehead

Energy Section Supervisor

Alabama Department of Economic and Community Affairs

Community Services Division

P.O. Box 5690

Montgomery, AL 36103-5690

TEL: 334-242-5365

FAX: 334-353-4311

E-MAIL: willie.whitehead@adeca.alabama.gov

WEB SITE: **http://216.226.178.189/txtlstvw.aspx?LstID=d9aead61-987c-4dae-a648-c48bcff32da9**

Ms. Hilda Frazier

Community & Social Services Operations Manager

Department of Community Affairs

Bureau of Housing and Community Development

Community Assistance Section

2555 Shumard Oak Boulevard

Tallahassee, FL 32399-2100

TEL: 850-922-1834

FAX: 850-488-2488

E-MAIL: hilda.frazier@dca.state.fl.us

WEB SITE: **www.floridacommunitydevelopment.org/liheap/index.cfm**

PUBLIC INQUIRIES: 850-488-7541

Mr. Jeff Blankenship
LIHEAP Coordinator
Division of Family and Children Services
Georgia Dept. of Human Resources
2 Peachtree Street NW, Suite 21-265
Atlanta, GA 30303-3180
TEL: 404-463-8047
FAX: 404-463-8046
E-MAIL: jlblanke@dhr.state.ga.us
WEB SITE: **www.heatga.org/assistance/assistance.asp**
PUBLIC INQUIRIES: 1-800-869-1150

Ms. Sharon Vinyard
Policy Analyst
Department for Community Based Services
Division of Family Support
Human Resources Building
275 East Main Street, 3E-I
Frankfort, KY 40601
TEL: 502-564-3440, Ext. 3023
FAX: 502-564-0405
E-MAIL: sharon.vinyard@ky.gov
WEB SITE: **http://chfs.ky.gov/dcbs/dfs/liheap.htm**
PUBLIC INQUIRIES: 1-800-456-3452

Ms. Tina Ruffin
Branch Director
Division of Community Services
Mississippi Dept. of Human Services
750 N. State Street
Jackson, MS 39202-4772

TEL: 601-359-4766
FAX: 601-359-4370
E-MAIL: truffin@mdhs.state.ms.us
WEB SITE: **www.mdhs.state.ms.us/cs_info.html**
PUBLIC INQUIRIES: 1-800-421-0762

Ms. Erica Jennings
Program Consultant II
Food & Nutrition Svcs. & Energy Programs
Department of Health and Human Services
Division of Social Services
325 North Salisbury Street
Raleigh, NC 27603-5905
TEL: 919-733-7831, Ext. 275
FAX: 919-733-5457
E-MAIL: erica.jennings@ncmail.net
WEB SITE: **www.ncdhhs.gov/dss/**
PUBLIC INQUIRIES: 1-800-662-7030 (CARE LINE)

Ms. Ashlie Lancaster
Director
Governor's Office of Economic Opportunity
Suite 358
1205 Pendleton Street
Columbia, SC 29201
TEL: 803-734-0662
FAX: 803-734-0356
E-MAIL: alancaster@oepp.sc.gov
WEB SITE: **www.oepp.sc.gov/oeo/programs.htm**

Ms. Regina Surber
Director, Community Programs
Department of Human Services
Citizens Plaza Building
400 Deaderick Street
Nashville, TN 37248-9500
TEL: 615-313-4762
FAX: 615-532-9956
E-MAIL: regina.surber@state.tn.us
WEB SITE: **http://state.tn.us/humanserv/adfam/afs_hea.html**
PUBLIC INQUIRIES: 615-313-4766

REGION 5

Mr. Larry Dawson
Managing Director
Department of Commerce and Economic Opportunity
100 West Randolph, Suite 3-400
Chicago, IL 60601
TEL: 312-793-4724
FAX: 312-793-2798
E-MAIL: larry.dawson@illinois.gov
WEB SITE: **www.liheapillinois.com**
WEATHERIZATION WEB SITE: **www.illinoisweatherization.com**
PUBLIC INQUIRIES: 1-877-411-WARM (9276)

Mr. Tom Scott
Community Development Administrator
Indiana Housing and Community Development Authority
30 South Meridian Street
Indianapolis, IN 46204

TEL: 317-232-7015
FAX: 317-232-7778
E-MAIL: ScottTJ@ihcda.IN.gov
WEB SITE: **www.in.gov/ihcda/2523.htm**
PUBLIC INQUIRIES: 1-800-622-4973

Ms. Barbara Anders
Director, Adult and Family Services
Michigan Department of Human Services
Grand Tower Suite 1306
P.O. Box 30037
Lansing, MI 48909
TEL: 517-335-6358
FAX: 517-335-7771
E-MAIL: andersb@michigan.gov
WEB SITE: **www.michigan.gov/dhs**
PUBLIC INQUIRIES: 1-800-292-5650

Mr. John Harvanko
Director, Energy Assistance Programs
Energy Division
Minnesota Department of Commerce
85 7th Place East, Suite 500
St. Paul, MN 55101-2198
TEL: 651-284-3275
FAX: 651-297-7891
E-MAIL: john.harvanko@state.mn.us
WEB SITE: **www.state.mn.us/portal/mn/jsp/content.do?id=-**
536881374&agency=Commerce
PUBLIC INQUIRIES: 1-800-657-3805

Mr. Nick Sunday
Chief, OCS/HEAP
Ohio Department of Development
P.O. Box 1001
77 South High, 25th Floor
Columbus, OH 43216
TEL: 614-644-6846
FAX: 614-728-6832
E-MAIL: nick.sunday@development.ohio.gov
WEB SITE: **www.odod.state.oh.us/cdd/ocs/heap.htm**
PUBLIC INQUIRIES: 1-800-282-0880 (TDD: 1-800-686-1557)

Ms. Susan Brown
Deputy Administrator
Wisconsin Department of Administration
Division of Energy Services
P.O. Box 7868
Madison, WI 53707-7868
TEL: 608-267-3680
FAX: 608-267-6931
E-MAIL: heat@wisconsin.gov
WEB SITE: **www.homeenergyplus.wi.gov**
PUBLIC INQUIRIES: 1-866-432-8947

REGION 6

Ms. Cathy Rowe
Manager, Home Energy Assistance Program
Office of Community Services
Department of Human Services
P.O. Box 1437/Slot 1330
Little Rock, AR 72203-1437

TEL: 501-682-8726
FAX: 501-682-6736
E-MAIL: cathy.rowe@arkansas.gov
WEB SITE: **www.arkansas.gov/dhs/dco/ocs/**
PUBLIC INQUIRIES: 800-482-8988

Ms. Darleen Okammor
Program Manager
Louisiana Housing Finance Agency
Energy Assistance Department
2415 Quail Drive
Baton Rouge, LA 70808
TEL: 225-763-8700, Ext. 205
FAX: 225-763-8752
E-MAIL: dokammor@lhfa.state.la.us
WEB SITE: **www.lhfa.state.la.us/programs/energy_assistance/low_in-come_energy.php**
PUBLIC INQUIRIES: 1-888-454-2001

Ms. Loretta Williams
LIHEAP Program Manager
Human Services Department
Income Support Division
Work & Family Support Bureau
P.O. Box 12740
Albuquerque, NM 87195-2495
TEL: 505-383-2495
FAX: 505-383-2551
E-MAIL: loretta.williams@state.nm.us
WEB SITE: **www.hsd.state.nm.us/isd/liheap.html**
PUBLIC INQUIRIES: 888-523-0051

Ms. Cari Crittenden
Program Field Representative
Oklahoma Department of Human Services
FSSD/LIHEAP
P.O. Box 25352
Oklahoma City, OK 73125
TEL: 405-521-4089
FAX: 405-521-4158
E-MAIL: cari.crittenden@okdhs.org
WEB SITE: **www.okdhs.org/programsandservices/liheap**
PUBLIC INQUIRIES: 1-866-411-1877

Mr. Michael DeYoung
Program Manager
Energy Assistance Section
Texas Department of Housing and Community Affairs
P.O. Box 13941
Austin, TX 78711-3941
TEL: 512-475-2125
FAX: 512-475-3935
E-MAIL: michael.deyoung@tdhca.state.tx.us
WEB SITE: **www.tdhca.state.tx.us/ea/index.htm**
PUBLIC INQUIRIES: 1-877-399-8939
LITE-UP TEXAS: 1-866-454-8387
PUBLIC UTILITY COMMISSION COMPLAINTS: 1-888-782-8477

REGION 7

Mr. Jerry McKim
Chief, Bureau of Energy Assistance
Division of Community Action Agencies

Department of Human Rights
Lucas State Office Building
321 W. 12th Street, 2nd Floor
Des Moines, IA 50319
TEL: 515-281-0859
FAX: 515-242-6119
E-MAIL: jerry.mckim@iowa.gov
WEB SITE: **www.dcaa.iowa.gov/bureau_EA/index.html**
PUBLIC INQUIRIES: 515-281-4204

Mr. Lewis A. Kimsey
Energy Assistance Director (LIEAP)
Social & Rehabilitation Services
915 SW Harrison, Suite 580
Topeka, KS 66612
PHONE: 785-296-0147
FAX: 785-296-6960
E-MAIL: lewis.kimsey@srs.ks.gov
WEB SITE: **www.srskansas.org/ISD/ees/lieap.htm**
PUBLIC INQUIRIES: 1-800-432-0043

Ms. Jeanna Machon
Assistant Deputy Director
Family Support Division
Department of Social Services
P.O. Box 2320
Jefferson City, MO 65102
TEL: 573-526-4836
FAX: 573-526-5592
E-MAIL: Jeanna.L.Machon@dss.mo.gov
WEB SITE: **www.dss.mo.gov/fsd/liheap.htm**

Mr. Mike Kelly
Program and Planning Specialist
Program Assistance Unit
Department of Health and
Human Services
301 Centennial Mall South, 4th Floor
P.O. Box 95026
Lincoln, NE 68509
TEL: 402-471-9262
FAX 402-471-9597
E-MAIL: mike.kelly@dhhs.ne.gov
WEB SITE: **www.hhs.state.ne.us/fia/energy.htm**
PUBLIC INQUIRIES: 1-800-430-3244

REGION 8

Mr. Todd Jorgensen
LIHEAP Director
Colorado Department of Human Services
789 Sherman Street, Suite 440
Denver, CO 80203
TEL: 303-861-0325
FAX: 303-861-0275
E-MAIL: todd.jorgensen@state.co.us
WEB SITE: **www.cdhs.state.co.us/leap**
PUBLIC INQUIRIES: 1-866-432-8435 or 303-861-0629

Mr. Jim Nolan
Chief
Intergovernmental Human Services Bureau
Department of Public Health and Human Services

1400 Carter Drive

Helena, MT 59620

TEL: 406-447-4260

FAX: 406-447-4287

E-MAIL: jnolan@mt.gov

Web site: **www.dphhs.mt.gov/**

PUBLIC INQUIRIES: 1-800-332-2272

Mr. Ron Knutson

Assistant Director of Energy & Nutrition

Department of Human Services

State Capitol Building, Judicial Wing

600 E. Boulevard, Dept. 325

Bismarck, ND 58505-0250

TEL: 701-328-4882

FAX: 701-328-1060

E-MAIL: rknutson@nd.gov

WEB SITE: **www.nd.gov/dhs/services/financialhelp/energyassist.html**

PUBLIC INQUIRIES: 1-800-755-2716

Mr. David Gall

Program Administrator

Office of Energy Assistance

Department of Social Services

206 West Missouri Avenue

Pierre, SD 57501-4517

TEL: 605-773-4131

FAX: 605-773-6657

E-MAIL: david.gall@state.sd.us

WEB SITE: **http://dss.sd.gov/energyassistance/index.asp**

PUBLIC INQUIRIES: 1-800-233-8503

Mr. Sherman Roquiero
Program Manager
HEAT & SNAPS
Department of Community & Economic Development
324 South State, Suite 500
Salt Lake City, UT 84111
TEL: 801-538-8644
FAX: 801-538-8615
E-MAIL: shermr@utah.gov
WEB SITE: **www.housing.utah.gov/seal/index.html**
PUBLIC INQUIRIES: 1-877-488-3233

Ms. Brenda llg
Program Manager
LIHEAP/Weatherization Programs
Department of Family Services
2300 Capitol Avenue
Hathaway Building, 3rd Floor
Cheyenne, WY 82002-0490
TEL: 307-777-6346
FAX: 307-777-6276
E-MAIL: BILG@state.wy.us
WEB SITE: **dfsweb.state.wy.us/fieldop/briefing5a.htm**
PUBLIC INQUIRIES: 1-800-246-4221

REGION 9

Ms. Sandra Mendez
LIHEAP Coordinator
Community Services Administration
Arizona Department of Economic Security
1789 W. Jefferson, Site Code 086Z

P.O. Box 6123
Phoenix, AZ 85007
TEL: 602-542-6607
FAX: 602-364-1756
E-MAIL: smendez@azdes.gov
WEB SITE: **https://egov.azdes.gov/cmsinternet/intranet.
aspx?id=2328&menu=34**
PUBLIC INQUIRIES: 1-800-582-5706

Ms. Kathy Ely
Senior Manager
Department of Community Services and Development
700 North 10th Street, Room 258
Sacramento, CA 95814
TEL: 916-341-4200
FAX: 916-327-3153
E-MAIL: KEly@csd.ca.gov
WEB SITE: **www.csd.ca.gov**
PUBLIC INQUIRIES: 1-866-675-6623

Ms. Patricia Williams
LIHEAP State Coordinator
SOH/BESSD/FAP
Benefit, Employment, and Support Services Division
Financial Assistance Office
820 Mililani Street, Suite 606
Honolulu, HI 96813
TEL: 808-586-5734
FAX: 808-586-5744
E-MAIL: pwilliams@dhs.hawaii.gov

WEB SITE: **www.hawaii.gov/health/disability-services/neurotrauma/
key-services-finance.html#liheap**
PUBLIC INQUIRIES: 1-808-586-5740

Ms. Lori Wilson
Chief
Energy Assistance Program
Employment & Support Services
1470 College Parkway
Carson City, NV 89706-7924
TEL: 775-684-0626
FAX: 775-684-0617
E-MAIL: lwilson@dwss.nv.gov
WEB SITE: **http://dwss.nv.gov/index.php?option=com_content&task
=view&id=116&Itemid=279**
PUBLIC INQUIRIES: 1-800-992-0900 (EXT. 4420]

REGION 10

Ms. Susan Marshall
LIHEAP Program Coordinator
Alaska Department of Health and Social Services
Division of Public Assistance
400 Willoughby, Suite 301
Juneau, AK 99801-1700
TEL: 907-465-3099
FAX: 907-465-3319
E-MAIL: susan.marshall@alaska.gov
WEB SITE: **www.hss.state.ak.us/dpa/programs/hap**
PUBLIC INQUIRIES: 1-800-470-3058

Ms. Chris Baylis
Program Specialist

Statewide Self Reliance Programs
Idaho Department of Health and Welfare
450 West State Street-2nd Floor
Boise, ID 83702
TEL: 208-334-5742
FAX: 208-334-5817
E-MAIL: baylisc@dhw.idaho.gov
INFORMATION ON APPLYING FOR ENERGY ASSISTANCE:
czamora@capai.org
WEB SITE: **www.healthandwelfare.idaho.gov**
PUBLIC INQUIRIES: 208-442-9991 or 208-442-9987

Ms. Melissa Torgerson
LIHEAP Program Coordinator
Oregon Housing and Community Services
North Mall Office Building
725 Summer Street NE, Suite B
Salem, OR 97301-1266
TEL: 503-986-2094
FAX: 503-986-2006
E-MAIL: melissa.torgerson@hcs.state.or.us
WEB SITE: **www.oregon.gov/OHCS/SOS_Low_Income_Energy_Assistance_Oregon.shtml**
PUBLIC INQUIRIES: 1-800-453-5511

Mr. Cinque R. Finnie
LIHEAP Contract Manager
Department of Commerce
906 Columbia Street, S.W.
P.O. Box 48350
Olympia, WA 98504-8350
TEL: 360-725-2855

FAX: 360-586-0489

E-MAIL: cinque.finnie@commerce.wa.gov

WEB SITE: **www.liheapwa.org**

SNAP Benefits – Toll-Free Numbers by State

The Supplemental Nutrition Assistance Program (SNAP) provides assistance to low-income families who have trouble being able to afford groceries. SNAP also provides information and education on nutrition, one of the reasons it recently changed its name from the "Food Stamp" program. Use the following numbers to get information on SNAP benefit questions in the states and areas of states listed. Most are toll-free numbers. Some of the numbers that are not toll-free will accept collect calls.

*Indicates numbers that are for in-state and out-of-state calls. All other 800 numbers are for in-state calls only.

STATE	PHONE #
Alabama	334-242-1700
Alaska	907-465-3347
Arizona	1-800-352-8401
Arkansas	1-800-482-8988
California	877-847-FOOD (3663)
Colorado	1-800-536-5298
Connecticut	1-800-842-1508
Delaware	1-800-372-2022 or 302-255-9500
District of Columbia	202-727-5355 (no collect calls)
Florida	1-866 762-2237
Georgia	1-800-869-1150 outside metro area 404-657-9358 inside metro area
Guam	671-735-7245
Hawaii	808-643-1643

STATE	PHONE #
Idaho	1-800-926-2588
Illinois	1-800-843-6154
Indiana	1-800-622-4932 *
Iowa	1-877-937-3663
Kansas	1-888-369-4777
Kentucky	1-800-931-9112
Louisiana	225-219-0351 1-888-LA HELPU (1-888-524-3578)
Maine	1-800-452-4643
Maryland	1-800-332-6347
Massachusetts	1-866-950-3663
Michigan	800-481-4989
Minnesota	1-800-657-3698 *
Mississippi	1-800-948-3050
Missouri	www.dss.mo.gov/fsd/fstamp/index.htm
Montana	1-800-332-2272
Nebraska	1-800-430-3244
Nevada	1-800-992-0900 (ext. 40500)
New Hampshire	1-800-852-3345 (ext. 4238)
New Jersey	1-800-687-9512
New Mexico	1-888-473-3676
New York	1-800-342-3009 upstate 1-877-472-8411 *NYC only*
North Carolina	1-800-662-7030
North Dakota	1-800-755-2716
Ohio	1-866-244-0071 *
Oklahoma	405-521-3444
Oregon	1-800-723-3638
Pennsylvania	1-800-692-7462 TDD 1-800-451-5886
Puerto Rico	1-800-981-5822; 1-787-725-7262; 1-787-725-1732; TTD 1-800-981-7641
Rhode Island	401-462-5300

330 What to Do When You Are Fired or Laid Off

STATE	PHONE #
South Carolina	1-800-768-5700
South Dakota	1-877-999-5612
Tennessee	1-866-311-4287
Texas	211 in state only; 1-512-973-9203 option 2
Utah	1-866-526-3663
Vermont	1-800-287-0589
Virgin Islands	340-774-2399
Virginia	1-800-552-3431; 1-804-692-2198 *in state only*
Washington	877-514-Food (3663)
West Virginia	1-800-642-8589
Wisconsin	1-800-362-3002
Wyoming	1-800-457-3659

OSHA Offices – To Report Whistleblower Discrimination

Workers who report practices on the job that are illegal or harmful to the public cannot be fired for that reason. To report whistleblower discrimination, contact your local OSHA office.

Occupational Safety and Health Administration (OSHA)
200 Constitution Avenue, NW
Washington, DC 20210
Tel.: 1-800-321-OSHA (1-800-321-6742)
TTY: 1-877-889-5627

Region 1

Connecticut | Massachusetts | Maine | New Hampshire | Rhode Island | Vermont
Regional Office
JFK Federal Building, Room E340
Boston, Massachusetts 02203
617-565-9860
617-565-9827 FAX

Region 2

New Jersey | New York | Puerto Rico| Virgin Islands
Regional Office
201 Varick Street, Room 670
New York, New York 10014
212-337-2378
212-337-2371 FAX

Region 3

District of Columbia | Delaware | Maryland | Pennsylvania | Virginia | West Virginia
Regional Office
U.S. Department of Labor/OSHA
The Curtis Center-Suite 740 West
170 S. Independence Mall West
Philadelphia, PA 19106-3309
215-861-4900
215-861-4904 FAX

Region 4

Alabama | Florida | Georgia | Kentucky | Mississippi | North Carolina | South Carolina | Tennessee
Regional Office
61 Forsyth Street, SW
Room 6T50
Atlanta, Georgia 30303

404-562-2300
404-562-2295 FAX

Region 5

Illinois | Indiana | Michigan | Minnesota | Ohio | Wisconsin
Regional Office
230 South Dearborn Street, Room 3244
Chicago, Illinois 60604
312-353-2220
312-353-7774 FAX

Region 6

Arkansas | Louisiana | New Mexico | Oklahoma | Texas
Regional Office
525 Griffin Street, Suite 602
Dallas, Texas 75202
972-850-4145
972-850-4149 FAX
972-850-4150 FSO FAX

Region 7

Iowa | Kansas | Missouri | Nebraska
Regional Office
Two Pershing Square Building
2300 Main Street, Suite 1010
Kansas City, Missouri 64108-2416

816-283-8745
816-283-0545 VOICE
816-283-0547 FAX

Region 8

Colorado | Montana | North Dakota | South Dakota | Utah | Wyoming
Regional Office
1999 Broadway, Suite 1690
Denver, Colorado 80202
720-264-6550
720-264-6585 FAX

Region 9

Arizona | California | Guam | Hawaii | Nevada
For issues involving federal agencies or private companies working for federal agencies in Arizona, California, Guam, Hawaii, and Nevada, call the numbers listed below.

Region IX Federal Contact Numbers
90 7th Street, Suite 18100
San Francisco, California 94103
415-625-2547 (Main Public - 8:00 AM - 4:30 PM Pacific)

800-475-4019 (For Technical Assistance)
800-475-4020 (For Complaints - Accidents/Fatalities)
Note: The 800 number for Complaints - Accidents/Fatalities is Regional only.

800-475-4022 (For Publication Requests)
415-625-2534 FAX

For issues involving private or state government employers in these states, refer to the appropriate state office:

Arizona
Arizona Division of Occupational Safety and Health (ADOSH)
Phoenix Office
800 W. Washington Street, 2nd floor
Phoenix, AZ 85007
602-542-5795
602-542-1614 FAX

Tucson Office
2675 E. Broadway Blvd. #239
Tucson, AZ 85716
520-628-5478
520-322-8008 FAX

California
Department of Industrial Relations
Office of the Director
455 Golden Gate Avenue
San Francisco, CA 94102
415-703-5050

Hawaii
Department of Labor & Industrial Relations
830 Punchbowl Street, Suite 321
Honolulu, HI 96813
808-586-8844

Nevada
Nevada OSHA
1301 N. Green Valley Parkway, Suite 200
Henderson, NV 89074
702-486-9020
702-990-0358 FAX

Region 10

Alaska | Idaho | Oregon | Washington
Regional Office
1111 Third Avenue, Suite 715
Seattle, Washington 98101-3212
206-553-5930
206-553-6499 FAX

Small Business Administration (SBA) offices

If you are considering starting your own business, either part-time until you find another job or as a new venture, contact your state's SBA office to get more information about their counseling and loan services.

Alabama District Office
801 Tom Martin Drive, Suite #201
Birmingham, AL 35211
Phone: 205-290-7101
Fax: 205-290-7404

Alaska District Office
510 L Street, Suite 310
Anchorage, AK 99501-1952
907-271-4022

Arizona District Office
2828 North Central Ave,
Suite 800
Phoenix, AZ 85004-1093
Phone: 602-745-7200
Fax: 602-745-7210

Arkansas District Office
2120 Riverfront Drive, Suite 250
Little Rock, AR 72202-1796

Phone: 501-324-7379
Fax: 501-324-7394

California - Los Angeles
District Office
330 North Brand, Suite 1200
Glendale, CA 91203
818-552-3215

California - Sacramento
District Office
6501 Sylvan Road, suite 100
Citrus Height, CA 95610
Phone: 916-735-1700
Fax: 916-735-1719

California - San Francisco
District Office
455 Market Street, 6th Floor
San Francisco, CA
94105-2420
415-744-6820

Colorado District Office
721 19th Street, Suite 426
Denver, CO 80202
303-844-2607

Connecticut District Office
330 Main Street, Second Floor
Hartford, CT 06106
860-240-4700

Delaware District Office
1007 N. Orange Street, Suite 1120
Wilmington, DE 19801-1232
302-573-6294

Florida - Jacksonville
District Office
7825 Baymeadows Way,
Suite 100B
Jacksonville, FL 32256 - 7504
904-443-1900

Florida - Miami District Office
100 S. Biscayne Blvd - 7th Floor
Miami, FL 33131
Phone: 305-536-5521
Fax: 305-536-5058

Georgia District Office
233 Peachtree Street, NE,
Suite 1900
Atlanta, GA 30303
404-331-0100

Hawaii District Office
300 Ala Moana Blvd
Room 2-235
Box 50207
Honolulu, HI 96850
Phone: 808-541-2990
Fax: 808-541-2976

Idaho District Office
380 East Parkcenter Blvd.,
Suite 330
Boise, ID 83706
Phone: 208-334-1696
Fax: 208-334-9353

Illinois District Office
500 W. Madison Street, Suite 1250
Chicago, IL 60661-2511
Phone: 312-353-4528
Fax: 312-886-5688

Indiana District Office
8500 Keystone Crossing, Suite 400
Indianapolis, IN 46240-2460
317-226-7272

Iowa District Office
210 Walnut St, Rm 749
Des Moines, IA 50309-4106
515-284-4422

Kansas District Office
271 W 3rd St, N Suite 2500
Wichita, KS 67202
316-269-6616

Kentucky District Office
600 Dr. Martin Luther King Jr
Place Rm 188

Louisville, KY 40202-2254
502-582-5971

Louisiana District Office
365 Canal St., Suite 2820
New Orleans, LA 70130
504-589-6685

Maine District Office
Edmund S. Muskie Federal Building, Room 512
68 Sewall Street
Augusta, ME 04330
207-622-8551

Michigan District Office
477 Michigan Avenue
Suite 515, McNamara Building
Detroit, MI 48226
313-226-6075

Minnesota District Office
100 North Sixth Street
Suite 210-C Butler Square
Minneapolis, MN 55403
Phone: 612-370-2324
Fax: 612-370-2303

Mississippi District Office
Regions Plaza
210 E. Capitol Street, Suite 900

Jackson, MS 39201
Phone: 601-965-4378
Fax: 601-965-5629
or 601-965-4294

Maryland District Office
City Crescent Building, 6th Floor
10 South Howard Street
Baltimore, MD 21201
410-962-6195

Massachusetts - Boston
District Office
10 Causeway Street, Room 265
Boston, MA 02222
617-565-5590

Missouri - St. Louis District Office
200 North Broadway, Suite 1500
St. Louis, MO 63102
Phone: 314-539-6600
Fax: 314-539-3785

Montana District Office
10 West 15th Street Suite 1100
Helena, MT 59626
Phone: 406-441-1081
Fax: 406-441-1090

Nebraska District Office
10675 Bedford Ave., Suite 100
Omaha, NE 68134

402-221-4691

Nevada District Office
400 South 4th Street
Suite 250.
Las Vegas, NV 89101
Phone: 702-388-6611
Fax: 702-388-6469

New Hampshire District Office
JC Cleveland Federal Building
55 Pleasant Street, Suite 3101
Concord, NH 03301
Phone: 603-225-1400
Fax: 603-225-1409

New Jersey District Office
Two Gateway Center, 15th Floor
Newark, NJ 07102
973-645-2434

New Mexico District Office
625 Silver SW Suite 320
Albuquerque, NM 87102
Voice: 505-248-8225
Fax: 505-248-8246

New York District Office
26 Federal Plaza, Suite 3100
New York, NY 10278
Phone: 212-264-4354

Fax: 212-264-4963

New York - Buffalo District Office
Niagara Center
130 S. Elmwood Avenue, Suite 540
Buffalo, NY 14202
Phone: 716-551-4301
Fax: 716-551-4418

New York - Syracuse District Office
401 S. Salina Street, 5th Floor
Syracuse, New York 13202
Phone: 315-471-9393
Fax: 315-471-9288

North Carolina District Office
6302 Fairview Road, Suite 300
Charlotte, NC 28210-2227
Phone: 704-344-6563
Fax: 704-344-6769

North Dakota District Office
657 2nd Avenue North, Room 218
P.O. Box 3086
Fargo, ND 58108-3086
Phone: 701-239-5131
Fax: 701-239-5645

Ohio - Columbus District Office
401 N. Front St. Suite 200
Columbus, OH 43215
614-469-6860

Oklahoma District Office
Federal Building
301 NW 6th St
Oklahoma City, OK 73102
405-609-8000

Oregon District Office
601 SW Second Avenue, Suite 950.
Portland, OR 97204-3192
Phone: 503-326-2682
Fax: 503-326-2808

Pennsylvania - Philadelphia
District Office
Parkview Tower
1150 First Avenue
Suite 1001
King of Prussia, PA 19406
610-382-3062

Pennsylvania - Pittsburgh
District Office
411 Seventh Avenue
Suite 1450
Pittsburgh, PA 15219
Phone: 412-395-6560
Fax: 412-395-6562

Rhode Island District Office
380 Westminster Street, Room 511
Providence, RI 02903

401-528-4561

South Carolina District Office
1835 Assembly Street, Room 1425
Columbia, SC 29201
803-765-5377 Fax: 803-765-5962

South Dakota District Office
2329 N. Career Ave., Suite 105
Sioux Falls, SD 57107
Phone: 605-330-4243
Fax: 605-330-4215
TTY/TDD: 605-331-3527

Tennessee District Office
50 Vantage Way, Suite 201
Nashville, TN 37228
Phone: 615-736-5881
Fax: 615736-7232

Texas - Dallas / Fort Worth
District Office
4300 Amon Carter Blvd. Suite 114
Fort Worth, TX 76155
Phone: 817-684-5500
Fax: 817-684-5516

Utah District Office
125 South State Street, Room 2227
Salt Lake City, UT 84138
801-524-3209

Vermont District Office
87 State Street, Room 205
Montpelier, VT 05601
802-828-4422

Virginia District Office
The Federal Building
400 North 8th Street, Suite 1150
Richmond, VA 23219-4829
804-771-2400 Fax: 771-2764

Washington District Office
2401 Fourth Avenue, Suite 450
Seattle, WA 98121
206-553-7310

Washington DC District Office
Washington Metropolitan Area
District Office
740 15th Street NW, Suite 300
Washington, D.C. 20005-3544
202-272-0345

West Virginia District Office
320 West Pike Street, Suite 330
Clarksburg, WV 26301
304-623-5631

Wisconsin District Office
740 Regent Street, Suite 100
Madison, WI 53715

608-441-5263 Fax: 608-441-5541

Wyoming District Office
100 East B Street
Federal Building, Room 4001
P.O. Box 44001
Casper, WY 82602-5013
307-261-6500
800-776-9144, Ext. 1

State Rapid Response Coordinators

Alabama

Ms. Susan Norman,
Associate Director
Field Services Division
Governor's Office of Workforce
Development (GOWD)
Workforce Development
Division (WDD)
Alabama Department of Economic
and Community Affairs (ADECA)
401 Adams Avenue
P.O. Box 5690
Montgomery, AL 36103-5690
1-800-562-4916 toll free
Fax: 334-242-5855
E-mail: DWU-Warn@adeca.alabama.gov

Alaska

Shawna Harper
TAA & Rapid Response Program
Coordinator
Department of Labor and Work-
force Development
907-465-1882
E-mail: shawna_harper@labor.
state.ak.us

Arizona

Ron Delgado
Coordinator
Dislocated Workers Unit
Arizona Workforce
1789 West Jefferson
Site Code 920Z
Phoenix, AZ 85007
602-542-2494
Fax: 602-542-2491
E-mail : radelgado@azdes.gov

Arkansas

Thomas Sheppard
Division Chief, Dislocated
Worker Services,
Arkansas Employment Security
Department
P.O. Box 2981

Little Rock, AR 72203
501-682-1818
E-mail: thomas.sheppard@arkan-
sas.gov

California

Cassandra Dunlap
Manager
CA Employment Development De-
partment
Workforce Services Branch
Workforce Services Division
P.O. Box 826880 (MIC 50)
Sacramento, CA 94280-0001
916-654-5181
Fax: 916-654-9586
E-mail: cdunlap@edd.ca.gov

Colorado

Terry Bohannon
State Rapid Response Coordinator
Colorado Department of Labor and
Employment
633 17th Street, Suite #700
Denver, CO 80202-3660
303-318-8840
Fax: 303-318-8930
E-mail: terry.bohannon@state.co.us

Connecticut

Andrea Slusarz
200 Folly Brook Blvd.
CT Department of Labor
Weathersfield, CT 06109
860-263-6588
Fax: 860-263-6039
E-mail: Andrea.Slusarz@po.
state.ct.us

Delaware

Betsy Archer
Division of Unemployment
and Training
P.O. Box 9828
4425 North Market Street
Wilmington, DE 19809
302-761-8114
E-mail: betsy.archer@state.de.us

District of Columbia

Susan Gilbert
Executive Assistant
Department of Employment
Services
602 H Street NE
Washington, DC 20002
202-698-3495
Fax: 202-673-8630
E-mail: susan.gilbert@dc.gov

Florida

Gene Rhodes
A. E. Rhodes, Administrator
REACT Program
107 E. Madison Street
Tallahassee, FL 32399-4137
850-921-3326
E-mail: gene.rhodes@awi.state.fl.us

Georgia

Laura Amaya
Acting Rapid Response Supervisor
Georgia Department of Labor
Suite 440
148 Andrew Young International
Blvd., NE
Atlanta, GA 30303
404-232-3505
Fax: 404-232-3503
E-mail: laura.amaya@dol.state.ga.us

Hawaii

Carol Kanayama
830 Punchbowl Street Room #329
Honolulu, HI 96813
808-586-8825
Fax: 808-586-8822
E-mail: ckanayama@dlir.state.hi.us

Idaho

Rico Barrera
Idaho Commerce and Labor
317 W. Main
Boise, ID 83735-0790
208-332-3570 ext. 3316
Fax: 208-332-7417
E-mail: Rico.Barrera@cl.idaho.gov

Illinois

Rebecca Harmon
Asst. Deputy Director
Bureau of Workforce Development
IL Department of Commerce &
Economic Opportunity
620 East Adams, 5th Floor
Springfield, IL 62701
217-558-2435
Fax: 217-557-5506
E-mail: Rebecca.Harmon@
illinois.gov

Indiana

Jennifer Long
Indiana Department of Workforce
Development
State Dislocated Worker Program
Coordinator
10 N. Senate Ave.

Indianapolis, IN 46204
317-232-7186
Fax: 317-233-2679
E-mail: jlong@dwd.in.gov

Iowa

Ted A. Harms
State Rapid Response Coordinator
Iowa Workforce Development
3420 University Avenue
Waterloo, IA 50701
515-669-0359
E-mail: Ted.Harms@IWD.iowa.gov

Kansas

Armand Corpolongo
Director
Kansas Department of Commerce
Curtis State Office Building
1000 SW Jackson, Suite 100
Topeka, KS 66612
785-296-7876
Fax: 785-296-1404
E-mail: acorpolongo@kansascom-
merce.com

Kentucky

Cecil Colliver
Rapid Response Team

Office of Employment and Training
Division of Workforce Services
275 East Main Street
Mailstop 2WA
Frankfort, Kentucky 40601
502-564-7456
Fax: 502-564-7459
E-mail: Cecil.Colliver@ky.gov

Louisiana

Bonnie McKneely
Louisiana Department of Labor
1001 N. 23rd Street
P.O. Box 94094
Baton Rouge, LA 70804-9094
225-342-7659
E-mail: bmckneely@ldol.state.la.us

Maine

Judith Pelletier
Rapid Response/TAA Coordinator
Bureau of Employment Services
Maine Department of Labor
55 State House Station
Augusta, ME
207-623-7993
E-mail: judith.a.pelletier@
maine.gov

Maryland

Scott Wallace
Director, Dislocated Workers Unit
Department of Labor, Licensing
and Regulations
Division of Workforce
Development
1100 North Eutaw Street
Room 209
Baltimore, MD 21201
410-767-2833
Fax: 410-333-5162
E-mail: swallace@dllr.state.md.us

Massachusetts

Ken Messina
Statewide Rapid Response Manager
Massachusetts Division of
Career Services
Charles F. Hurley Building
19 Staniford Street, First Floor
Boston, MA 02114
617-626-5703
Fax: 617-727-8671
E-mail: kmessina@detma.org

Michigan

Chong-Anna Canfora
Director, Rapid Response Unit

Michigan Department of Labor &
Economic Growth
611 West Ottawa, 4th Floor,
PO Box 30004
Lansing, MI 48909
517-335-1943
Cell: 517-242-4452
Fax: 517-373-4648
E-mail: canforac@michigan.gov

Minnesota

Filiberto (Fil) Chairez
Rapid Response Coordinator
Economic Development
1st National Bank Building,
Suite E200
332 Minnesota Street
St. Paul, MN 55101
651-259-7534
Fax: 651-215-3842
E-mail: filiberto.chairez@state.
mn.us

Mississippi

Gloria Neal
Department Chief
Mississippi Department of Employment Security
1235 Echelon Parkway

Jackson, MS 39213
601-321-6554
Fax: 601-321-6598
E-mail: gneal@mdes.ms.gov

Missouri

Dawn Busick
Director
Division of Workforce
Development
P.O. Box 1087
Jefferson City, MO 65102
573-751-3349
Fax: 573-751-8162
E-mail: dawn.busick@ded.mo.gov

Jacqulin Johnson
State Rapid Response Coordinator
Division of Workforce
Development
PO Box 1087
Jefferson City, MO 65102
573-751-9700
E-mail: Jacqulin.Johnson@ded.
mo.gov

Montana

Suzanne Ferguson
Dislocated Worker/Rapid

Response Unit

Statewide Workforce Programs Bureau

Workforce Services Division

Montana Department of Labor and Industry

P.O. Box 1728

Helena, MT 59624

406-444-4513

Fax: 406-444-3037

E-mail: sferguson@mt.gov

Nebraska

Jan Sovereign

Rapid Response/Dislocated Worker Unit Coordinator

Nebraska Workforce Development

Nebraska Department of Labor

550 S. 16th Street

PO Box 94600

Lincoln, NE 68509

402-471-9878

Fax: 402-471-3050

E-mail: jsovereign@dol.state.ne.us

Nevada

Shannan Canfield

Rapid Response Statewide

Coordinator

500 E. Third Street

Carson City, NV 89713

775-684-0362

Fax: 775-687-1073

E-mail: SLCANFIELD@nvdetr.org

New Hampshire

Bobby Stephen

Rapid Response and Dislocated Worker Director

Dept. of Resources & Economic Development

P.O. Box 1856

Concord, NH 03302-1856

603-271-2341

Fax: 603-271-6784

E-mail: bstephen@dred.state.nh.us

New Jersey

Joseph Dombrowski

Acting Assistant Director

NJ Dept of Labor and Workforce Development

Office of Employer Services

John Fitch Plaza, P.O. Box 933

Trenton, NJ 08625-0933

609-984-3519

Fax: 609-777-3202

E-mail: Joseph.Dombrowski@dol.state.nj.us

New Mexico

Mark Remington
State Coordinator for Rapid
Response
New Mexico Department of Work-
force Solutions
1596 Pacheco Street, Suite 201
Santa Fe, NM 87505
505-827-6895
Cell: 505-699-2767
Fax: 505-827-6812
E-mail: mark.remington@state.
nm.us

New York

Rick Grossi
Rapid Response Supervisor
New York State Department
of Labor
State Office Campus, Building 12
Albany, NY 12240
518-457-9880
E-mail: Richard.Grossi@labor.
state.ny.us

North Carolina

Russell Doles
Governor's Rapid Response
Team Manager

North Carolina Department
of Commerce
Division of Workforce
Development
313 Chapanoke Road, Suite 120
4316 Mail Service Center
Raleigh, NC 27699-4316
919-329-5284
Fax: 919-662-4770
E-mail: rdoles@nccommerce.com

North Dakota

Elaine Wentz
Program Administrator
Dislocated Worker Office
Job Service North Dakota
1000 E Divide Avenue
P.O. Box 5507
Bismarck, ND 58506-5507
701-328-3066
E-mail: ewentz@state.nd.us

Ohio

Michael Valentine
4020 East Fifth Ave
P.O. Box 1618
Columbus, OH 43216
614-644-0793
E-mail: michael.valentine@jfs.
ohio.gov

Oklahoma

Lynda Baird
Oklahoma Employment Security Commission
2401 N. Lincoln
Oklahoma City, OK 73152
405-557-5395
Fax: 405-557-1478
E-mail: lynda.baird@oesc.state.ok.us

Oregon

Laura J. Roberts
Rapid Response Coordinator
Community Colleges and Workforce Development
255 Capitol Street NE
Salem, OR 97310
503-378-8648, ext. 238
Fax: 503-378-3365
E-mail: laura.j.roberts@state.or.us

Pennsylvania

Christine Enright
Director
Rapid Response Coordination Services
Bureau of Workplace Development Partnership
12th Floor, Labor & Industry Building
651 Boas Street
Harrisburg, PA 17121
717-787-4811
Fax: 717-783-7115
E-mail: cenright@state.pa.us

Puerto Rico

Yolanda Rivera Ortiz
Directora Auxiliar, UETDP
Edificio Compañía Fomento Industrial, Piso 2 Avenida F.D. Roosevelt #355, Hato Rey, P.R. 00918
P.O. Box 192159, San Juan PR 00919-2159
787-754-5504 ext. 339
Fax: 787)754-7052
E-mail: yrivera@cdorh.org

Rhode Island

Connie Parks
Acting Chief of Business Services and Rapid Response
Rhode Island Department of Labor & Training
Center General Complex Bldg.73-3
1511 Pontiac Avenue
Cranston, RI 02920-4407
401-462-8724

Fax: 401-462-8722

E-mail: cparks@dlt.ri.gov

South Carolina

Ms. Michelle Paczynski
Dislocated Worker Unit Manager
South Carolina Department
of Commerce
1201 Main Street, Suite 1600
Columbia, SC 29201-3200
866-721-7867 or 803-737-3828
Fax: 803-806-3505
E-mail: mpaczynski@SCcommerce.com

South Dakota

Michael L. Ryan
WIA Program Administrator
700 Governors Drive
Pierre, SD 57501-2291
605-773-5017
Fax: 605-773-3216
E-mail: mike.ryan@state.sd.us

Tennessee

Joe W. Fults
Director
Dislocated Worker Unit/Rapid Response Team

Tennessee Workforce Development
Davy Crocker Tower, 12th Floor
500 James Robertson Parkway
Nashville, TN 37245-0658
818-253-5868
Fax: 615-741-3003
E-mail: joe.w.fults@state.tn.us

Texas

Juan Garcia
Texas Workforce Commission
101 E. 15th Street, Room 506T
Austin, TX 78778
512-936-0429
Fax: 512-936-0331
E-mail: Juan.Garcia@twc.state.tx.us

Utah

Dawn Lay
Dislocated Worker Unit
Coordinator
Utah Department of
Workforce Services
140 East 300 South, Suite 500
Salt Lake City, UT 84111
801-526-4312
Fax: 801-526-9662
E-mail: dlay@utah.gov

Vermont

Andrea M. Hussey
DLW Coordinator, Workforce Development
Vermont Department of Labor
5 Green Mountain Drive
P.O. Box 488
Montpelier, VT 05602
802-828-4177
Fax: 802-828-4374
E-mail: andrea.hussey@state.vt.us

U.S. Virgin Islands

Deborah Johnson
Virgin Islands Department of Labor
2203 Church Street, Christiansted
St. Croix, VI 00820
340-773-1994
Fax: 340-773-0094
E-mail: debfocus@yahoo.com

Virginia

Willie Blanton
Administrative Manager
VCCS Workforce Development Services
101 N. 14th Street
Richmond, VA 23219
Phone: 804-819-4946
Fax: 804-819-1699
E-mail: wblanton@vccs.edu

Washington

Bob Hughes
Washington State Employment Security Department
P.O. Box 9046
Olympia, WA 98507-9046
360-438-4627
Fax: 360-438-4666
E-mail: bhughes@esd.wa.gov

West Virginia

Martha Craig-Hinchman
Manager
Workforce West Virginia
Dislocated Worker Services Unit
112 California Avenue, Room 409
Charleston, WV 25305-0112
Phone: 304-558-8415
Fax: 304-558-7029
E-mail: mcraig-hinchman@workforcewv.org

Wisconsin

Ron Danowski
Division of Workforce Excellence
Wisconsin Department of Work-
force Development
201 E. Washington Avenue
Madison, WI 53707-1784
608-266-7406
Fax: 608-267-0330
E-mail: ron.danowski@dwd.state.
wi.us

Wyoming

Kellie Moreno
Department of Workforce Services
Wyoming Department of
Employment
P.O. Box 2760
Casper, WY 82602
307-235-3270
Fax: 307-235-3293
E-mail: kmoren@state.wy.us

APPENDIX D

Resources

The following resources will help you learn more about how to deal with unemployment and how to move on toward bigger and better things. These useful resources include assessment tools, guides to developing a new career path or creating your own job by becoming an entrepreneur, and résumé and tax tips.

Books

Kirk, J.L. (2007). *The ParentPreneur Edge: What Parenting Teaches About Building a Successful Business*. New York: Wiley.

Bolles, R. (2008) *What Color is Your Parachute? A Practical Manual for Job-Huntes and Career-Changers*. Berkeley: Ten Speed Press.

Career Assessment and Interest Assessment

Myers-Briggs Type Indicator
www.myersbriggs.org

ElementK
www.elementk.com

DISC Assessment from Leading Insight
www.leadinginsight.com

360° Reach Assessment
www.reachcc.com/360reach

Information About Job Types

Bureau of Labor Statistics

Occupational Employment Statistics

www.bls.gov/oes/

Job Listings

www.TheLadders.com

www.RobertHalf.com (accounting)

www.CareerBank.com

www.Execunet.com

www.Monster.com

www.craigslist.com

Job Search Tips

Job Hunter's Bible

Dick Bolles, author of *What Color is Your Parachute?*

www.jobhuntersbible.com

Magazines

Personal Branding Magazine

www.personalbrandingmag.com

Résumé and Cover Letter Tips

Pongo - Résumé and Cover Letter Tools, Templates, and Support

www.pongoresume.com

Monster.com Résumés & Letters

http://career-advice.monster.com/resumes-cover-letters/careers.aspx

Tax Issues

Tax Information with a Mother's Touch

www.TaxMama.com

APPENDIX E
Bibliography

Employment Law Guide, Whistleblower Protection Provisions Enforced By OSHA. U.S. Department of Labor. May 2009. **<www.dol.gov/compliance/guide/whistle.htm>**

Employment Situation Summary, USDL 09-0224. March 6, 2009. U.S. Department of Labor/Bureau of Labor Statistics. Accessed May 2009. **<www.bls.gov/news.release/empsit.nr0.htm>**

Energy Savers Booklet, Tips on Saving Energy & Money at Home. U.S. Department of Energy. Accessed May 2009. **<www1.eere.energy.gov/consumer/tips/pdfs/energy_savers.pdf>**

Essential Elements of an Effective Job Search. U.S. Department of Labor. Accessed May 2009. **<www.dol.gov/odep/pubs/ek97/element.htm>**

Housing information – mortgage and foreclosure prevention information. Housing and Urban Development. Accessed May 2009. **<www.hud.gov>**

OSHA Regional and Area Offices. Occupational Safety and Health. Accessed May 2009. <www.osha.gov/html/RAmap.html>

Recovery Act Overview. Small Business Administration. Accessed May 2009. <www.sba.gov/idc/groups/public/documents/sba_homepage/recovery_act_overview_033009.pdf>

SBA Local Offices. Small Business Administration. Accessed May 2009. <www.sba.gov/localresources/index.html>

Unemployment Insurance. U.S. Department of Labor. Accessed April 2009. <workforcesecurity.doleta.gov/unemploy/>

Workforce Investment Act, "Plain Language" Text. U.S. Department of Labor. Accessed April 2009. <www.doleta.gov/usworkforce/WIA/Runningtext2.htm>

AUTHOR BIOGRAPHY
PK Fontana

PK Fontana is a freelance writer and trainer, specializing in business communications and entrepreneurial topics. Based in Cary, North Carolina, her clients include businesses and individuals from across the country. She has earned a master's in English, with a concentration in Technical and Professional Communications, from East Carolina University, and plans to continue teaching at the community college level, helping students develop professional writing skills before they enter the workforce or start their own businesses. PK is married, the mother of two and the stepmother of four. She grew up on the beaches of the Gulf Coast of Florida and plans to eventually retire on the beach of the Jersey Shore. Learn more about PK's writing and training at **www.pkwriting.com**.

INDEX